KU-265-955

Contents

Unit 4 Italy

Unit 5 International relations

Unit 6 The United States of America

3 8017 00118 9604

on file

DAN
4/06
£9.95

AS/A-LEVEL

19th & 20th Century
European and World History

Patrick Walsh-Atkins

Exam
Revision
Notes

Philip Allan Updates
Market Place
Deddington
Oxfordshire
OX15 0SE

tel: 01869 338652
fax: 01869 337590
e-mail: sales@philipallan.co.uk
www.philipallan.co.uk

© Philip Allan Updates 2001

All rights reserved; no part of this publication may be reproduced, stored in a retrieval
system, or transmitted, in any form or by any means, electronic, mechanical,
photocopying, recording or otherwise without either the prior written permission
of Philip Allan Updates or a licence permitting restricted copying in the United
Kingdom issued by the Copyright Licensing Agency Ltd, 90 Tottenham Court Road,
London W1P 9HE.

ISBN 0 86003 435 6

Cover illustration by John Spencer
Printed by Raithby, Lawrence & Co. Ltd, Leicester

CROYDON COLLEGE
LIBRARY

COPY 06118 9604

CLASS 909·8 WAL[s]

Introduction

About this book

Before you read this book, you should already have read the recommended textbooks, made detailed notes and produced answers to examination questions. These revision notes comprise:

- the main **factual material** — this is organised in a way which will be easy to remember and revise from
- **margin notes** — advice about what to expect in examinations and how to use the factual material contained in the book

About the AS and A2 examinations

These notes cover the major AS and A2 modules of the three main examination boards: AQA, Edexcel and OCR. Check with your teacher or examinations officer at your school or college to find out which examination board specification you are studying. Also check which units you will be examined on.

The specification which you are studying will outline the format the examination will take. Some modules/units require you to answer several questions based on **source material**. You might, for example, have to compare material from several sources, or assess the reliability, usefulness or value of a source to a historian, or explain why different historical interpretations appear in different sources.

Other modules/units require you to **explain a historical term** within the context of the topic you have studied. Most examination papers will require you to engage in **extended writing**. This could be a question based solely on your own knowledge. Other questions require you to combine source material and your own knowledge to produce an analytical answer.

Finally, you may have to write an essay based on your own knowledge. In AQA AS module 3 you will be required to write a course essay. You will be given the title beforehand but you will have to write the answer under examination conditions using your own notes.

The standard of the AS examination is meant to be between GCSE and A-level. You might be asked questions which require you to explain causation, e.g. 'Why did … occur?' You might also have to explain the main problems facing politicians or governments, and the degree to which they were successful. The A2 examination is of GCE A-level standard, requiring you to write balanced, analytical answers by evaluating evidence.

The AS and A2 examinations have some important features.

- They all require you to demonstrate **knowledge and understanding** of history. This book of revision notes will assist you in remembering the main factual information required to answer both AS and A2 questions.
- You should be able to identify and explain **different historical interpretations**. Most of the chapters in this book cover topics which have encouraged considerable historical debate. It is important to know why historians have differed. They might have based their judgements on different evidence, written at different times or might have a different philosophy or view on history.

- You will also be asked to study and assess **sources in historical context**. To do this you have to have good factual knowledge of the topic.
- In the A2 examination you will be expected to engage in **synoptic assessment**. This will require you to draw together different aspects of history to make a historical judgement. You might have to identify different political, social, economic and cultural reasons why a historical event occurred. You will also be expected to assess the role of the individual.

How to prepare for the examinations

Effective planning of your revision will enable you to get the best out of the examination. Use a diary or calendar to plan the amount of time you will allocate for revision. It is much better to engage in revision over a period of time rather than all at the last minute. **Steady, methodical revision is always the best strategy.**

Examinations take place either in the morning or in the afternoon. Try to revise at a similar time. It is unwise to revise in the evening or late at night. You might eventually end up sleeping into the late morning. This will alter your body time clock. As a result, when you take an examination you might be mentally tired and your body clock might be telling you to go to sleep.

You will need to exercise self-discipline. Keep evenings free if at all possible. Passive learning will take place at this time when you can relax to take in the material you have revised during the day. There will be plenty of time to go out and celebrate once you have sat your modular/unit examination.

Just before the examination

If you face a morning examination, give yourself plenty of time to get up and get organised. To prevent last minute hitches, pack all you will need for the examination the night before.

In the examination room

- Always take time to **read the examination paper carefully** to make sure that you answer the question on the paper.
- What are the **command instructions**? You may be required to explain 'why' or 'how' in an AS paper. In an A2 paper you might be asked to explain 'how far...?' or 'to what extent...?'. You might also have to assess the validity of a statement.
- Are you being asked to cover a **particular period**? If the question states 1815–30, you will need to confine your answer to these years.
- Does the question contain any words or phrases which require **definition**? Make sure, for example, that you can define such terms as 'revolutionary', 'liberal' and 'conservative'.
- If the question is on a social or economic topic, try to include **statistical data** to support your case.
- Take a short time to **plan your answer**. This might be little more than writing down, in list form, the points you wish to cover. This will stop you forgetting important points.
- **Pace yourself.** Allocate your time so you spend an appropriate amount on questions which carry different marks. If, for example, you are sitting a 1-hour examination and one question is worth 30 marks and the other is worth 60, spend one-third of the time (20 minutes) on the first question and two-thirds on the second (40 minutes).

A The unification of Germany to 1871

Key questions

What were the origins of German nationalism in the nineteenth century and why did it grow?

Why did early attempts at German unification fail?

What led to the dominance of Prussia in the nineteenth century?

How important was Bismarck to German unification?

GERMANY IN 1815

Napoleon had a major impact on German nationalism.

While there had been some German unity under the Holy Roman Emperor, the eighteenth-century situation was one of 314 separate states, which were fragmented and disunited except perhaps for their language. Napoleon I had changed much of that, partly by defeating both Prussia and Austria, and partly by bringing about the Confederation of the Rhine and introducing the same liberal and nationalistic ideas as he had in Italy.

THE VIENNA SETTLEMENT

Ensure you have a clear picture of the territorial expansion of Prussia up to 1815.

While this restored legitimacy as much in Germany as elsewhere, it led to a considerable increase in Prussian territory, particularly near the Rhine. Successful participation in the Fourth Coalition also increased the status and prestige of Prussia. Austria gained much from the Vienna Settlement, and the scene was set for real rivalry between the two. The work of Stein and Hardenburg in abolishing serfdom and improving the army and education in Prussia was important for the modernisation of Prussia and in its development of a leadership role in central Europe.

THE GERMAN CONFEDERATION

This grouping of 39 German states, including major ones such as Austria and Prussia, was important as a first step towards unity. It enabled communication to take place between those states and gave an impression of unity, although it had little power and was largely controlled by Metternich.

METTERNICH AND GERMAN NATIONALISM

Metternich, an Austrian, was never keen on the aspects of German unification which threatened Austrian control.

Metternich would have done better to accept that German nationalism was a fact of life and try to harness it.

Metternich feared German nationalism as a rival to Austrian supremacy in Europe, and he did his best to contain it. Napoleon had given nationalism real impetus, partly by uniting Germans in their desire to expel him, and partly through his nationalist ideas. The growing Romantic movement also encouraged ideas of freedom and unity, as well as the development of a specifically German culture. Metternich did his best to repress liberal ideas through the Carlsbad Decrees, which imposed censorship and restricted political debate. The fact that the enemy of German unification was an Austrian added to the movement's attractiveness.

The Zollverein must be seen as a vital part of the process of unification.

THE ZOLLVEREIN

The Zollverein included most German states by the early 1840s, with the exception of Austria. The idea of working together economically had an impact which is much debated: economic unity was bound to lead to greater political unity; this raised Prussian status and lowered Austrian status in Germany. The growth of a uniform railway network around Germany also aided unification. Although still politically repressed, Germany had made significant moves towards economic and cultural unity by 1848.

It is important to note that the nationalists and liberals did not work well together and that this was a weakening factor in the unification process.

THE REVOLUTIONS OF 1848: AUSTRIA

Although they were eventually repressed, the initial successes of the revolutions in the Austrian Empire were to have a significant effect on German unity. The revolutions weakened Metternich and his system, and significant concessions were made to the nationalist demands. The revolutions also fed liberal hopes for social and economic change.

There is still a debate on the impact of the revolution in Prussia.

THE REVOLUTION IN PRUSSIA

The impact that the Prussian revolution had on German unification is controversial. Certainly the adoption of a liberal regime by King Frederick William IV helped, as did his open support for unification with Prussia. It also led to a growing split between German liberals and nationalists and to growing support for nationalism by the right. In other words, nationalism became an illiberal force.

The Frankfurt Parliament was central to the unification process.

THE FRANKFURT PARLIAMENT

The Frankfurt Parliament revealed the split between liberalism and nationalism in Germany, and perhaps weakened both. Although the parliament failed, it clarified thinking about German nationalism and what would have to be done to achieve unity. The relationship between states and a possible federal government was analysed and the *Kleindeutsch* versus *Grossdeutsch* debate (i.e. the debate between those who wanted a 'smaller' or 'greater' Germany) also had implications for the future.

Ensure you know the positive and negative aspects of the 1848 revolutions.

THE IMPACT OF THE 1848 REVOLUTIONS ON GERMAN UNIFICATION

Hopes were raised and dashed. The growth of a more authoritarian government in Prussia gave Bismarck the ability to dominate policy and thwarted the Austrian aim of stopping German unification. Bismarck made nationalism aggressive and populist, and German nationalism became the tool for politicians to further their own aims. The Olmütz agreement of 1850, which restored the German confederation, might have set the clock back superficially to 1815, but it was not to last.

Note the strength of the Prussian economy.

THE GROWTH OF PRUSSIA AS THE DOMINANT FORCE IN GERMANY AFTER 1848

Prussia had been the economic leader of Germany since its acquisition of economically useful territory in 1815. It had a well-run economy (thanks to the early reforms of Stein and Hardenburg) and benefited from its sensible participation in the Zollverein and the growth of free trade in Germany. The Prussian education system and a banking system geared to capital investment provided the necessary infrastructure for an industrial revolution. Progressive economic policies led to a growth of rail, iron and steel and chemicals.

THE IMPORTANCE OF PRUSSIAN ECONOMIC GROWTH TO GERMAN UNITY

Economic factors are vital in explaining Prussian military supremacy.

Bismarck's dreams could not have been realised without the support of a modern state. Prussia's economic leadership of Germany led to a sympathy for its politicians. Although Austria still seemed to have political leadership in Germany, Prussia had the economic muscle sufficient to support a large army and an efficient government.

DEBATES ABOUT THE UNIFICATION OF GERMANY

Ensure you have evidence to back up all three views.

There are three broad ideas about German unification. Bismarck encouraged the first interpretation, which is that he planned and implemented it throughout. The second is that unification was more by accident than by design, and was the result of Austrian ineptitude compounded by the acquiescence of France and Britain. The third view holds that Bismarck took advantage of a range of linguistic, cultural and economic forces.

THE RISE OF BISMARCK

Bismarck's ability to master detail and have a broad view was exceptional.

Bismarck was known as the 'man of blood and iron'. He was well educated and rose through the Prussian military and civil service. During the 1848 revolutions Bismarck absorbed many lessons about liberalism, nationalism and Austria and, above all, about the attitudes which different German states and classes had towards the idea of unity. He had no wish to be driven out of office as Metternich had been by the revolutions of 1848 in Vienna. Although hostile to liberalism, Bismarck had the awareness to manage popular pressures. He was appointed minister/president as a result of the dispute between the Landtag (parliament) and the expansionist military ideas of von Roon and von Moltke, the army commanders. Bismarck solved the situation by ignoring the Landtag and giving the army what it wanted.

BISMARCK AND GERMAN UNIFICATION, 1862–63

There is evidence here of real planning by Bismarck.

Bismarck's long-term goal was German unity under Prussia rather than Austria. In 1863 he defeated the *Grossdeutschland* proposal of Schmerling (the Austrian prime minister between 1860 and 1865), while gaining the support of the liberal nationalists for the *Kleindeutsch* idea. His support for Russia during a Polish revolt gained him an ally and tended to isolate Austria. Bismarck's able conduct of foreign policy during the Schleswig-Holstein dispute further strengthened his hand.

BISMARCK, SCHLESWIG-HOLSTEIN AND THE DANISH WAR OF 1864

Further evidence of Bismarck's planning and execution.

The mixture of Prussian military might and Bismarckian diplomacy was significant during the events of 1864. With Russia friendly because of Poland, and Austria supportive (note the joint invasion of Schleswig and Holstein in the war against Denmark), Schleswig was incorporated into Prussia. This established Prussia as the leader of German nationalism. Bismarck noted the suspicion that grew between France and Britain over the affair. He was astute in manipulating the press in a quest for moral justification, which helped forestall intervention by other countries. The peace agreement at Gastein in 1865 confirmed Prussian dominance.

THE PRUSSIAN–AUSTRIAN WAR OF 1866: THE BACKGROUND

Note the careful
diplomatic preparations.

The rivalry for the leadership of Germany had been there for decades, and Gastein was likely to lead to further division. As with Denmark, clever diplomacy ensured Austria was isolated diplomatically. The friendship with Russia continued, Napoleon III — convinced that Prussia was no threat — was hoodwinked at his Biarritz meeting with Bismarck over Belgium, and Italy was negotiated with in order to tie down Austrian troops there. The Italians were persuaded to appear as a major threat to the Austrian possessions in northern Italy.

THE PRUSSIAN–AUSTRIAN WAR, 1866

Note the planning,
anticipation and
effective execution.

After longstanding tension between Austria and Prussia, further friction arose over Schleswig-Holstein. Bismarck was clever in provoking the showdown with Austria. He deployed his usual mix of press manipulation and reasonable-seeming demands for a German parliament, which he knew would appear as an unacceptable ultimatum to the Austrians. Underpinning this strategy was the development of a superb Prussian army, which took Holstein quickly and then defeated the Austrians at Sadowa (Königgrätz).

RESULTS OF THE PRUSSIAN–AUSTRIAN WAR

Compare Bismarck's
stance here and his later
work with France.

The Prague Treaty of 1866 revealed Bismarck's intentions and methods, for while Austria was not humiliated or alienated permanently, Prussia annexed more territory. Schleswig and Holstein were incorporated into Prussia along with further territories such as Hesse Cassell and Hanover. The North German Confederation was set up with Prussia very much the dominant unit in all Germany and secure as the leader of German nationalism.

THE NORTH GERMAN CONFEDERATION, 1867–71

The impetus towards
both Prussian domina-
tion and German unity is
clear.

The North German Confederation was a stepping stone towards both Prussian domination and German unity, and provides further evidence of Bismarck's motives and attitudes. The Confederation confirmed the leadership of King William I of Prussia over much of north Germany, gaining him control of all military and diplomatic matters. There was a semblance of autonomy and federalism, but Prussia ruled with a superficial democracy which, in practice, was highly authoritarian.

THE FRANCO–PRUSSIAN WAR: THE CAUSES

The range of skills
shown by Bismarck in
his preparation for the
war was remarkable.

Bismarck saw France as an enemy which needed defeating. He was aware that Napoleon III (the French leader, 1852–70) was reluctant to allow Prussia to become the dominant force in Europe and that the remaining German states outside Prussian control, such as Bavaria, looked to France for protection against encroachment. In addition, the Prussian intelligence service alerted him to Napoleon's ambitions in Belgium and Luxembourg. The Hohenzollern candidate to the throne of Spain provided Bismarck's excuse to provoke the French. The French were not keen on having a German on the Spanish throne. Bismarck was aware of Napoleon's weak personality and knew he could provoke him easily. Bismarck edited the famous Ems Telegram carefully — he achieved the objective of provoking Napoleon into declaring war on Prussia. Bismarck did not therefore appear as the aggressor.

Note the systematic detachment of possible French allies.

THE FRANCO~PRUSSIAN WAR: THE DIPLOMATIC PREPARATIONS

Bismarck's mastery of diplomacy ensured that France had no allies, and Napoleon's ineptitude did not help the French cause. Bavaria was encouraged into the Prussian orbit when Bismarck leaked French acquisitive tendencies towards it. A similar leak about Belgium alienated Britain from France. Austria had been carefully pacified in 1866 and Russia had always been supported in its tough management of Poland. The Italians were unhappy with the French withdrawal from the war with Austria after the battles of Magenta and Solferino in northern Italy, and by the French army's protection of the papacy. France was on its own.

Note the military achievement after the diplomatic success in isolating France.

THE FRANCO~PRUSSIAN WAR, 1870~71

The French planned for attack but found defence against the Prussian military machine an impossibility. Defeats at Metz, Sedan and finally Paris led to Napoleon's humiliation. The Second Reich was proclaimed in the Hall of Mirrors at Versailles and the Second French Empire ended with an indemnity and the loss of Alsace and Lorraine. The resulting Treaty of Frankfurt in 1871 contains perhaps some of the key causes of the First World War.

WHY WAS PRUSSIA THE MAJOR FORCE IN GERMAN UNIFICATION?

Was German unification Bismarck's personal achievement, or was he merely exploiting existing forces?

Prussian progressiveness and conservatism established an efficient and effective government which appealed to the many other independent German states. The Zollverein, for example, prepared the way for economic unity and the Frankfurt Parliament offered leadership to Prussia as early as 1849. Bismarck and King William I offered stability and leadership and the unaffiliated states could see the advantages of integration with Prussia. The only alternative was Austria, and Austria was economically backward and administratively archaic, and had little sympathy with either liberal or nationalistic ideas. In addition, the Austrians lacked Bismarck's understanding of German nationalism and how to manage it.

Key factors behind the failure of early unification
- the Vienna Settlement
- the restoration of regimes determined to repress liberalism and nationalism
- Metternich
- the tradition of separation
- Austria
- the failure of 1848
- the Frankfurt Parliament

Key factors in German unification
- the legacy of Napoleon
- the German Confederation
- the Zollverein
- the 1848 revolutions
- the Frankfurt Parliament
- the rise of Prussia
- the role of Bismarck

- the role of the Prussian military
- Prussia's economic progress
- the North German Confederation
- the wars with Denmark, Austria and France

B Germany, 1871–90: domestic policy

Key questions

How united was Germany in the period 1871–90?

How successful were Bismarck's domestic policies?

In what ways and with what success did the rulers of Imperial Germany deal with economic change and political opposition between 1871 and 1918?

IMPERIAL GERMANY IN 1871: THE CONSTITUTION OF THE REICH

It is vital to note the Emperor's power.

The constitution created for the Second Reich was distinctly authoritarian and dominated by King William I, who was now known as the German Emperor. He controlled a powerful central executive and appointed key ministers and the military, who were responsible to him and not to the legislature. There was a two-chamber legislature, the Bundesrat and the Reichstag, and the new Emperor could veto legislation and dissolve the Reichstag. There was a federal structure, with the individual state governments such as Bavaria controlling areas like education and police, whilst broad policy in defence and foreign policy lay with the Emperor.

PRUSSIAN DOMINATION OF THE SECOND REICH

Resentment in some parts of Germany at Prussian domination was the weak link in German unity.

In addition to a Prussian emperor, and with Bismarck installed as first chancellor, Prussia was the biggest single unit in the united Germany. Its group in the Bundesrat could block any change it wanted and the *Junker* aristocracy dominated the army and much of the federal civil service, particularly the Foreign Office. Prussian social values and attitudes permeated all aspects of German life and forced the other states to conform to Prussian dominance.

HOW LIBERAL WAS BISMARCK'S GERMANY?

Bismarck was wise enough not to go for a full totalitarian system of government.

Some of the ideas of 1848 had been taken on board in Prussia, notably the education and public administration reforms of the 1850s and the introduction of adult male suffrage within the North German Confederation. Under the federal system, elected state governments had autonomy in many areas. The Reichstag had some budgetary control and was in a position to oppose the Imperial Executive, if not call it to account. A large number of political parties, including liberals and socialists, existed in Germany and were represented in the Reichstag. There is a debate as to whether Bismarck's Germany was a limited liberal or limited authoritarian system.

HOW AUTHORITARIAN WAS BISMARCK'S GERMANY?

The German inheritance was an authoritarian one with a history of autocratic monarchy and a strong Prussian *Junker* military caste. Prussia and its values dominated the Imperial Executive and the military, and there was no accountability to the legislature by the executive. When the Imperial Government wanted to go to war or make a treaty, it did. The system was fundamentally authoritarian with limited and ineffective consultation by what some might see as constitutional monarchy. Political parties were not involved in government, except as critics or supporters. It is, however, important to note that Bismarck always found it necessary to work with the political groupings in the Reichstag, in order to get legislation through.

> The system was authoritarian, but there had to be political support in Germany for any major moves.

BISMARCK'S DOMESTIC POLICIES: THE BROAD AIMS

There are two major themes running through the domestic policy of Bismarck. The first was to ensure that German unity was complete in every sense, and the second was to prevent threats to what he perceived as his Germany. These threats could come from different quarters: the separatism of some states; a too liberal Kaiser; an internationalist Catholic Church; dangerous and radical socialists; or free traders who disliked Bismarck's tariffs. To maintain his conservative ideals, Bismarck had to work closely with different political parties in the Reichstag, and he demonstrated considerable political skills in the process. He had also to adapt to huge economic and political changes, such as the development of democracy and socialism and the impact of industrialism in Europe as a whole.

> Note the vision that Bismarck had for Germany.

BISMARCK AND THE POLITICAL PARTIES

To an extent, Bismarck had to adapt to party politics in order to get his policies through. Examples are the alliance with the Liberals in the 1870s to secure the final stages of unification and the management of the centre during the *Kulturkampf*, when conflict between the Catholic Church and the state came out into the open. He resorted to repression of the Social Democrats with the Anti-Socialist Laws and then tried to undermine their power base with legislation which benefited their working-class supporters. His dealings with the right-wing political groups of the *Kartell* were initially successful, though their ultimate alienation played a part in his downfall.

> The manipulative skills of Bismarck's early diplomacy are in evidence again here.

BISMARCK AND THE KAISERS

Bismarck had to deal with three Kaisers, all of whom were very different. William I (1861–88) supported him, grateful for the fact that it was Bismarck who had brought him prestige and glory by making him Emperor of Germany. The more liberal Crown Prince Frederick challenged Bismarck's conservatism and Bismarck started to develop the *Kartell* in order to get himself more Reichstag support on the right. With Frederick's death in 1888, William II's accession to the throne led to Bismarck's reluctant departure from power in 1890.

> Without the support of the Kaiser, Bismarck had limited power.

BISMARCK AND THE *KULTURKAMPF*

Having completed the necessary unification stages by introducing a common currency, legal system and commercial codes, Bismarck attacked the Catholic Church. He viewed Catholicism as a challenge to his Protestant and conservative

> The *Kulturkampf* episode reveals the nature of Bismarck's power and his vision for Germany.

views and to Prussian domination of Germany, as well as a threat to the type of state he wanted. He viewed Catholic ideas as internationalist and separatist. Falk's May Laws, where the state got extensive control over the Catholic Church, were a typical Bismarckian mix of liberalism and conservatism.

BISMARCK AND TARIFF REFORM

This is an example of Bismarck's political astuteness.

Pressure from agriculture and industry to end free trade appealed to Bismarck and he agreed to implement a protectionist policy. Tariffs increased the state's revenue, which was needed to maintain a growing military machine. The liberals strongly opposed tariffs, but as they had now served their purpose for him during the completion of the unification process, Bismarck gave up the *Kulturkampf* and formed an alliance with the conservative and centre parties. The alliance enabled him to achieve the protectionist measures he sought and is a good illustration of how Bismarck played party politics to achieve his objectives.

BISMARCK AND THE RISE OF SOCIALISM

A good example of the limits of Bismarckian power and the way he managed opposition.

Bismarck saw socialism as a serious threat to his vision for Germany. He tried repression first with the Anti-Socialist Laws of 1878 and, when these failed, he embarked on his state socialism of the 1880s and tried to kill the Socialist Party of Germany (SPD) with kindness. This, although expensive, failed to limit the growing support for the SPD, and Kaiser William I's sympathy for the SPD's policies did not make Bismarck's life any easier.

WAS BISMARCK'S DOMESTIC POLICY A SUCCESS?

Overall, Bismarck was a successful leader, particularly bearing in mind that his leadership followed a long and difficult unification process.

Bismarck's fall in 1890 revealed his lack of widespread support. By then he had few political allies and was becoming out of touch with current views in Germany. The *Kulturkampf* had been abandoned, some of the more intolerant measures of the 1870s had been repealed in the 1880s, and his wish to prevent the rise of socialism had not been fulfilled. On the success side, unification had been completed, free trade had been introduced on Bismarck's terms, his welfare policies had made Germany a model for other countries and he had been able to manage the peculiar mix of authoritarianism and liberalism of the German political and constitutional system.

Key elements in German domestic policy under Bismarck
- the constitution of the German Empire
- Prussian domination of the German Empire
- the role of the Reichstag
- the role of the Chancellor
- the role of the Kaiser
- the role of the *Junkers*
- the relationship between the church and state
- socialism
- the role of the political parties
- the management of opposition
- the *Kulturkampf*
- tariffs
- social reform

C Bismarck's foreign policy

Key questions
How successful was Bismarck's foreign policy?
What were the main influences on Bismarck's foreign policy?
What was the nature and extent of Bismarck's colonial policy?

THE AIMS OF BISMARCK'S FOREIGN POLICY

> It was perhaps an error to impose such harsh terms on France in 1871.

After the Franco-Prussian War, Bismarck wanted to avoid further open conflict and had no wish for more territory. Given the French desire for revenge, he wished to keep France isolated. Good relations with Austria and Russia were also vital, partly to avoid a conflict in the Balkans and partly to stop France getting an ally and threatening Germany with a war on two fronts.

INFLUENCES ON BISMARCK'S FOREIGN POLICY

> Public opinion and contemporary events always had to be taken into consideration.

Public opinion crept into Bismarck's calculations, prompting a greater focus on prestige and the colonies than he might have wished. The imperialist ideas sweeping many countries also had an impact on his policies, as did the growth of Slav nationalism in the Balkans and pan-Slavism in Russia. French politics influenced Bismarck too, particularly when the more militant right was in power in the 1870s, and he used the threat of French aggression to help his position at home, particularly in the 1875 French war scare.

THE *DREIKAISERBUND*

> The first stage of a long process which was to play a major part in the causes of the First World War.

Bismarck had always been friendly with Russia for unification reasons, and this continued after 1870. Along with the pro-German Count Gyula Andrassy in Austria, he started regular informal meetings with Russia in 1872. The maintenance of the status quo was the main objective, with the suppression of socialism as a subsidiary aim. The *Dreikaiserbund* between Germany, Austria and Russia was not a formal agreement, but more an understanding to help each other in the event of an unprovoked attack, and it set the scene for the alliances and counter-alliances which were to come.

THE BALKAN CRISIS OF 1875–78

> Bismarck always had mixed views on the Balkans.

Bismarck had no wish to be drawn into the Balkans, but he was well aware that conflict here could spread. He played a vital role in brokering a peace in Berlin in 1878 after the war between Russia and Turkey. He prevented a major conflict when Austria and Russia were at loggerheads and Britain moved its fleet to support the Turks. He worked in conjunction with Britain to pacify Austria and Russia, but this did not solve the Balkan problems. Russia felt betrayed, and the Turks were humiliated and sought revenge. None of the Balkan nationalist groups was content either, particularly the Serbs and the Bulgars.

THE DUAL ALLIANCE, 1819

> The Dual Alliance was a triumph of statecraft, but held potential dangers.

Bismarck feared both Russia and France. Seeing Austria as his most likely ally, Bismarck formalised an agreement with Austria in 1879. This was quite an achievement, considering that only 5 years earlier the Prussian army had

humiliated the Austrians. The Dual Alliance was secret, valid for 5 years and could be renewed. It committed each country to assist the other if attacked by Russia and to remain neutral if attacked by a country apart from Russia. There was an element of risk in a strategy which might encourage Russia to ally with France, or Austria to get over-confident about German backing in the Balkans. This alliance was to be a central feature of German foreign policy until 1914.

THE TRIPLE ALLIANCE, 1882

> The Triple Alliance was a central part of Bismarck's foreign policy.

The Triple Alliance between Germany, Austria and Russia was a secret treaty to last 3 years initially. If any one of the three nations was involved in a war, the other two would remain neutral. Bismarck hoped that it would calm the Balkans and please Russia to the extent that the Russians would look less favourably at Germany's defeated enemy, France. This alliance bound together the three most conservative nations in Europe.

THE LATER YEARS OF BISMARCK'S FOREIGN POLICY

> Some of the flaws were beginning to show.

By and large, Bismarck's ambition of security survived his tenure of office. However, the Bulgarian crisis of 1885–97 threatened his system by bringing Russia to the point of war and forcing Germany to choose between its two allies, Russia and Austria. By the First Mediterranean Agreement of 1887, Britain, Italy and Austria agreed to retain the status quo in the Mediterranean. Bismarck's suspicion of France is very evident here. The Triple Alliance was renewed in 1887 and the Reinsurance Treaty of 1887 revealed Bismarck's hope of restoring a relationship with Russia which had been badly damaged during the Bulgarian crisis. The Second Mediterranean Agreement of 1887 was geared towards containing Russia more than France.

WAS BISMARCK'S FOREIGN POLICY A SUCCESS OR A FAILURE?

> Compare this with Bismarck's work before unification and his domestic policies.

Bismarck didn't want to gain any more territory. Peace was maintained and he had firm allies. However, it could be argued that Bismarck's foreign policy was too complex, was created too much as a reaction to events and may also have been driven too much by domestic concerns. Any benefits were very short term. Hostility to France seemed inbuilt and was to lead to war. The Balkan issue was never solved and continued to cause international problems. Russia linked with France soon after Bismarck's departure and his alliance system played a central role in creating the tension which led to the First World War.

BISMARCK'S COLONIAL POLICY

> Given the limited gains and the potential for conflict, colonial policy is perhaps not one of Bismarck's success stories.

Bismarck's colonial policy was perhaps more reactive than directive and was carried out in response to internal social, economic and political pressures. Initially, Bismarck had little interest in colonies, but he permitted considerable territorial gains in South and East Africa and in islands in the Far East. The reasons are varied, ranging from popular pressure and enthusiasm to industrial demands for fresh markets. Bismarck's colonial stance was, to some degree, an extension of his foreign policy, as is shown by the Berlin Conference of 1884 where he helped to lay down rules about the further colonisation of Africa. German colonial activities could affect relationships with France, Italy and Britain, so he was anxious to avoid conflict.

Key factors in Bismarck's foreign and colonial policy
- the need for security
- the relationship with France
- the fear of *revanche* (revenge by France for the defeat of 1871)
- the relationship with Russia
- the relationship with Austria
- the attitude to the Balkans
- the *Dreikaiserbund*
- the alliance system
- the Balkan Crisis of 1875–78
- the Treaty of San Stefano and the Congress of Berlin
- the Dual Alliance
- the Triple Alliance
- the Mediterranean Agreements
- the Reinsurance Treaty
- the Berlin Conference on colonies

D German domestic politics, 1890–1914

Key questions

How authoritarian was the rule of William II in Germany?

How well was Germany ruled between 1890 and 1914?

THE ROLE OF THE KAISER

The personality and views of the Kaiser are of central importance to both German and international history in this period.

With the departure of Bismarck and the accession of William II, German policy-making changed. The Kaiser undermined chancellors such as Hohenloe and he took advice from whom he wished, listening to the military in particular. Some historians doubt the Kaiser's grip over Germany, seeing him as the mouthpiece of the Prussian officer corps, the landed aristocracy and big business. There is also an argument that much policy was a result of pressure from an urban working class demanding reform and social justice, and that an active foreign policy was part of the Kaiser's bread-and-circuses political approach. The *Daily Telegraph* affair (where his words to a British journalist offended many in Germany and Britain) and the Zabern crisis (where the Kaiser supported the arrogant behaviour of German officers towards the new Germans of Alsace) are examples of the Kaiser at work.

THE GOVERNMENT OF GERMANY

Germany was simply not well governed from 1890 to 1914.

Under the Kaiser, who is generally recognised as having been both authoritarian and incompetent, a good working relationship between executive and legislature was never established. Chancellors Caprivi, Hohenloe and Bethmann-Hollweg were less able than Bismarck, and military men such as Turpitz and favourites such as Eulenburg emerged as powerful figures. Foreign ministers such as Bülow were able to work apart from the chancellor, pursuing different policies. Meanwhile, the military emerged as a law unto itself, with rival administrations to the civil ones, producing schemes such as the Schlieffen Plan without thinking through the implications. The Reichstag became progressively more difficult to manage and a force which increasingly had to be reckoned with and conceded to.

THE ECONOMY

Limited government regulation was the key to a sound economy.

Overall the economy was healthy, but this was probably due more to the laissez-faire tradition in Germany than to good management. Growing industrialisation and sensible taxation meant a balanced budget. Commercial treaties initially made sense as they helped exports and reduced the price of food. However, the treaties antagonised the aristocratic landowners in the Agrarian League, and tariffs were reintroduced to the detriment of industry and the urban working class. It was largely a reactive policy, but Germany was to start the First World War with a reasonably healthy economy.

SOCIAL REFORMS

Make sure that you know the motivation for the reforms.

Current views are that although social reforms were extensive, they were brought in as a result of pressure from below. Fear of revolution was a major factor, and the preference at the top was for a reintroduction of Bismarck's anti-socialist legislation. However, the gains for the working class were considerable. Hours of work, employment of women and children, the relationship between employers and employees, sick pay and accident compensation were all covered. Whether or not the government was motivated by an improving zeal, Germany was seen very much as a leader of social reform.

DEFENCE

The Kaiser's inability to control the military and its spending was one of his major failings.

There was a rapid growth in both the navy and army. Military expenditure prompted huge struggles with the Reichstag and led to its worsening relationship with the executive. Although the centre could be relied on for some support, the SPD opposed the amounts of money being poured into armaments. There was a 500 million mark budget deficit by 1905 caused by high defence spending, and this inevitably led to more taxes for all.

WAS WILLIAM II'S DOMESTIC POLICY A SUCCESS OR A FAILURE?

Make sure that you know both the points for and against William II .

There was social progress, the country overall was competently administered, areas such as education improved and Germany became one of the major industrial powers in the world. However, there was little coherence in a domestic policy which arguably became reactive and dependent on foreign policy. On the other hand, the dominance of the military, the increasing whimsicality of the Kaiser and the lack of a link between the executive and a representative legislature made the system potentially unworkable.

Key features of domestic affairs after Bismarck's departure
- the personal rule of the Kaiser
- the influence of the military
- the role of the élites

- the chancellorships of Caprivi, Hohenloe and Bethmann-Hollweg
- the changing role of the Reichstag
- industrial development
- social reforms
- arms spending and the arms race

German foreign policy, 1890–1914

Key questions

What were the main influences behind Germany's foreign policy between 1890 and 1914?

How responsible was Germany for causing the First World War?

THE CHRONOLOGY OF EVENTS

1890	Dismissal of Bismarck
	No renewal of Reinsurance Treaty
1894	Franco–Russian Alliance
	Disputes with Britain over Africa and the Far East
1895	Kruger telegram
1898	Naval arms race begins
1899	Open support for Boers against the British
1900	Failure of third attempt at alliance between Germany and Britain
1904	Anglo–French entente
1905	Björko agreement with Russia
1906	Britain and France work together over Algeciras
1907	Anglo–Russian convention
1908	Germany backs Austria over Bosnia and Serbia
1911	Britain and France work together over Agadir incident
1914	German support for Austrian ultimatum to Serbia
	German ultimatum to Russia and declaration of war
	German declaration of war on France — Schlieffen Plan operational
	German invasion of neutral Belgium

THE RELATIONSHIP WITH FRANCE

Central to the whole period was the German assumption that France was determined on revenge for its defeat in the Franco–Prussian War. After Bismarck's brief attempt to encourage French colonial growth in Africa, there was no attempt to pacify France. The policy of ensuring French isolation lapsed and France was to gain powerful allies in Britain and Russia, neither of which necessarily shared common aims with the French. German military planning was directed against France, and a policy of almost deliberate provocation was adopted towards France, as the attempted German 'invasion' in Morocco in 1905 showed.

Mismanagement of the French relationship was one of the biggest errors in German policy-making.

UNIT 1   Germany

This was a flaw in German policy-making which helped cause the First World War.

THE RELATIONSHIP WITH AUSTRIA

Bismarck had always seen the Balkans as having the greatest potential for European conflict and he did his best to remain uninvolved; his successors were not as wise. The close Austro–German relationship that developed was under-pinned by Austrian assumptions that an uncritical Germany would support its aggression in the Balkans. The Bosnian crisis of 1908 duly sucked Germany into an area where it had no real interest, and which was bound to lead to conflict with Russia, the ally for decades of Austria's Serbian enemy.

Note the lack of any coherent strategy.

THE RELATIONSHIP WITH RUSSIA

Bismarck's legacy of not antagonising the Russians dissipated and the working arrangements he had established ended with the Franco–Russian Alliance in 1894. The German fear of being attacked on two fronts grew from then on and was to dominate German military thinking. A brief attempt to reconcile with the Russians was made at Björko in 1905, but the Kaiser failed to press it through and the race for hostile alliances continued. German thinking from 1905 onwards was dominated by the need to plan for war against Russia and France.

There was no real reason for antagonism between the two nations.

THE RELATIONSHIP WITH BRITAIN

There were several attempts to establish good relations with Britain along the lines of the deals that Bismarck had struck with Disraeli in Berlin. In addition to the various colonial compromises, there was cooperation over China and three sets of negotiations between 1898 and 1901. Although there were no obvious grounds for conflict between Britain and Germany, the Kaiser's ambitions seemed antagonistic. The German naval programme, the rivalry in East Africa, the German dealings with the Boers and a Berlin-to-Baghdad railway which threatened British interests in the Middle East combined to provoke British fears. The closer ties which Britain had with Russia and France, and its long-standing interest in Belgium, should have encouraged caution on the Kaiser's part.

It is important to consider German responsibility, as opposed to that of the other major powers.

GERMAN RESPONSIBILITY FOR CAUSING THE FIRST WORLD WAR

There is a strong case for arguing that Germany must take the bulk of the blame for the outbreak of war in 1914. The case rests on many factors: the desire for *Weltpolitik* (a dominant role for Germany in the world); the abandonment of Bismarck's system of peace and caution; the antagonism of Britain; provocative diplomacy such as at Agadir; the alienation of Russia through support of the aggressive and unstable Austria; Germany's dominant role in the arms race; and a general lack of awareness of the tension it was causing. All these factors were topped off by the Schlieffen Plan with its inherent lack of political control. In July and August 1914, continued German support for Austria, the declaration of war against Russia and the invasion of Belgium precipitated catastrophe.

Perhaps there is a case for blaming all the major powers.

OTHER FACTORS THAT CAUSED THE FIRST WORLD WAR

There is an equally strong case for arguing that Austria, Russia, Britain and France must share blame for the outbreak of war. There was the ambition of Austria in the Balkans, the French obsession to avenge defeat in the Franco–Prussian War and the failure to realise what German reactions would be to a Franco–Russian alliance. The French and the Russians were easily provoked, and both heightened tension by building up their armies. The British too were oversensitive, and the British government did little or nothing to defuse chauvinism and xenophobia.

Given the Kaiser's constitutional power, there is a strong argument that he bears considerable responsibility for Germany's stumbling towards the First World War.

WAS IT SIMPLY THE KAISER?

There are debates about whether Germany drifted or rushed towards war, and the extent to which the Kaiser formed policy or responded to pressures from within. There was general support amongst a reasonably free press for *Weltpolitik*. Further pressure came from Germany's élites in the military–industrial complex and from an aggressively nationalist population at large. The Kaiser was certainly powerful in matters of defence and foreign policy, and he listened to advice from the military more than from civilians. Military dominance worked in tandem with the Kaiser's ambitions, as he allowed the Schlieffen Plan to take a central role in policy.

Key factors in Germany's responsibility for the outbreak of war
- the relationship with France
- the support for Austria
- the relationship with Russia
- Germany's role in the arms race
- Germany's role in developing the alliance system
- Germany's relationship with Britain
- Germany and colonial rivalry
- the Schlieffen Plan
- the Kaiser's personality
- popular pressure
- the international atmosphere in 1914

F The Weimar Republic, 1919–33

Key questions

How strong was the Weimar Republic and why did it collapse?

How was the Weimar Republic able to overcome its early problems?

How important was Stresemann to the success of the Weimar Republic?

The complex internal politics of 1918 need careful analysis.

THE NEW SYSTEM OF GOVERNMENT

In 1918 there were two revolutions in German government, one from above and the other from below. The civilian government which ran Germany in 1914 had been replaced in 1916 by the military dictatorship of Ludendorff, but the failure to win the war by summer 1918 meant that Germany faced disaster. The dismissal of Ludendorff in 1918 led to the re-creation of a constitutional monarchy, with Max of Bavaria as the chancellor subject to the Reichstag. There were two reasons for the change from a military to a civilian government. The first was that the Allies would not negotiate with the military. The second was that the German

UNIT 1

Germany

military government could leave it to civilians to take the humiliation of surrendering to the Allies.

THE INTERNAL CRISIS IN GERMANY IN 1918

It is vital to remember that the Kaiser and his military aides had left government before the war ended.

It was not just military failure which prompted the end of rule by the Kaiser and Ludendorff. There were a series of naval and army mutinies, there was appalling hunger among the civilian population in Germany, and there was particular anger among the German working class, who had been promised a military victory. These factors, together with the proclamation of a soviet republic in Bavaria by Eisner, led to the resignation of Max of Bavaria and the abdication of the Kaiser. The republic was proclaimed by Scheidemann of the SPD before the war ended and this new civilian government took on the task of trying to end the war.

THE REVOLUTIONS OF 1918 AND 1919

Consider carefully why these revolutions failed.

The successful revolution in Russia inspired German revolutionaries, who were urged on by the despair of defeat, the hunger and the misery caused by the war and the Allies' blockade. Although Luxemburg and Liebknecht of the Spartacus League offered inspirational leadership, there was a lack of co-ordination amongst the left and, while Germany was ready to reject the Kaiser, it was not ready to accept communism. Ebert and the other Weimar leaders were assiduous in dealing with the mutinies, the armistice and the outbreak of revolutions in various parts of Germany, and they enabled Groener, the army leader, to suppress the revolutions and deploy the Freikorps to smash the Spartacists.

THE WEIMAR CONSTITUTION

Consider the merits of giving a liberal and democratic system to a nation unused to such freedoms.

Popular sovereignty was built into the Weimar constitution, where the key institution was a directly elected Reichstag. The president was also elected, and he appointed a chancellor and the executive, which had to command a majority in the Reichstag and were responsible to it. The constitution also guaranteed a range of civil liberties by extending unparalleled democracy and social justice to the German people. Its principal weakness, which many see as the cause of its failure, was in Article 48, which gave the president emergency powers and was to prove vital to the rise of Hitler. In addition, a proportional representation election system led to indecisive coalition governments.

THE TERMS OF VERSAILLES

You should be able to debate the merits and demerits of Versailles and be aware of its longer-term implications.

The debate about the fairness or unfairness of Versailles echoes on. Germany suffered a range of territorial losses, including Alsace-Lorraine and part of Poland, and was also subjected to military clauses that restricted its army and naval activity. It was forced to sign a 'war guilt clause' accepting responsibility for causing the war, and also to accept a ban on *Anschluss* — that is, on uniting Germany with Austria. In addition, it was made to pay reparations to the Allies for losses they had suffered in the war. Bearing in mind the terms which Germany imposed on the Russians at Brest-Litovsk — and what it would have imposed on the French and British had it won — Versailles was perhaps not unreasonable. However, it provided huge leverage for later critics of the regime, such as Hitler. Revision of the treaty was a central part of German foreign policy from 1919 onwards.

THE IMPACT OF VERSAILLES ON GERMANY

Consider the Allies'
alternatives and the
political pressures on
them.

Within Germany there was bitter resentment against those who signed the Treaty of Versailles (particularly their acceptance of the war guilt clause), and a lack of understanding of the alternatives they faced. The treaty gave the Weimar critics, especially those on the nationalistic right, a popular stick to beat the Weimar politicians with. Economically Germany did not suffer hugely — the Germans recovered faster than either France or Britain and soon achieved full employment. The greatest impact was psychological. Each item of the treaty was perhaps acceptable on its own, but collectively they proved too much for the Germans.

THE POLITICAL INSTABILITY OF WEIMAR

You need to consider
whether Weimar was
doomed to failure.

There is much debate as to whether political instability was built into the Weimar Republic, or resulted from later political developments. The elections of 1919 need careful assessment, as do all the elections between 1919 and 1933. In 1919 most political parties accepted democracy and the republic, but this was not the case thereafter. Can any system survive when the majority of voters are hostile to its very basis? Perhaps what kept Weimar going was an opposition split between the far left and far right. Proportional representation (PR) is often blamed for weak governments, but this view needs balancing against the view that PR does not cause political instability in itself and reflects opinion more accurately than a first-past-the-post system such as Britain's.

OPPOSITION TO WEIMAR FROM THE LEFT

Consider why the left,
in spite of quite large
support, was unable to
make much impact on
Weimar politics.

The mutual loathing of the right and left was an important reason for the survival of Weimar. The left was brutally smashed in 1919. The Communist Party of Germany (KPD) — which commanded a large vote through to 1933 — was always alienated from the Socialist Party of Germany (SPD) and would not work with it to defeat the threat from the right in 1932–33. Socialist and communist views were unacceptable to the majority of the German people, so the left stood no chance of success. The left's failure to compromise and work with centre groups led to its leaders being among the first to be incarcerated in Nazi concentration camps.

OPPOSITION TO WEIMAR FROM THE RIGHT

While the left split over
issues, the right tended
to weaken itself over
clashes of personality.

The right was discredited by the loss of the war and the humiliating abdication of the Kaiser, and most of its leaders saw Weimar as a necessary evil which had to be tolerated for lack of an alternative. There were attempts to overthrow the regime, such as those by Kapp and Hitler in Munich, but they lacked legitimacy or coherence. The plight of the German people was not serious enough to engender much support for them. The fact that there were many strong supporters of the nationalistic right in the army, the judiciary, the civil service and among many survivors of the old regime helped the right and weakened Weimar.

THE ECONOMIC PROBLEMS OF WEIMAR

In many respects the German economy recovered faster than that of either France or Britain. German territory had not been fought over as in France; nor had Germany lost a vital component of its economy compared with Britain's diminished export markets. Full employment was achieved much faster in Germany than elsewhere. While many Germans blamed the hyperinflation of

Consider whether the inflation was more important psychologically than economically.

the early 1920s on Versailles, reparations payments and the French occupation of the Ruhr, speculation and the printing of paper money to service debts and fund public services were also major causes. The speed with which Germany solved its inflationary crisis undercuts the interpretation that inflation was caused from the outside.

THE IMPACT OF THE INFLATIONARY CRISIS

Opponents of the Weimar Republic made political capital from inflation and used it to gain international sympathy. In 1924 the Dawes Plan reduced the burden of reparations and in 1926 Germany was admitted to the League of Nations. Within Germany, the middle-class loss of savings alienated it from Weimar and secured support for Hitler when the next economic crisis hit Germany in 1929. Although there were dramatic images of German citizens being paid with piles of bank notes, the overall impact of inflation was perhaps limited and, despite the fall of the government in 1923, there was no noticeable radicalisation of voters.

The deflation of 1929 onwards was to hit Germany harder than the earlier hyper-inflation.

THE ECONOMIC RECOVERY

Consider how deep economic recovery actually went.

Stresemann, Marx and Schacht were the key figures in an economic recovery between 1923 and 1925. Stability was restored rapidly with a new currency and American support via the Dawes and Young Plans. Reparations became less important, at least until 1929 when Hitler resurrected the issue. American investment was used in productive industry and by 1929 Germany was the major European industrial power with an economy larger than it had been in 1913. With economic health always a central factor in political stability, Weimar was looking like a real success story. Germany enjoyed an economy in substantially better shape in terms of employment and investment than Britain.

THE ECONOMIC COLLAPSE OF WEIMAR

Consider whether economic collapse was fundamental to the rise of Hitler.

The role of the Depression in Weimar's collapse and the rise of Hitler is much debated. The Wall Street Crash caused an American recall of loans, as did the collapse of the Credit Anhalt bank and much of the German banking system. Why the impact on Germany was so severe is a very technical debate, but it certainly was severe. Unemployment soared to over six million and there was no effective social security system to cope with that degree of destitution. Bankruptcy hit the middle classes and deflation proved to be much more painful than inflation. The situation could have been eased had Schacht's remedies of taxation and spending on public works been adopted, but the government lacked the political will to implement them.

THE IMPLICATIONS OF WEIMAR'S ECONOMIC COLLAPSE

Note the unwillingness of major politicians to take the decisions necessary for economic recovery.

The political implications were vast. The collapse highlighted the inability of the democratic process to deal with disaster and created the demand for authoritarian government. It gave Hitler propaganda material and demonstrated the inability of other politicians to cope. The increased use of Article 48 (which allowed rule without the Reichstag), the growth of Nazism, and the defection of the middle classes to Hitler and of the working class to the KPD all heightened the weakness of Weimar and the sense of crisis. Without the Depression and the way it was managed by German politicians after 1929, Hitler would not have stood a chance.

THE FOREIGN POLICY OF WEIMAR, 1919–24

Versailles dominated German foreign policy from 1919 onwards, with reluctant and partial co-operation as the initial policy. Meanwhile, Germany continued to be viewed as a criminal nation, was excluded from the League of Nations and was invaded by the French in 1923 for non-payment of reparations. The first significant German foreign policy initiative was the Rapallo agreement with Russia in 1922 when two international outcasts agreed to co-operate industrially and commercially. It was a marriage of convenience and provided an opportunity for the Germans to bypass some of the military limitations of Versailles. With Stresemann in control of foreign policy by 1923, reparations were modified favourably by the Dawes Plan of 1924.

STRESEMANN'S ROLE

Gustav Stresemann was a right-wing politician who became the dominant figure of the successful years of Weimar, and gave it credibility and legitimacy. Although only chancellor briefly, Stresemann played a central role in the rehabilitation of Germany in the eyes of the world. He also played an important role in gaining acceptance for Weimar amongst a significant proportion of the Germans. The economic recovery, the intellectual and artistic renaissance and the enjoyment of the freedoms and rights that came with Weimar are partially ascribed to his benign overview. The idea that he tolerated Weimar as it fulfilled his ambitions, and that the German people tolerated Weimar for want of a better alternative, needs consideration.

FOREIGN POLICY, 1924–29

Stresemann dominated German foreign policy in the mid-1920s. Revisionism was his main theme and he paid considerable attention to the idea of collective security and to German borders, in both the east and the west. At Locarno in 1925 he got the western borders of Germany guaranteed, but was promised a review of those in the east. The Treaty of Locarno was vital in international relations in the 1920s and may be considered as a link between the expansionist ideas of the Second and Third Reichs. Stresemann was awarded the Nobel Peace prize for his work at Locarno and for gaining German admission to the League of Nations in 1926, but his reputation as a peace-maker is also based on the Treaty of Berlin with Russia (and its link with the later Nazi–Soviet Pact), his role in the Kellogg–Briand Pact and his contribution to the Young Plan, which appeared at the time to bring the reparations issue to a close. Stresemann's overall contribution to both the peace of the 1920s and the tension which grew after 1929 needs careful and balanced consideration.

FOREIGN POLICY, 1929–33

The focus in the years of economic crisis between 1929 and 1933 was inevitably on domestic affairs, and frequent changes of government led to a lack of consistency. Reparations were halted at Lausanne in 1932, so part of the Versailles settlement disappeared. However, the growth of the right in politics engendered a more aggressive nationalism and there was increasing German resentment about the eastern boundaries of Germany laid down by Versailles. The military started serious planning to end the military limitations of Versailles, which later enabled Hitler's rapid rise to power.

Rapallo made the surprising 1939 Russo–German pact more likely. Note the similarities between the foreign policy of Weimar and that of the 1930s.

Consider how important Stresemann was to the survival of Weimar.

You need to be able to cope with questions which cover German foreign policy between 1919 and 1939.

It is important to note the continuity between the Weimar Republic and Hitler.

Consider whether the foundations of the Weimar Republic were so flawed that it was simply unable to survive real pressure.

An understanding of German politics from 1929 to 1933 is vital to any study of the rise of Hitler.

THE WEAKNESSES OF WEIMAR

The reluctance of the German élites in the army and judiciary to accept Weimar was a factor which helped the growth of extremist parties of both left and right. Even Hindenburg, the elected president, was no strong supporter. Article 48, which allowed rule without the Reichstag, became damaging. Proportional representation produced coalitions which, although initially able to govern, proved incapable in the face of the Depression. There was always a strong anti-democratic feeling in a German political system that had been imposed in a post-war rush and had not evolved slowly, as in other countries. The essential belief in the democratic process was not ingrained.

WHY DID WEIMAR COLLAPSE?

The work of Hitler and the Nazis was vital, and this will be considered later. The unwillingness of the political parties to co-operate to solve the economic crisis was another critical factor. Communists saw the SPD as a greater enemy than the Nazis, and many in the centre would rather have been Nazi than Red. The inability of the political leaders, especially Papen and Schleicher, to work effectively to solve problems was critical, as was simple self-interest. Both the middle and working classes were looking for radical solutions once they had accepted that Weimar would not provide for them. In the end, the Nazis beat the Communist Party to the prize.

Key factors behind the success of Weimar

- the collapse of the military government
- the abdication of the Kaiser
- the failure of revolutions
- the leadership of Ebert and Scheidemann in the early years
- the role of the army and the Freikorps in smashing the left
- the constitution of Weimar
- the granting of civil liberties
- the split opposition
- the ability to solve problems
- the role of Stresemann
- the successful ending of the inflationary crisis
- Locarno and the successful revisionist foreign policy
- the work of Schacht in improving the economy
- the Dawes and Young Plans, which eased the burden of reparations

Key factors behind the collapse of Weimar

- the Treaty of Versailles
- coalition governments
- the novelty of popular democracy and extensive civil liberties
- the use of those freedoms by anti-democrats
- the lack of support from the élites
- the role of the army
- the opposition of the KPD and the right
- the flawed economic foundations
- the Wall Street Crash and the collapse of the banking system
- the skills of Hitler

- the support for Hitler
- the death of Stresemann in 1929
- the ineptitude of leadership after 1929
- the impact of the Depression
- the role of Hindenburg in failing to provide effective leadership
- the use of Article 48, which undermined the democratic process

G The rise to power of the Nazis

Key questions

Why was the Nazi Party weak in the 1920s?

How and why did the Nazis come to power in 1933?

What were the main policies of the Nazi Party between 1919 and 1933, and what was the nature of its appeal?

How important was the role of Hitler in the Nazi accession to power in 1933?

THE ORIGINS OF THE NSDAP

Many of the ideas which Hitler put into practice in the 1930s were in the party he joined in 1919.

The National Socialist German Workers' Party (NSDAP) was created in 1919 by Anton Drexler, a rather limited politician who led one of many similar right-wing groups in the ferment of early Weimar. The party was hostile to Versailles, Jews, communists and big business. Initially it had a tiny membership, among whom there was a strong ex-service mentality from men who had survived the trenches and felt bitter and betrayed by Germany's defeat. When the German army sent Hitler to monitor the NSDAP, he joined it and found he had the political skills to dominate it.

CHANGING NAZI TACTICS, 1919–23

The willingness to adapt and learn was always vital to Hitler's success.

Hitler formalised what had begun as vague prejudices into the 20-point programme of 1920. Its key points were anti-Semitism, anti-communism and anti-Versailles sentiments allied with nationalistic and socialist elements. Hitler became the NSDAP's theorist and principal speaker and honed his skills as an orator and propagandist with a critical understanding of the crowd and of crowd psychology.

THE MUNICH PUTSCH

Consider why Hitler failed in 1923 and yet was able to gain power a decade later.

The Munich Putsch was an illegal attempt to seize power in 1924, modelled on Mussolini's March on Rome in 1922. It was Hitler's first — and possibly his only — tactical error during his rise to power, and revealed an overconfident attitude. Hitler's hope for mass support and help from the Bavarian authorities was dashed. Hitler was jailed, but he received a light sentence for what was high treason and he made full use of the trial for propaganda purposes. He must have noted the sympathy of the judiciary for his nationalistic views, but he learned from this episode that henceforth he had to operate within a legal framework.

Although written off after the failed putsch, Hitler took full advantage of every opportunity to achieve his objectives.

THE DEVELOPMENT OF THE NAZI PARTY BETWEEN 1924 AND 1929

While in jail Hitler wrote *Mein Kampf* (My Struggle). Anti-Semitism dominates a book which has been called the 'intellectual detritus of history' and which sets out a domestic and international blueprint for what Hitler intended to do when in power. He anticipated a popular yet autocratic party operating within the law under a single leader. The growth of the Führer principle starts here and the ideas of *Mein Kampf* were soon to be put into practice.

THE ELECTORAL DEVELOPMENT OF THE NAZI PARTY, 1924–29

Without the preparation of the years after 1924, Hitler would not have stood a chance of attaining power in 1933.

The election results of 1924–28 (especially those of 1928) were a disappointment to a Nazi Party which appeared to be little more than a group on the far right fringe. However, it was a key period of development. Vital subordinates such as Goebbels and Goering came aboard, press barons such as Hugenburg were wooed, and business was contacted with a view to raising funds. The Nazi Party was organised both to present a legal and respectable front and to destroy opponents illegally. The SA (*Sturmabteilung*) was formed and its role developed in order both to smash Nazi opponents by force and to help spread the Nazi message. The country was divided up into *Gaue* (areas) under the *Gauleiters*, who were responsible for spreading Nazism in each area. It was a critical stage in the Nazi take-over of power.

THE CHOICE OF HITLER BY THE CONSERVATIVE RIGHT, 1932–33

Consider the responsibility of the politicians of Weimar for the rise of Hitler.

The Depression and the inability of the governments of the 1929–33 period to tackle it or provide the confidence needed to underpin a recovery was vital for Hitler. His ability to use every opportunity that came his way was exceptional. He exploited the Young Plan to attack Versailles and the shame it brought on Germany and used his connections with the right, his fund-raising abilities, the deployment of the SA and the intrigues and rivalry between politicians such as Brüning and von Schleicher to gain power. The ageing Hindenburg and electoral success also helped the Nazis on their journey from the lunatic fringe of politics.

CENTRAL FEATURES IN THE RISE OF HITLER

A large number of questions centre on how Hitler attained power in Germany in 1933.

Both the weaknesses of Weimar and the skills, planning and appeal of Hitler were vital. He presented himself as all things to all men. The inability of Weimar to solve problems was critical, as was Hitler's ability to present himself as an alternative in ways which eluded the communists and his other opponents. The support of the nationalist right, convinced that it could contain the upstart, was a key element. Also working in Hitler's favour was the growing authoritarianism of Weimar, and the strong anti-democratic ideas of the army, judiciary, police and civil service. The opposition to Hitler was weak. In addition, there was the appeal of the Nazis, their electoral success, the fear of the breakdown of law and order, Hitler's effective propaganda and his sense of what the German people actually wanted.

SUPPORT FOR HITLER: SOCIAL CLASS

One of the most remarkable features about the rise of Hitler was his ability to get so many different types of support.

Although Hitler never gained a majority of votes or parliamentary seats before 1933, he attracted considerable electoral success across the German social spectrum. The aristocratic and the rich liked his anti-communism plus his nationalism and support for big business. The upper middle class, who swung to him

in large numbers from 1931 onwards, liked his anti-communism, his stance on law and order, his authoritarianism and the possibility of his dealing with the deflationary crisis. The lower middle class, always key Nazi supporters, felt he would provide a better alternative than either capitalism or communism and would stop their social and economic decline. The working class, dominant in the vital SA and over a third of the party membership, appreciated Hitler's rabid nationalism and anti-Semitism and felt he would protect them from economic depression and exploitation.

SUPPORT FOR HITLER: OTHER FACTORS

The sheer breadth of Hitler's appeal needs to be stressed once again. The military favoured his expansionist ideals and nationalists liked his ideas on national unity and the revision of Versailles. Hitler's grip on German youth was strong and he gained a larger student following than the communists ever succeeded in gaining. The SA's brutal tactics on the streets were mainly directed against communists and created an impression of the breakdown of law and order. However, Hitler offered scapegoats and solutions and was able to sell the idea that he could solve a problem that he was, in fact, doing much to create.

THE OPPOSITION TO HITLER

Hitler's ability to present himself so as not to appear threatening to the ambitions of others was critical here. Also, his insistence that things were always done legally was vital to the reduction of opposition. There were many opponents or potential opponents to Hitler and he consistently calmed the fears of the latter while neutralising the former. The central reason for the lack of an effective opposition to Hitler was its inability to work together. The communists would not work with the SDP, and the Jews would not work with the Catholics (and vice versa). There was no co-operation either inside or outside the political process of the various groups which opposed Hitler and the Nazis. The wealth and effectiveness of the Nazi organisation were difficult to overcome, and the sheer brutality of the SA was another factor in destroying opposition.

THE OVERALL ROLE OF HITLER IN THE NAZI RISE TO POWER

Hitler's influence is central, and inevitably subject to huge debate. Was his work more important than the weaknesses of Weimar and the scheming incompetence of the politicians of the right? Those who favour 'Big Man' historical interpretations say he was the central figure behind the party organisation and its propaganda. Hitler formed the Nazi policies and dictated the strategies. He made the decisions after the disaster of Munich and determined the nature of the Nazi appeal after 1929, and it was his insistence on a superficial legality which was critical to electoral success in 1933. By this analysis, the Nazi Party would be a footnote in history without Hitler.

THE ROLE OF KEY SUPPORTERS

Obviously other personalities must be considered, for without many key individuals there were limits to what Hitler could have done on his own. Goebbels' propaganda skills — and his use of the radio in particular — were critical. So too were the organisational skills of Goering and his links with the aristocracy. The support of press barons like Hugenburg and machine politicians like Strasser

Hitler understood the people's wishes and allayed their fears by appealing to their prejudices.

Consider how important the incompetence of potential opposition was to the rise of Hitler.

You need to analyse the importance of Hitler's political skills in comparison to other factors.

Another of Hitler's skills was to command great loyalty from competent supporters.

was vital. Röhm and the SA bosses were also fundamental to Nazi advances, while the cash contributions made by business helped electoral success from 1929 onwards, and made the Nazis into a force to be reckoned with in 1932–33.

THE FINAL STAGES

During the latter stages of the Nazi's accession to power in 1932–33, the degree of their electoral success began to wane and Hitler failed to win the presidency against Hindenburg. By this time, Hindenburg was dependent on his son and others, and intrigues and petty rivalries between right-wing politicians like Kurt von Schleicher and Franz von Papen rendered the elected government ineffective. Hitler, resisting pressure from his own supporters for a coup, was eventually invited into office in 1933, with von Papen as vice-chancellor. Von Papen was one of many who thought he could manage Hitler.

> The events of late 1932 and January 1933 have to be learned carefully.

Key factors in the rise of Hitler

- the evolution of his ideas before Munich
- the Munich Putsch
- the writing of *Mein Kampf*
- the reorganisation of the Nazi Party after 1924
- the development of the *Führerprinzip*
- the recruitment of able supporters
- fund raising
- mass unemployment
- Hitler's skills as a propagandist
- Hitler's understanding of crowd psychology
- Hitler's oratorical skills
- Hitler's ability to convince others he could be managed
- the range of his support
- the attitudes of the élites — especially the army
- the role of the SA
- the use of terror and intimidation
- the appeal of his ideas
- Hitler's insistence on the appearance of legality
- key supporters such as Hugenburg
- the role of Hindenburg and von Papen

H The creation of a Nazi state

Key questions

How was Hitler able to create a dictatorship in Germany?

How were the Nazis able to maintain their position in power?

HITLER'S MOTIVES AND THE LEGACY OF WEIMAR

Hitler always saw the legal acquisition of power as the first stage in the Nazi revolution. Once in power, the real revolution would follow. Initially he was

There was a tradition of authoritarian rule, and the last months of Weimar had heightened the need for it.

chancellor, subject to all the limitations of the Weimar constitution, and the only other Nazis in the Cabinet were Frick and Goering. The use of Article 48, which enabled rule without the Reichstag, lay with Hindenburg, but it had been increasingly used and the Reichstag was increasingly marginalised in the 18 months before January 1933.

THE ELECTION OF 1933

The need to attain and retain power legally, through elections, needs noting.

Although the Nazis' 44% share of the vote did not secure a majority in the Reichstag, the 1933 election was a critical stage in the complete take-over of power. The election result was enough to give Hitler the ability to use the main organs of the state — especially the police — to contain opponents, to exploit Article 48 and then to suspend civil liberties after the Reichstag fire. Opponents were intimidated and imprisoned.

THE ENABLING ACT 1933

The Enabling Act was a central plank of Nazi dictatorship.

The Enabling Act removed all key limits to Hitler's power and was thus a vital component in establishing the Nazi dictatorship. The fact that it was an act of the Reichstag gave Hitler the legitimacy he required, though the methods used to get the necessary two-thirds majority included the expulsion of all communist deputies and a coercive pressure on politicians of the centre. After 1933 Hitler could make law and was above the law.

THE ELIMINATION OF OPPOSITION IN 1933

Note that Hitler was still not secure enough in 1933 to eliminate all opposition.

The Enabling Act placed Hitler and his agents in the Gestapo and the SS (Hitler's own army/police force) above the law and accountable to no-one but himself. Intimidation of all possible opponents started and parties apart from the NSDAP were banned. Elections were totally controlled to the extent that only Nazis were elected. The Catholic centre, which was electorally and socially too strong to be destroyed in the same way as the Communist Party, was bought off with promises.

THE ELIMINATION OF OPPOSITION, 1934–35

The Night of the Long Knives illustrates Hitler's political skills and understanding of his opponents.

The SA had been vital in Hitler's rise to power, but it became an embarrassment and an encumbrance. The SA leader Ernst Röhm was impatient at the lack of a real revolution and was worrying the army with his desire for military power using the SA as a base. Hitler dealt with Röhm by organising his murder in June 1934 during the Night of the Long Knives, which was part of a larger plan initially to win the support of the army and then to dominate it. The way in which the SS was used and the way in which possible rivals, such as Strasser, were killed along with other SA bosses should be noted. At this stage, Hitler was selective in his use of terror, in contrast with the incompetence of Mussolini or the indiscriminate cruelty of Stalin.

THE SUBORDINATION OF THE ARMY

Having dealt with the Reichstag, the communists and the SA, Hitler was well aware that the army was the only major group that could seriously threaten his power. He also wanted its total support to enable him to achieve his territorial ambitions. The repression of the SA naturally appealed to the army, and his replacement of Hindenburg by himself as head of state also appealed to short-

Again, note the skill and the varying methods with which Hitler controlled his rivals.

Note Hitler's differing methods to gain support — the mix of the carrot and stick and the use of propaganda.

Consider how important terror was to the establishment and survival of Nazism in Germany.

term military interests. The way in which Hitler discredited the army leadership with clever attacks on Werner von Fritsch (the commander-in-chief, 1934–38) and Werner von Blomberg (the *Wehrmacht* commander-in-chief, 1933–38) was a subtle blend of carrot and stick. He rearmed, which the army loved, but he took increasing control and used both the Gestapo and the SS to watch over and intimidate the generals. Hitler, as the later plots against him revealed, was never totally successful in dominating the army.

OTHER GROUPS OF POTENTIAL OPPONENTS

Hitler was conscious of the limits to his power during the years of peace. He took care not to antagonise the prejudices of major groups, such as the Catholics, and stopped the euthanasia programme when it led to an outcry. He proceeded cautiously on his anti-Semitic policies, not wishing to appear extreme or to resort to outright illegality. He did not confront other religious groups, such as the Protestants, and preferred to absorb the civil service, police and judiciary into the Nazi system. Education and indoctrination and a complete control of the media helped ensure that his message predominated and that none of his opponents' ideas got an airing.

THE USE OF TERROR

Any legal check on Hitler and his agents had gone with the Enabling Act. They could now make the law themselves and the entire judicial process became subordinate to what Hitler defined as the needs of the state. There was small protest on the part of the judiciary. The rights of individuals achieved by Weimar vanished with little apparent regret. Meanwhile, the expanding Gestapo gained in internal power, and the SS became more or less a state within a state under Himmler. The SS had played the key role in killing Ernst Röhm, and was developing concentration camps to deal with opponents of Nazism. All Germany was aware that underneath the veneer of legality lay a system of great brutality which was willing to torture and kill without compunction.

Key factors in establishing the Nazi dictatorship
- the appearance of legality
- the legacy of Hindenburg and Article 48
- the election of 1933
- the Reichstag fire
- the Enabling Act
- the elimination of opposition
- the Night of the Long Knives
- the treatment of the SA
- the treatment of the army
- the relationship with the Church and the élites
- the use of terror
- the control of the police
- the use of propaganda and indoctrination

German foreign policy, 1933–39

Key questions

To what extent did Nazi foreign policy imitate earlier German foreign policy?

How responsible was Hitler for causing the Second World War?

What were the main influences on Nazi foreign policy?

THE LEGACY OF WEIMAR

Revisionism set in with Dawes, Young and Locarno, all of which had modified the terms of Versailles. A working relationship with Russia had been established by the Rapallo and Berlin Treaties. Stresemann had made Germany more respectable at Locarno again, and entrance to the League of Nations was important to German rehabilitation. Germany had signed the Kellogg–Briand Pact, but revisionism had not been neglected either with the eastern clauses of Locarno, which indicated that the boundaries between Germany and its eastern neighbours might be redrawn in Germany's favour. Allied troops were withdrawn and Germany attended the Lausanne Conference of 1932 in the hope of ending the reparations issue. It also attended the Disarmament Conference at Geneva, while secretly making plans to rearm. It could be argued that the foundations for what Hitler intended to achieve were laid in the years before he came to office, and that there was considerable continuity between Weimar and Nazi Germany in this respect.

HITLER'S INTENTIONS

Mein Kampf, although incomprehensible in places and frequently contradictory, contains foreign policy objectives along with the racial ones. The book calls for the subordination of eastern Europe to German interests. Hitler's determination to destroy communism and his craving for land and resources in the East led inevitably to a conflict with Russia and Poland and to the Ukraine's absorption into Germany. Austria and the German speakers of countries like Poland and Czechoslovakia would also be absorbed into the Reich. However, Hitler did not anticipate conflict in the West. He felt that the interests of France and Britain in the destruction of communism need not conflict with those of Germany.

NAZI FOREIGN POLICY, 1933–35: THE INITIAL IDEAS

At first, caution was the main feature of Hitler's foreign policy. He had no military power because of Versailles, no alliances, no secure power base at home and powerful French and Russian armies to consider. The French had allies in eastern Europe, Italy was hostile, and collective security and disarmament were preoccupied with the order of the day. It was not a time for bold ventures. However, the Nazis found encouraging signs. Potential opponents of German expansionism were preoccupied with the Depression. Japan had showed earlier how easy it was to get away with aggression in Manchuria and in doing so had demonstrated that collective security had very obviously not worked. The USA was becoming

Note the continuity between the Second Reich, Weimar and the Nazi regime in foreign policy.

The basic foreign policy ideas of Hitler were always fairly clear.

There was evidence that Hitler could get away with bold moves in foreign and military policy.

more isolationist, divisions between Britain and France were apparent during disarmament talks and the Soviet Union was sinking into the nightmare of the Terror.

THE FIRST STEPS, 1933–35

Note the reasons for Hitler moving carefully at first.

Withdrawal from the League of Nations followed the breakdown of disarmament talks in Geneva. A German non-aggression pact with Poland showed a concilia-tory and diplomatic German face to counter the facts of rearmament, the intro-duction of conscription and the ignoring of the Versailles military clauses. The Nazis had to watch other developments, particularly the Stresa Front, where the British, French and Italians made it clear they were unhappy with German diplo-macy, the Franco–Russian Pact of 1935 and the strong Italian reaction to Hitler's involvement in Austria, when Chancellor Dolfuss was assassinated by Nazis in 1934 and a Nazi seizure of power was attempted. Nazi progress had been made, but it was more limited than Hitler would have wished.

CRITICAL DEVELOPMENTS, 1936

Many see 1936 as the turning point in Nazi foreign policy, with Hitler having secured his power base at home and built up the army, and the economy being in a position to support his strategy. This is linked in with the Four-Year Plan at home and the ideal of self-sufficiency. The Anglo–German naval deal of 1935 (which undermined Stresa, as it encouraged German naval rearmament), the success of Mussolini in Abyssinia, the diversion of Spain, the Anti-Comintern Pact and the start of the Rome–Berlin Axis combined to encourage Germany to remilitarise the Rhineland. It was a small step, considering the Rhineland was part of Germany, but the fact that Hitler got away with it so easily overrode the fears of his generals and enhanced Hitler's position. The open split between Britain and France on how to react to events in the Rhineland, and an apparent reluctance of any major power to act against Germany, were also encourage-ments. The League of Nations had proved useless and collective security was dead.

With the period of consolidation over, Hitler could act decisively. Note also his involvement in the Spanish Civil War, in clear breach of League of Nations rulings.

DEVELOPMENTS, 1937–38

Note the mixture of planning and opportunism.

The year 1937 was vital for Hitler's consolidation and control of the army into a subordinate and less independent agent of the German state. The Hossbach Memorandum revealed Hitler's aggressive military intentions in the East. During 1938, the Nazi movement in Austria was developed to undermine the democratic government and the *Anschluss* came into existence. The work of Seyss-Inquart, the Austrian Nazi ordered to destroy democracy in Austria, and the insistence on at least the appearance of some legality by Hitler ran true to past form. The inability or unwillingness of France, Britain or any other major power to inter-vene in response to the *Anschluss* played a vital role in encouraging Nazi ambitions.

MUNICH

This was perhaps the most significant series of events in the build-up to the Second World War.

A glance at the European map indicated that Czechoslovakia would be the next gain that Germany needed to realise the Polish/Russian ambitions that Hitler had written about in *Mein Kampf*. Encouraged by the inactivity of other powers, and yet still warned to be cautious by his military, Hitler demanded the Sudetenland.

Methods tried and tested during the *Anschluss* were used in Czechoslovakia — unrest was stirred up and unrealisable demands were placed on the Czech leadership. Using Mussolini as the nominal conference head, Hitler got what he wanted at Munich. He ignored the warnings of his military that he might face the united armies of France, the Soviet Union, the Czechs and Britain, and his audacity paid off once again. The impact was far-reaching. The Soviet Union was so disgusted with France and Britain that it moved towards signing the pact with Germany in 1939. This, of course, did nothing to check Hitler's eastward ambitions. The drive that Munich gave to the British rearmament programme should also be noted.

1939

The take-over of the remainder of Czechoslovakia led to the Polish guarantee by Britain and France. But Hitler's experience of Munich led him to believe that he still had a free hand. With the Russian pact sealed and another pact with Italy securing mutual support, Hitler's Germany had the confidence to invade Poland.

THE NAZI–SOVIET PACT

The Nazi–Soviet Pact in 1939 was seen as an amazing *volte face*. How could an anti-communist Nazi state actually do a deal with the head of a regime that it was committed to destroying? Bearing in mind the earlier deal at Rapallo in 1922 when Weimar Germany made an agreement with Russian communists, the deployment of another big lie was not that surprising. The pact gave Hitler security in the East, in case he had to fight in the West. It gave him a large slice of Poland and a much easier spring-board from which to invade the Soviet Union later. The fact that Germany gained access to vital raw materials made further sense.

HITLER'S FOREIGN POLICY: THE GREAT DEBATE

There are many debates on Hitler's foreign policy, particularly as to whether there was continuity with German policy under the Second Reich and during the Weimar years. The extent to which Hitler followed a thought-out plan laid down in *Mein Kampf*, or merely seized opportunities to expand Germany as they came along, is much debated. The extent to which it was Hitler's own policy or the wishes of the German people and the German élites has also been the subject of much debate, as has the question of whether he had continental or global ambitions.

Key factors in German foreign policy to 1935

- the tradition of eastern expansion of the Second Reich
- the Treaty of Brest-Litovsk
- the Treaty of Versailles
- the Treaty of Rapallo with Russia in 1922
- the earlier revisionism of Locarno, especially the eastern boundary clauses
- disarmament
- the ideas expressed in *Mein Kampf*
- Hitler's opposition to the Young Plan, which implied agreement with the Treaty of Versailles
- Manchuria
- the failure of collective security

Consider whether the invasion of Poland was where Hitler made his biggest error.

The Nazi–Soviet Pact was one of the greatest errors that Stalin made.

You won't be expected to know the truth here, but at least be aware of the issues.

- leaving the League of Nations in 1933
- German rearmament
- the Stresa Front — the British/Italian and French attempt in 1935 to contain Hitler
- the Franco–Russian Pact
- the murder of Dolfuss in Austria — the first attempt at a German/Nazi take-over
- the Anglo–German Naval Agreement, which encouraged German rearmament

Key factors in German foreign policy, 1936–39

- the remilitarisation of the Rhineland
- Abyssinia — Mussolini's illegal seizure of another country
- the Hoare–Laval Pact — the British/French agreement which allowed Mussolini to keep Abyssinia
- Hitler's illegal support of the fascists in Spain
- the Hossbach Memorandum, which showed Germany's aggressive eastern policies
- Seyss-Inquart and the *Anschluss* — the illegal take-over of Austria
- the Sudetenland
- Munich
- the Anti-Comintern Pact — the treaty with Italy and Japan
- the brutal friendship with Italy
- the invasion of Czechoslovakia
- the Polish guarantee by Britain and France
- Danzig and the Polish corridor — Hitler's final attempt to expand eastwards without a full war
- the Nazi–Soviet Pact
- the invasion of Poland

J Nazi economic policy

Key questions

To what extent did the Nazis transform German society?

How successful were Hitler's economic policies?

THE NAZI ECONOMY

Mein Kampf talks of the need for German self-sufficiency, but not of how it might be achieved. Apart from promising to end the Depression — and in doing so giving conflicting ideas to industrial workers, students, business people, industrialists and farmers — Hitler was simply not interested. Economics to him was a means to an end. If economic policies won acceptance and enabled him to implement his aims, he was unconcerned about methods. If they involved an unbalanced budget, deficit financing or an adverse balance of payments, he was likewise unconcerned. Economic matters were not things Hitler thought about or discussed in depth and he had no coherent economic policy.

Economics was never a central part of Nazi thinking.

THE EARLY ECONOMIC POLICY

The first 3 years of Nazi power were a mixture of state control and free enterprise. Hjalmar Schacht, president of the Reichsbank, is the key figure here.

He had played a central role in the German economy in the 1920s and produced a variety of ideas on how the Depression might be solved. Hitler was the leader with the political will to implement these ideas. Jobs were created, Germany was rearmed, wages were controlled and union power was broken. The growth of confidence led to a growth of investment. Schacht wanted to stabilise the economy and ensure growth before a huge programme of rearmament started, but he was able to satisfy Hitler's needs and eliminate the worst of the Depression by 1936.

THE FOUR-YEAR PLAN

In 1936, Hitler and Schacht parted company. Hitler's ambitions overrode Schacht's economic realism and he was replaced by the economically illiterate Goering. He aimed for self-sufficiency and a powerful war machine — highly ambitious targets given that vital war materials such as oil and rubber had to be imported. One reason for the eventual failure of Hitler was the lack of resources needed to wage war against the Soviet Union and the USA as well as Britain and France.

THE WARTIME ECONOMY

Hitler failed to improve radically the living standards of most Germans and by 1939 many real wages had dropped in comparison to the 1920s. However, Hitler was seen to have provided jobs and economic stability, although the underlying trends in German economics by 1939 were pointing well away from this direction. Once war started, looting — be it of French lorries or Soviet grain — was central to Nazi survival. There was no serious attempt to use the resources and people of the occupied territories effectively, and it was not until Albert Speer took control of war production that economic efficiency prevailed. If the German economy had been as well organised in 1938 as it was in 1944, then there might (in spite of the bombing) have been a different outcome to the Second World War.

THE IMPORTANCE OF THE ECONOMY TO NAZISM

Economic management and mismanagement were central to the Nazis' rise to power, retention of power and final defeat. The Depression of 1929–33 helped Hitler gain power, his ability to solve unemployment consolidated his position and his failure to use the resources of Germany and the vast occupied territories played a crucial part in his defeat. Tanks ran out of fuel in the Ardennes offensive and he gassed key munitions workers as they were Jews. Logic did not come into it.

THE ECONOMIC IMPACT OF NAZISM

The Depression was solved by 1938. That said, the standard of living for most Germans rose only if 1933 is taken as the starting point (and not 1928). Industrial workers suffered from a decline in real wages, the union ban and longer hours brought on by wartime needs. Employment was virtually guaranteed, however, and there were some benefits to workers from the Nazi unions, such as subsidised holidays. In rural areas, the rich benefited and the agricultural worker suffered as German agriculture remained backward and unproductive. Big business benefited enormously from the war and profits rose massively. Women were initially pushed out of the labour force in order to massage the

The rapid growth in employment from 1933 onwards showed what could be done if the will was there.

A fundamental weakness in Nazism was the lack of resources to implement its ideas.

Do not view the German economy as a model of efficiency. It was not.

Such economic success as existed was essentially short term.

unemployment figures, and then brought back when needed. This provides a good example of the poor use that the Nazis made of German resources.

Key factors to consider about Nazi economics
- not discussed in *Mein Kampf*
- no coherent Nazi economic policy
- disinterest of Hitler
- seen as a means to an end
- work of Schacht
- the easing of unemployment
- the impact of the Depression in Hitler's accession to power
- rearmament
- the Four-Year Plan
- the role of Goering
- the incompetent use of resources
- the overlapping administrations, where several ministries might be given the same task
- the failure to use the resources of captured territories well
- the dream of self-sufficiency

K Nazi racial policy

Key questions
What were the motives behind Nazi racial policy?
How and why was Hitler able to implement his racial policies?

THE INITIAL IDEAS

Note the selective anti-Semitism in the years before the Nazis gained power.

Racism was fundamental to Nazism. Hitler grew up amidst the endemic anti-Semitism of prewar Vienna and anti-Semitism is the main theme of *Mein Kampf*. The book spelled out a wider agenda of total Aryan dominance and it became the Nazi mission to enslave or eliminate other racial and social groups including the alcoholic and the disabled. Racism gave the Nazi system a sense of purpose which almost amounted to a religion; it provided a kind of social cohesion by identifying scapegoats. Racism was not just a part of Nazism, it was its essence.

THE EARLY YEARS

Anti-Semitism was an integral part of Nazism.

In the campaigns of 1929–33, Jewish people were cast as scapegoats rather than a prime target of Nazism. The SA placed more of a focus on the open enemies of the Nazis, such as the communists and the SPD, and there was more anti-Semitic rhetoric than action. There is evidence to suggest that anti-Semitism was down-played officially in order not to antagonise the respectable vote that Hitler was anxious to win. Although anti-Semitism ran deep in German society, Hindenburg was known for his tolerance and the Nazis could not afford to antagonise him at this stage.

THE SEIZURE OF POWER

In early 1933, the SA organised an initial outburst of violence against the Jews. The disorder provoked hostility from people whom Hitler was anxious not to antagonise until he was in absolute control. Hitler saw anti-Semitism as a long-term project which needed to be managed with care. He never got officially involved with extreme SA activities and he restricted Röhm to organising boycotts. There is very little in official documentation of the 1930s that directly links Hitler to the anti-Semitic programme.

Note Hitler's early hands-off approach.

THE FIRST PHASE: INDOCTRINATION

A programme of indoctrination lasted up to 1939 and used all the resources of a totalitarian state to convince the German people that the Jews were a huge problem demanding a solution. The Nazis deployed the propaganda skills of Goebbels, the education system and the Hitler Youth. Many of the finest talents in writing, radio, journalism and film seemed happy to assist in conjunction with the universities and the judiciary. There was no opposition from the Christian churches either in a programme that prepared ordinary German people and soldiers to play their part in the Final Solution.

Massive resources, including state education, were subject to anti-Semitic indoctrination.

THE FIRST PHASE: LEGALISM

Once the Enabling Act had been passed in 1933, Hitler was able to exclude Jews from key posts in the civil service and the judiciary. This was followed by the Nuremberg Laws, when anti-Semitism was made government policy. There was no strong reaction to these measures. The only bar to more rapid progress was a reluctance by Hitler and the top Nazis to offend Hindenburg and the other élites. At the time of the 1936 Olympics, Hitler wished to showcase Nazi Germany without revealing Nazism's brutal aspects. There was therefore a pause in the programme and some restriction was put on the obsessive Julius Streicher, who led the anti-Semitic campaign. Amongst some of the top Nazis there was the attitude that anti-Semitism was just a disadvantage they would have to put up with.

Again, note the flexible — even inconsistent — attitude towards anti-Semitism in the years to 1939.

THE SECOND PHASE

There was a speeding up of the anti-Semitic tempo after 1937, as Hitler felt more secure at home and abroad. The treatment of the German Jews became progressively more barbaric, and more accepted by the German people. The protection of the law was removed from Jews, and the *Kristallnacht* attacks on Jews and their property in 1938 showed what the Nazi regime could do to its citizens and get away with. Evidence of careful news management is the way Goebbels used the murder of a German diplomat by a Jew in Paris to make escalating excesses appear as a spontaneous outbreak of anger by the German people. Meanwhile, Hitler appeared to remain detached from anti-Semitism and there was still some caution in the Nazi approach.

Just as with his foreign policy, the greater security felt by Hitler in the late 1930s led to a more aggressive policy.

THE THIRD PHASE

Nazi intentions were clear in the Polish invasion of 1939 when extermination groups followed the German army with the sole intention of killing Jews. War was also used as a justification for accelerating the murder of German Jews and other groups such as communists and the mentally handicapped. The early

The evidence is that there was widespread involvement by many Germans in the killing process.

Again, though Hitler was not directly involved, there is no way an operation of this size could have been mounted without his involvement.

butchery was inefficiently managed and haphazard, and frequently had very damaging psychological results for those who participated in it. Yet there was no sign of opposition from either the German army or, where they were involved, German civilians.

THE FINAL PHASE

After the German invasion of the Soviet Union, millions more Jews and communist 'undesirables' were brought into the Reich, and Himmler's SS was ordered to take on the Jewish 'problem' in a much more systematic way. Ideas of sending all Jews to Madagascar were now no longer viable, and the Wannsee Conference of 1942 led to the creation of Eichmann's SS organisation to exterminate the Jews and to the full horror of the Holocaust.

Key elements in Nazi racial policies

- Hitler's early experiences in Vienna
- the tradition of German anti-Semitism, which went back to the nineteenth century
- the ideas of the NSDAP advocating anti-Semitism
- *Mein Kampf*
- Aryan race beliefs
- anti-Semitism in Hitler's programmes up to 1933
- the boycott of 1933 — the first open attack on the Jews in Germany
- the indoctrination programme
- the Nuremberg Laws — the state starting to practise anti-Semitism
- the work of Goebbels and Streicher in indoctrinating Germans
- the social exclusion of the Jews after the Enabling Act
- the murder of a German diplomat by a Jew in Paris
- *Kristallnacht* — the mass attack on Jews and their property
- the euthanasia programme
- the *Einsatzgruppen* — the killing squads
- the final extermination programme laid out at Wannsee in 1942

L Nazi opposition and support

Key questions

Why was there so little opposition to the Nazis?

Who supported the Nazis after 1933?

OPPOSITION

There was no tradition of legitimate political opposition in Germany.

There was no tradition of a loyal opposition in German politics, and the need to establish an appearance of legitimacy explains Hitler's anxiety to gain power legally. Social, political and economic opposition to the Nazis before 1933 came from nationalists, the SPD and the communists, but they were unable to keep the Nazis out of power partly through a disunity which, for example, had groups

such as the communists defining the SPD as greater enemies than the Nazis. Throughout this early period, Hitler had a great ability to appear unthreatening.

REASONS FOR THE LACK OF OPPOSITION

All the reasons need to be known, as they are all important. There is no one overriding reason for the lack of opposition to the Nazis.

Hitler's ability to appeal to potential opponents such as the army was remarkably skilful. Big business was also carefully wooed. Propaganda, or what today might be called marketing, was combined with the effective use of terror. At first, terror was not the vast industry in Germany that it was in the Soviet Union, but it existed — as the Night of the Long Knives showed — and all knew it was there. The fact that Hitler was elected to power, appointed by Hindenburg and worked hard to convince the Germans that he was acting in their interests, was vital. Once the war started, then opposition inevitably became even more treasonable and difficult than it had been in peacetime.

OPPOSITION TO THE NAZIS: THE LEFT

A divided and purged left was a major reason for Nazi success.

The left was the largest group, but it was bitterly divided. Communist opposition was weakened by the Nazi–Soviet Pact, and Stalin killed several key leaders of the German Communist Party as part of his purges. It was not until too late that the communist leadership realised how dangerous an enemy Nazism was. At the same time, brutality, propaganda and the law banning political parties made it difficult for groups like the SPD to organise on anything other than a tiny scale.

OPPOSITION TO THE NAZIS: THE RIGHT

The broad support for many Nazi policies among the upper classes was another important factor in the lack of opposition.

Much of the German aristocracy disliked Hitler as an upstart Austrian corporal, but his endorsement by Hindenburg and the alliance with von Papen in the coalition government of 1933 gave him enough respectability. The Oath of Loyalty taken by the officer corps also helped. The fact that Hitler reunited Germany and left the traditional élites in the army and the Foreign Office alone was clever. On the whole, the right did not oppose Nazism because it posed no real threat to their social status and Hitler's anti-communist, anti-Semitic policies had their support. There were no Jews in the upper ranks of the army or the Foreign Office.

THE MILITARY OPPOSITION

Military opposition was both limited in objective and isolated. This perhaps indicated support for the regime and its motives.

The military was the only group to pose a major threat to Hitler, and he knew it. The Gestapo watched military leaders carefully, and the way in which Fritsch and Blomberg were publicly humiliated shows an astute understanding of military threats from within. Attempts by one or two soldiers to remove Hitler before the war failed as, by and large, he was doing what the officer corps wanted him to do. Once the war started, there was little sign of opposition, apart from heroic gestures like that of the Munich students who formed the White Rose movement in an attempt to stop the war. It was not until it was clear that the war was going to be lost that serious opposition started. Von Moltke and his aristocratic friends could have provided some leadership, but they could do little without middle-class support. The strongest opponents of the Nazis were always the communists, but middle-class and aristocratic Germans would not work with them. The July Plot to assassinate Hitler in 1944 needs noting, but it is worth remembering that the plotters only wanted to stop the war in the West, not the East, and that nothing was mentioned about ending the Holocaust. Perhaps the lack of military opposition was mainly due to the fact that most of its leaders were, at the very least, tacit Nazis.

Consider how difficult it
was to oppose Nazism.

OTHER POTENTIAL OPPONENTS

Apart from successful Catholic opposition to the Nazis' euthanasia programme, there was little effective response from the churches. Hitler's anti-communism had an appeal, and carefully directed propaganda managed to avoid offending too many Christian sensibilities. The Concordat agreement between the Nazis and the Roman Catholic Church was an example of the highly ambivalent relationship between Nazism and the Christian churches. Other key leaders of society, in education, law, the civil service and the police, seemed broadly in agreement with the main direction of Nazi policy, or preferred to ignore it. The majority of these groups joined the Nazi Party and certainly gave the appearance of open endorsement. The lack of any tradition of opposing the legitimate government was important here, as was Hitler's care in preventing any possible focus for opposition by not alienating key groups. Whereas Stalin killed powerful opponents, Hitler tried to prevent opposition.

SUPPORT FOR THE NAZI REGIME

Central to Nazi success was the fact that until the war Hitler gave most Germans what they wanted. He marketed himself brilliantly, solved the Depression, brought status back to Germany and overthrew the Versailles Treaty. The army expanded, and this delighted the officer corps; the rich got richer; and the status of the upper middle class was not threatened by deflation or inflation. A mixture of carrot and stick kept the urban and rural working classes in order, and propaganda convinced women of the importance of their role. Care was taken to see how the interests of each group in society could be matched with the current needs of the Nazi state.

Was the main reason
for the lack of
opposition the lack of
any alternative?

Key factors in the lack of opposition to Hitler

- the lack of a tradition of political opposition
- the divisions within and between his opponents
- the broad appeal of Nazism
- Hitler's legality
- Hitler's ability to fulfil the aspirations of many Germans
- the endorsement of Hindenburg and the politicians of the right
- Hitler's skilful propaganda
- Hitler's use of terror
- Hitler's ability to seem harmless initially

M The Nazi system of government

Key questions

How effectively was Germany governed under the Nazis?

What type of government did Hitler create in Germany?

DUPLICATION AND CHAOS

In some cases the Nazis left existing institutions and officials in place, as long as they were loyal and obedient to the Nazi state. In other cases Hitler appointed Nazis to key roles, such as police chiefs, and ensured control in that way. The Nazis also created new and rival administrations which would conflict with the old ones: for example, pitting the Reich governors and *Gauleiters* against existing local government structures. Who had control of what was never worked out and there was duplication and chaos. Goering was put in charge of the Four-Year Plan, but his relationship with the economics ministry and the Reichsbank was never clarified. Nazi youth leaders argued endlessly with the education department which, in turn, clashed with Goebbels' propagandists.

The government of Nazi Germany was not a model of efficiency.

AN ANALYSIS OF NAZI GOVERNMENT

Historians debate whether the Nazis operated a deliberate divide and rule policy or were simply incompetent. A brief look at *Mein Kampf* does not reveal evidence of an ordered or rational mind, so it is hardly surprising that the Nazi movement reflected a lack of interest in anything to do with administration. There is a strong argument to say that if German resources had been effectively organised, then the Second World War might have had a very different outcome.

There is a case to be made out for Hitler deliberately creating rival administrations in order to divide and rule.

INDOCTRINATION AND PROPAGANDA

The breadth and depth of Nazi indoctrination was remarkable and spread throughout education and culture. One of the Nazis' first actions when in power was the creation of the Ministry of Enlightenment and Propaganda. This was the world's most systematic attempt to gain control of the minds of a people. Culture was dictated from the top and what was defined as music or poetry or art was laid down by a government determined to use culture as an instrument for gaining domination by influencing the thinking of its people.

Goebbels' control of both education and the media shows the overarching nature of Nazi propaganda.

CONTROL OF THE MASS MEDIA

The Nazis were the first to realise the propaganda potential of a radio network that transmitted to over 16 million radios in Germany. Journalists became instruments of state propaganda, artists had to paint themes which followed Nazi guidelines, and writers and poets had to subordinate their work to state directives and echo anti-Semitic or social Darwinist (survival of the fittest) guidelines. In a comprehensive attempt to dominate the thinking of a people, the Nazis aimed to educate, persuade and influence, rather than relying totally on terror as Stalin did.

Consider how important control of the media was to the success of the Nazi regime.

EDUCATION AND THE YOUTH MOVEMENTS

Under Hitler, German education became the first twentieth-century attempt at mass indoctrination. All forms of schooling were subordinated to the Nazi machine and the syllabus was rewritten to encourage anti-Semitism and to indoctrinate with other racist ideas. The study of biology, for example, was subordinated to racial theory, and history books were rewritten to prove Hitler's theories correct. Good Nazis were more important than educated citizens in a system where the objective was to create efficient and loyal fighting men and to turn women into Third Reich breeding machines. When not being

Hitler was prepared to sacrifice potentially important parts of the curriculum, such as engineering, in order to inculcate Nazism's racial ideals.

indoctrinated at school, children had to be involved in the Hitler Youth and its female equivalent.

HOW TOTALITARIAN WAS THE SYSTEM CREATED IN NAZI GERMANY?

Could Hitler be described as a 'popular' dictator?

Nazi Germany embodied all the hallmarks of a totalitarian system: terror, censorship, secret police, racism, aggression, barbarism and the appalling treatment of any opposition. The wish of one individual was dominant and opponents — whether Jews or generals — died. The crucial question is whether Hitler could have behaved as he did without massive support. The media echoed and praised Hitler's views and he was able to indoctrinate the young and intimidate the various élites. But does this explain the lack of real opposition or was Hitler operating on the basis of genuine support?

Key issues in Nazi government

- the inefficiency of the system of administration
- the duplication of administrative jobs
- the indoctrination of the people
- the rigorous control of education
- the use of education for indoctrination
- the Nazi youth movements and their indoctrination programmes

A Russia, 1815–55

Key questions

What problems and challenges faced the tsars of Russia in the period?

To what extent did the reign of Nicholas I represent 30 wasted years?

How much did political authority change in Russia in this period?

THE BACKGROUND TO RUSSIA IN REVOLT

Remember Russia's size, that its population was the largest of any European power and that — having absorbed the Cossacks, Ukrainians and Mongols — it was an Asiatic power as well. It was an almost totally agricultural nation where 96% of the population were peasants, about half of them serfs. The remaining 4% of the population was split between the aristocracy and the middle class. There was a strong tradition of autocracy going back for centuries. Though influential, the Church was subordinate to the state's needs, and the tsars had divine rule, a vital factor in their autocracy.

> Russia was fundamentally different from any other European country.

ALEXANDER I

Tsar Alexander I (1777–1825) provides an example of how Russian events were a reflection of autocratic power. His two main motives were a wish to improve and a fear of disorder, and this odd mixture of the liberal and the reactionary dominated his reign at home and abroad. Personally well educated, Alexander I put through superficial reforms such as army modernisation and the expansion of universities, the latter measure being potentially dangerous because an educated middle class deprived of power can prove difficult to govern.

> Note the mixture of liberalism and repression and see later how it was to return.

ALEXANDER I'S FOREIGN POLICY

As a victor against Napoleon Bonaparte, Alexander I was determined to repress any further invasions or the spread of revolutionary ideas. The Quadruple Alliance and above all the Holy Alliance, with its determination to repress revolution, were dominant influences in this thinking. He saw opposition to revolution as a divinely inspired role, and played a part in the repression of revolution — and liberal and nationalistic ideas — in Greece, Spain, Portugal and Naples. Russian expansionism continued (Poland and territories around the Black Sea were gained), and this continued to be a worry to Western powers. Ironically, after taking over Poland, Alexander granted the Poles a constitution and a parliament, and there is an idea that these might have been a blueprint for Russia itself. However, the Poles continued to loathe Russian rule.

> Russia became a significant force in international relations.

THE REIGN OF NICHOLAS I AND THE DECEMBRIST REVOLT

The Decembrist revolt took place just after the death of Alexander I. The plotters were a mixture of army officers, middle-class intellectuals and dissident nobles with freemason links. They had many differing aims, including a constitutional monarchy, elections, the ending of serfdom and legal reform. Though they were united by hostility to autocracy and influenced by the ideas of revolutionary

> The Decembrist revolt was the first of many against tsarist autocracy. Note the reaction to it.

and Napoleonic France, there was a split between the northern and the southern groups and the divided movement had no leadership. The revolt, however, had a great influence on Nicholas I and gave revolutionary Russia its first martyrs.

NICHOLAS I'S PERSONALITY

Note the nature and extent of Nicholas I's autocracy.

Strongly influenced by the Decembrist revolt and also by the French revolution and Polish revolt of 1830, Nicholas I's initial mildness disappeared rapidly. Orthodoxy, autocracy and nationality were his watchwords and the policy of Russification (imposing Russian ideas, language and practices on non-Russian nations such as the Georgians) was a paramount concern. Otherwise Nicholas was opposed to any change, obsessed with military matters and convinced of the divine backing for his mission. Under his rule there was a codification of the legal system. The other important factor to note was the restraining influence allowed to Nesselrode (Foreign Secretary, 1815–56) in foreign policy, where he did much to keep the Tsar out of war.

NICHOLAS I'S GOVERNMENT

Incompetence was the hallmark of Nicholas I's administration.

Autocracy proved inefficient. All decisions had to be taken by the Tsar in a corrupt and centralised system which had an unwieldy bureaucracy. The issue of how one person could run such a vast country was not raised, for Russia was a police state, with censorship, informers, and arrest and imprisonment without trial. There were no actual plots — bar mild nationalistic demonstrations in the Ukraine and the discovery of the Petrashevsky circle (a debating society of radicals and reformers) in 1849. In 1826 Nicholas created the Third Section, the secret police designed to keep down political unrest. They were initially to have welfare as well as repressive functions, but the former were rapidly forgotten.

THE ARMY UNDER NICHOLAS I

The Russian army was not the major force that many western European powers feared it might be.

Military matters dominated Nicholas I's life. He loved dressing up in military uniform and having parades. The huge conscript army was brutally run and highly inefficient and had a weak officer corps, which was recruited from a nobility that valued rank above military skills. Some competence in artillery and fortifications was offset by a strong belief that it was the bayonet which won wars and this proved expensive in the Crimea, when thousands of infantrymen were killed in battles like Inkerman. Victory over the Persians, which gained Persian Armenia for Russia, and the Turks at Sinope, came about because their armies and navies were even more incompetently run. During these campaigns more men died of disease and neglect than in battle.

FOREIGN AND MILITARY POLICY BEFORE THE CRIMEAN WAR

Note the vital role of Russia in 1848.

The Polish revolt of 1830 was crushed, but incompletely, and the problem returned. Persian Armenia was gained by 1830, and Asiatic Russia was consolidated. Russia helped destroy the Turkish fleet at Navarino in 1827, which moved Greece towards independence (a fact often omitted from British history textbooks), but then helped Turkey smash a nationalist revolt in Romania. In 1848 the Tsar played a major role by intervening in Austria-Hungary to restore the Habsburgs and Metternich.

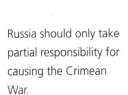
THE CRIMEAN WAR: THE RUSSIAN ROLE IN ITS CAUSES

Russia should only take partial responsibility for causing the Crimean War.

Nicholas I did not have the acquisitive tendency of which the British suspected him. He did not want Constantinople, but did not want anyone else to have it either. He wanted to influence rather than fight Turkey, and did not want Austria to dominate the Balkans. He feared the disruptive impact of breaking up the Turkish empire, and was only partly responsible for the outbreak of the Crimean War. For prestige and moral reasons he felt he had to protect the Orthodox Christians in the Turkish empire. His intervention in the Danube provinces and at Sinope was seen as provocative by the British and French, but — given the issues in the region — as necessary preventive action. With the Turkish empire collapsing, Russia was not going to allow another power to take over Turkey.

THE CRIMEAN WAR: COURSE AND RESULTS

You should have a basic knowledge of the geography of the region.

Russian military incompetence lost it most of the military battles against Britain in the Crimea, though its army proved a match for the even more disorganised Turks in the Caucasus. Where fortification and artillery came into play at the siege of Sevastopol, then the Russians did better. Given the course of the war, the Peace of Paris in 1856 was not too damaging, though the loss of a Russian fleet on the Black Sea was humiliating and there was a loss of initiative in the Danube area. This led to the creation of a Romania less susceptible to Russian influence. The overall loss of status amounted to a clear statement to the world that Russia was not yet a great power.

THE IMPACT OF THE CRIMEAN WAR ON RUSSIA

The Crimean War was significant in bringing change to Russia.

Just as the British disasters in the Crimea led to reform, so the same happened in Russia. The failings of the army at all levels led to a questioning of the system which lay behind it. There was not only a demand for change but a realisation at the top that change had to come. This challenged basic assumptions about the autocracy of the tsars, the system of conscription and the serfdom which underlay it. The inability of the Russian economy to cope with the attacks and the resources of the sophisticated economies of countries like Britain was also noted. The domination of conservative forces in Russia began to be weakened.

NICHOLAS I'S REIGN

It is important to note the very different development in Russia compared to the rest of Europe in this period.

There is a tendency to view Nicholas I's reign as '30 wasted years'. Given the huge social, intellectual and economic progress made by most of Europe, Russia was stuck in an autocratic time warp, with the signs of change that had been apparent under Alexander I disappearing. Russia continued to expand territorially, but did not show any sign of creating the political institutions capable of extending government. There were really only two significant developments: the first was the growing system of repression by the Third Section; and the second was the growth of an educated minority which was more prepared to challenge the system.

Key factors during Nicholas I's reign

- the Decembrist revolt
- the Polish revolt
- the focus on orthodoxy, autocracy and nationalism
- the Crimean War and its impact

Key changes during the reigns of Alexander I and Nicholas I
- the army under Alexander I
- education under Alexander I
- the Holy Alliance — the attempt to repress liberalism and nationalism in Europe
- Poland
- expansionism and interventionism in foreign policy
- the Third Section — the secret political police
- the role of the army under Nicholas I

B Alexander II's reign

Key questions

Why did the reforms of Alexander II fail to make the Romanovs more popular?

How much did political authority change in Russia under Alexander II?

How much were social, economic and religious changes linked to political changes?

THE ROLE OF THE TSAR

Alexander II (1855–81) has had a mixed press ranging from 'Tsar Liberator' to 'medieval autocrat'. He was well educated, widely travelled and sophisticated, and there were many reforms during a rule which saw considerable economic and social change, such as the emancipation of the serfs. He stayed out of war on the whole, yet there was considerable expansion of Russian territory. However, the big question mark over him was his reluctance to consider how Russia was governed from the top. Was he tinkering with the regime's peripheral problems rather than taking on the central issue?

EMANCIPATION OF THE SERFS: THE BACKGROUND

One thing which the Russians shared with the Americans in 1855 was slavery. The serfs were a neglected section of the population who could be bought and sold. They had only been a factor in Russian history when, as with Pugachev, they had revolted, and barbaric repression was the result. The serfs had an obligation to work for their noble masters with no reciprocal benefits and no tradition of concern for their welfare. Note the role of the *Mir* (the village organisation), the allocation of common land and the essential conservatism of the serfs, which was reflected in their dislike of any modernisation of agricultural practices. The whole social structure was archaic and led to a highly uneconomic and inefficient use of land in a system where agricultural improvement was rendered virtually impossible.

THE EMANCIPATION

Even in autocratic Russia, serfdom was becoming an anachronism. The fear of another Pugachev plus the realisation of the need to modernise were major factors behind emancipating the serfs. The state could not be modernised with slavery for a base. The basic principles of reform were that serfs should get a

You need to focus on the nature of the change under Alexander II.

The serfs, and later the peasants, were a conservative and regressive force.

Serf amancipation was a major reform which alienated many from the regime.

measure of freedom and land tenure; there should be compensation for the landlord/owner; and no landless proletariat should be created. The demerits of the system were that there was simply not enough good land to satisfy both freed serf and landlord, and that an impoverished peasantry was in no position to compensate landlords. This produced an embittered nobility (even though compensated by government) and an embittered peasantry which felt it had to pay for what it saw as its own.

EMANCIPATION: THE RESULTS

In what ways could emancipation of serfs be seen as a success?

Emancipation satisfied few. The nobles feared loss of status and property, and although compensated they felt that the compensation was insufficient. Few of the peasants actually paid, partly because they couldn't and partly through a refusal to pay for what they saw as communal land. Little land improvement was possible and most holdings were small and inefficient. Subsistence farming was the norm and the low output of Russian agriculture remained, in spite of some of the most fertile soil in the world. The embittered peasantry became much more prone to disorder. Whether a better solution could have been devised is arguable.

THE ECONOMY AND INDUSTRY UNDER ALEXANDER II

As in other countries, economic change was to lead to social and then political change.

Under Nicholas I, the demand for a balanced budget and a fear that industrialisation would produce a dangerous revolutionary force in an industrial proletariat were the major influences on economic policy. Only the railways made progress. Under Alexander II, there was a fundamental change in attitude. Starting with tariff reform, there was encouragement to develop local industries in textiles, iron and steel, coal and oil. Foreign entrepreneurs were brought in and a mixture of state help and private enterprise helped development. The great acceleration was to start later, but the positive change of attitude by the state was important.

LEGAL REFORMS

Legal reforms were to Alexander's II's credit, but may have weakened his regime.

The Russian judicial system under Nicholas I had become even more archaic, incompetent, confused and cruel. Alexander II's reforms of 1864 introduced the legal right to a defence, developed a jury system of trial, increased the supply and quality of independent judges and allowed free speech in court. Although there were loopholes which benefited the state, the popular legal reforms are generally judged Alexander II's greatest success. They also weakened the government as the Zasulich case showed, with its public humiliation of the whole tsarist system of repression.

MILITARY REFORMS

With long frontiers and neighbours like the Turks, a standing army — albeit an expensive and incompetent one — was a necessity. Military disasters in the Crimea prompted calls for reform, and the speedy destruction of the French army by Russia's neighbour, Prussia, also reinforced the need for change. Note the work of Milyutin (the war minister in 1861–81) in areas such as conscription and officer training. Conscription was drastically changed and the service for life altered. The right to become an officer was extended to all classes — a reform hated by the

Russia was too undeveloped to support a modern army.

nobles and middle classes. Better military education was brought in, administration and logistics were improved and a staff college was created. However, the economic infrastructure was not sufficiently developed to support an army to rival industrialised nations — as the wars with Japan and Germany were to show in the next century — and a lack of sufficient resources was a serious failing.

EDUCATION

The issue of how to develop education, while at the same time retaining total obedience to the state, was not resolved. Initially restricted after the unrest of 1861, universities were expanded and allowed greater freedom. Secondary education was also developed and literacy rose considerably. There was a literary revival, with Tolstoy, Turgenev and Dostoyevski producing some of the greatest works of Russian literature. The change here was both a relaxation and a reform, but it did not produce contentment, only demands for much more radical reform and change.

LOCAL GOVERNMENT REFORM

The role of *zemstva* (locally elected assemblies) needs to be seen as part of Alexander II's whole reform programme. The reforms had some effect in education, health and welfare and there was a limited participation in decision-making. Arguably the changes were too little and happened too late to establish any form of democratic process. Others argue that the local government reforms were the first step towards a modern liberal state.

ALEXANDER II'S FOREIGN POLICY

Alexander II was concerned by pan-Slavism and the rise of Prussia. He also got Russia involved in a war against the Turks to help the Christians in the eastern European/Balkan part of the Turkish empire. He listened too much to the aggressive Milyutin (war minister, 1861–81). Apart from defeating the Turks at Plevna in 1877, the Russian army was ineffective. Russia initially did well out of this war by the Treaty of San Stefano in March 1878, particularly in Bulgaria. However, these gains were wiped out later in 1878 at the Treaty of Berlin, and Russia got virtually nothing from an expensive war. Russian prestige was lost, and the Tsar's popularity suffered.

THE GROWTH OF REVOLUTIONARY IDEAS IN THE 1860S

The development of the universities and the growth of an intelligentsia was bound to lead to challenges to the system. The ideas of Herzen (a radical writer and socialist thinker) spread rapidly. Various student groups evolved after the outburst of radicalism in the universities in 1863. There were many different and often contradictory strands of radicalism emerging in the 1860s, including the ideas of the anarchist Bakunin, and the nihilists who opposed everything. The Polish revolt of 1863 and the Land and Liberty movement — which wanted to give all land to the peasants and abolish the state — were also important influences.

REVOLUTIONARY IDEAS IN THE 1870S: THE POPULISTS

The populists, also known as the *Narodniki*, propounded a revolutionary socialism based on the peasants, in an anti-capitalistic idealisation of the traditional agricultural communes and the *Mir*. Their non-violent approach was opposed by more violent radicals such as Bakunin. The peasants declined to be radicalised and their minds were not won over. The *Narodniki* mostly ended up in Siberia, free to practise agriculture as they wished. Their failure naturally led to an increased focus on more radical and revolutionary methods.

An expanded education system and autocracy proved incompatible.

Were changes to local government damaging to autocracy?

Alexander II's foreign policy damaged Russia.

Consider how radical ideas could have best been managed by Alexander II.

Note the inability of the revolutionaries to make much impact on the peasants.

REVOLUTIONARY IDEAS IN THE 1870S: THE RADICALS

The other main strand of radical development was the Land and Liberty group, which was more prepared than the *Narodniki* to use violence. Land and Liberty was weakened by personality clashes and divisions between those who were prepared to kill opponents and those who were not. A serious campaign of violence started in 1880, and they killed the Tsar in 1881. The populist movement was ended by this act and the course was firmly set for 1917, by which time a revolutionary leadership had learned that westernisation and socialist ideas did not appeal to the peasantry.

This was a vital step towards 1917.

Alexander II's key reforms

- emancipation of the serfs and its impact on agriculture, the nobility and the serfs
- the legal system
- the military
- education
- local government

Key changes in the period

- the reforming atmosphere
- territorial expansion
- industrial growth
- the impact of emancipation
- foreign investment
- development of civil rights and liberties
- modernisation of the military
- growth of an educated middle class
- the literary revival
- increased participation in government
- the growth of revolutionary ideas and activities
- increased militarism

C Alexander III's reign

Key questions

How did political authority change in Russia during Alexander III's reign?

What was the significance of the reign of Alexander III to the development of revolution in Russia?

By what means did Alexander III attempt to maintain his regime?

ALEXANDER III'S REIGN

Note the complete contrast with Alexander II.

Alexander III's reign between 1881 and 1894 was in marked contrast to that of Alexander II. He was a much tougher and firmer character who did not believe in concession. His advisers were more strongly conservative, he was determined to uphold autocracy and equally determined to destroy the liberalism which he felt had led directly to his predecessor's assassination.

THE REASSERTION OF AUTOCRACY

Alexander III realised how dangerous education could prove to autocracy.

More power was given to the police, especially in cases seen as political. The press was more tightly controlled. Universities were more carefully scrutinised with access restricted to all but a few from the upper classes. There was a radical change of attitude by the whole government to anything that hinted at dissent, and Siberian exile grew rapidly. The Third Section, the secret police, became a more dominant part of government.

THE CHANGE IN LOCAL GOVERNMENT

Major long-term causes of the Russian Revolution can be seen here.

The short tradition of devolving power to the locality was altered and centralisation — with all its incompetence and delay — returned. The roles of the *zemstva* (locally elected assemblies), in the countryside, and their urban counterparts, the municipal *dumas*, were restricted and care was taken to ensure that their membership was restricted to approved classes of people. The slowly growing middle class was excluded from government and restrictions were reimposed on the peasants, with the Land Captain system enforcing discipline in rural areas. These impositions on the peasants reduced their status and lost the regime a strong conservative ally. The regime was beginning to base its support on a tiny, if wealthy, minority.

THE GROWTH OF RUSSIAN NATIONALISM

Russification was a major cause of the revolution.

The growth of Russian nationalism was significant in Alexander III's reign. In an official policy known as Russification, there was discrimination against all non-Russian minorities, including Jews, Armenians and Finns. Local liberties were taken away and direct control from the Russian capital was established. This was damaging to the regime because it encouraged disadvantaged minorities to get involved in opposition and fuelled the Bolshevik appeal to separate nationalities.

THE INFLUENCE OF POBEDONOSTSEV

Note another link between the forces of reaction and the revolution.

The influence of K. P. Pobedonostsev — the procurator general of the Holy Synod — on Tsar Alexander III was crucial. A profound conservative, Pobedonostsev stressed Alexander's divine mission and the need to retain autocracy. His opposition to any sort of reform or economic progress was crucial, and it could be argued that by the time of Alexander III's death it was too late to adapt the system to modern conditions. Reaction was now too great a part of tsarism.

THE ECONOMY IN ALEXANDER III'S REIGN: AGRICULTURE

There is clear evidence here of the economic causes of the later revolution.

There were significant changes in agriculture which were to have a great impact on tsarism as well as on the peasants. The growth of the landless peasant was a destabilising factor in the countryside, and more land fell into the hands of the rich. Huge pressure on land came through a growing population, falling world food prices and a decline in the peasantry's purchasing power. Taxation was also high on the peasants, and their poverty led to the alienation of an important conservative group. Remember that the peasantry still made up the vast bulk of a population where famine was common, and where limited industrialisation meant there was little alternative work away from the land.

THE ECONOMY IN ALEXANDER III'S REIGN: INDUSTRY

The growth in Russian industry may have been large by Russian standards, but

it was small when measured against what was going on in Britain and Germany. Although Russia acted like an industrial state, it was not in a position to compete in times of war. Sergei Witte (the finance minister 1892–1903 and prime minister 1905–06) mixed foreign and state intervention, with the aim of establishing self-sufficiency and great power status. However, a disregard for the living and working conditions of industrial workers proved a barrier to industrialisation. As unions were outlawed and the government sided with employers, so more hostile groups were created, and the industrial workers began to emerge as the spearhead of revolution.

The capacity of the Tsar to make enemies grew.

GROWTH OF RADICAL OPPOSITION TO THE TSAR'S AUTOCRACY

The major developments came after Alexander III. The impact of Marxism on leaders like Plekhanov — one of the early radicals of the 1870s — grew, as did the organisation and coherence of the more moderate liberals in the *zemstva*. Opposition was fuelled by banning many talented young men from universities, thus forcing them into opposition. The attacks on minorities such as the Jews created more opponents, as did mistreatment of the urban proletariat.

By the end of Alexander III's reign there were opposition leaders, and plenty prepared to follow them.

Key changes during Alexander III's reign

- the return of autocracy
- police powers
- repression
- education restricted
- peasant status declined
- rise of an aristocratic élite
- Russian nationalism
- discrimination against minorities
- the increasing influence of the Church in society
- agricultural decline
- industrial growth
- radical opposition

D Nicholas II's reign

Key questions

What problems and challenges faced Nicholas II?

How stable was the Russian state in the period 1906–14?

How and why was Nicholas II able to survive the 1905 revolution?

NICHOLAS II'S REIGN

The reign of Nicholas II between 1894 and 1914 is always seen as part of the build-up to the revolution in 1917. At the beginning of his rule, autocracy still had its supporters and there was no uniform demand for change because opposition groups were divided about means and ends. The regime made many errors and was seemingly bent on antagonising its opponents, though many have argued that, until the pressure of the First World War, it was in a position to have survived. But whereas Alexander III realised the wisdom of staying out of war, Nicholas II involved himself in two disastrous campaigns.

ECONOMIC CHANGES UNDER WITTE

Although he was appointed under Alexander III, Witte's work had greatest impact in Nicholas II's reign. The focus on heavy industry and railways brought about rapid change and revealed Russia's potential. Economic advances could have been used to strengthen and adapt the regime, but potential gains were lost. An angry and hungry industrial workforce, damaged by inflation, listened to radical messages from Marxists and perhaps also inspired too much confidence in Russia's leaders about their war-making potential.

THE 1905 REVOLUTION

There is much debate about the causes and significance of the 1905 revolution. The regime was badly damaged by Russia's feeble naval and military perform-ance against Japan. This mobilised a range of opposition from industrial workers under Father Gapon marching to the Winter Palace in 1905, to city-wide strikes in Moscow and Petersburg, to serious military unrest, to a revolt of hungry peasants deprived of land. The first soviets were created and demonstrated the spread of Marxist and other socialist ideas.

THE IMPACT OF 1905

Perhaps the only comfort that the regime obtained from 1905 were the divisions amongst its opponents — the Bolsheviks and Mensheviks, the Constitutional Democrats, the Social Revolutionaries and the Union of the Russian People. Their ideas ranged through all shades of left-wing thinking from the moderate liberal to the anarchist. The Tsar reacted savagely and both the police and the military were brutal. However, there were constitutional concessions which, if carefully managed, could have split the radical and constitutional opponents and provided the basis for more gradual change.

CONSTITUTIONAL CHANGES AFTER 1905

Awareness of the need for change was forced home after the widespread dissent shown in 1905. The decision had to be made as to whether to follow the methods of Alexander III or the zemstva/mir tradition of Alexander II. The historical consensus is that Nicholas II was determined to retain his autocracy, and that the changes made were only token concessions to buy off opposition until the regime became stronger. Note on one side the contents of the October Manifesto, which promised reform, and on the other the role of the Duma and the State Council, the elections and the parties which participated (and those which did not). The Fundamental Laws of 1906 showed the true spirit of the regime and revealed an autocracy that sought a superficial cloak of liberal respectability.

ECONOMIC CHANGE AFTER 1905

There was a period of rapid growth after the 1905 revolution. This was fuelled by private enterprise and less government restriction, combined with more of a focus on consumer goods and less on heavy industry and infrastructure. However, the heavy industrial sector did not expand rapidly enough and Russia was still in no

---

Do not assume that the Russian Revolution was inevitable.

Economic changes both strengthened and weakened the regime.

The 1905 revolution shocked the regime and inspired its opponents.

The chance of realistic change to save the regime was perhaps lost in 1905.

The tsarist regime could have adapted to meet the wishes of many Russians.

There were signs of both optimism and pessimism for the regime here.

position to compete effectively with Germany and Britain. There were beneficial agricultural changes, with improvements to the peasants' redemption payments and the creation of the Land Bank to help investment in agriculture. Agricultural techniques were also improved, particularly where land holdings increased in size. However, these reforms tended to benefit mainly the richer peasants and left a desperately poor and potentially dangerous social group among the very poor.

SOCIAL CHANGE UNDER NICHOLAS II

Was this the Tsar's biggest missed opportunity?

There were signs of awareness that the regime had few friends, bar the rich and powerful. Alienation had gone deep and wasn't lessened by the lifting of restrictions on unions and associations, or the introduction of health insurance after 1905. There was limited factory reform and increased spending on education, but these social advances were too limited and too late.

THE DUMAS

Note the determination to retain the principles of autocracy by Nicholas II and his advisers.

The Dumas (Parliaments) attempted to provide an alternative to tsarist autocracy. They lacked any of the powers or autonomy of, say, the French Assembly and had no ability to control money, policy or ministers. There was a veto over their actions and electoral law was changed to ensure maximum compliance. The differing parties which did attend the Dumas were unable to work together and couldn't provide alternative leadership to the tsars. The incompetent bureaucracy remained uncontrolled. No links were established between the *Dumas* and the *zestva*, and their essential tokenism became increasingly apparent.

THE WORK OF STOLYPIN

Note Stolypin's importance to tsarism after 1905.

P. A. Stolypin, the Russian prime minister from 1906 to 1911, was the most able of Tsar Nicholas II's servants. He did more to keep the regime going than most and yet was remarkable for the number of enemies he attracted, from both left and right. The former were alienated by a conservative supporter of autocracy; the latter felt he was an upstart who was making too many concessions to peasants and workers. Nonetheless, Stolypin must take the credit for the main agricultural and social reforms of the period. He is best remembered for his assassination in 1911, and for the Stolypin Neckties, which were the hangings he insisted on for many of the regime's opponents.

REVOLUTIONARY MOVEMENTS DURING NICHOLAS II'S REIGN

Radical groups managed to survive, but not to flourish, in the period to 1914.

Note carefully the growth of the various Marxist groups, especially the Bolsheviks and the Mensheviks and the issues which united and divided them. The work of Plekhanov (an early socialist), Martov (the Menshevik who opposed Lenin) and, above all, Lenin was crucial. Note what happened also to the populist groups who wanted to give power to the peasants.

NICHOLAS II TO 1914

You are likely to get questions on the strength of the regime and the likelihood of its survival.

The prevailing historical consensus is that tsarism could have survived without the pressure of the First World War. The 1905 revolution had given the system a shock and the regime had shown itself capable of adapting constitutionally on a modest scale. There were some healthy signs of social and economic improvement and Stolypin showed that an intelligent mixture of the carrot and the stick might have enabled the regime not only to survive, but possibly also to flourish. Opposition

was present, but so disunited on both left and right as to make any alternative to tsarism unviable.

Key problems and challenges under Nicholas II

- war
- the radical opposition of the Marxists
- the 1905 revolution
- peasant poverty
- the growth of an urban proletariat
- the failure of the Russian armed forces in the war against Japan
- the demand for change

Key issues under Nicholas II

- the work of Witte
- economic development
- the Russo–Japanese War and the resulting humiliation for the regime
- the impact of the 1905 revolution
- agricultural change
- social improvements
- constitutional change
- the Fundamental Laws, which in theory made the regime more liberal
- the *Dumas* — the elected assemblies
- the work of Stolypin
- the alliances with France and Britain and entry into the First World War against Germany

E The Russian Revolution

Key questions

How likely was a revolution in Russia in 1914?

Why were there two revolutions in Russia in 1917?

Why were the Bolsheviks able to seize power in 1917?

REVOLUTION IN 1914: THE CASE AGAINST

The system had reformed itself and shown itself responsive, through a less regulated economy and important political and social shifts. Although Witte was killed, the Okhrana (the secret police) was becoming proficient. The press was controlled, but not in an overbearing way. There was a growing middle class which was responding to liberalisation and seemed likely to adhere to the regime if it continued to reform. The conservative nobility was declining in power and there were some improvements in the lot of the peasants. The vigour of the Cadets (the moderate democratic liberals) revealed a growth in moderate liberal democratic parties, and the radical opposition was bitterly divided. The blind reaction of Alexander III appeared to be a thing of the past and the army was loyal. Memories of 1905 were fading.

This is the basis of the case for arguing that there was little chance of a revolution in 1914.

Consider whether this case is stronger than the one above.

REVOLUTION IN 1914: THE CASE FOR

This case considers Russia's unwieldy and unresponsive bureaucracy, which was over-dependent on one not very bright man for leadership. It points to the reluctance of the Tsar to change any fundamentals and the minimal nature of the concessions. To modernise, Russia had to westernise and that was not possible with concessionary — rather than genuinely improving — reforms. The opposition was increasingly convinced that violence was the only solution. An all-pervasive secret police had a malign influence, as did the limited intelligence of the Tsar and the damaging influence of the Tsarina. Illustrations of what was fundamentally wrong with the regime are in the role of Rasputin (a monk who had a major influence over the Tsarina) and the naval supply scandals, where shortages and corruption led to naval mutinies.

THE DECISION TO GO TO WAR

How responsible should the Tsar have been for the decision to go to war?

While Russian public opinion was aggressive, few in government were keen on war in 1914. Russia's economic weakness and its humiliation in the Balkan and Japanese wars meant that the Russian foreign ministry advised caution and favoured alliances. However, it was the alliances with the French and the British which gave Tsar Nicholas II the confidence to act firmly. Partial mobilisation against Austria was designed to ease tension in the Balkans — a strategy that failed when the Tsar's generals told him that this was not possible. Mobilisation had to be all or nothing and — as with the Schlieffen Plan in Germany — the planners took control. The Tsar reluctantly ordered full mobilisation, then cancelled it, then restored it again. He could not climb down without further humiliation.

THE FIRST WORLD WAR AND THE RUSSIAN REVOLUTION: THE MILITARY IMPACT

The First World War was the biggest single cause of the revolution and the collapse of the regime.

Russia's entry into the First World War resulted in a military failure that led to eventual political collapse. From every point of view the army failed. Its leadership was weak, its organisation dreadful, and the troops were ill-trained, poorly led and under-equipped. The army was regularly defeated — from Tannenburg and the Masurian Lakes in 1914 onwards — and, amidst a catalogue of horror, it was remarkable that it lasted so long. The decision by the Tsar to take command caused responsibility for further failure to fall directly on him and further weakened his regime. Some military success would have helped, but there was none. Russia simply did not have the ability to fight a war against the Germans and was bled dry.

THE FIRST WORLD WAR AND THE RUSSIAN REVOLUTION: THE ECONOMIC IMPACT

The effect of the shortages on the army was critical.

Russia's weak economic and industrial infrastructure did not have the capacity to wage war against Germany and its allies. The small-scale conflict against the Japanese in 1905 should have indicated that a larger conflict was unsustainable. There was a shortage of all the necessary material for war, from medical supplies to grain, and from bullets to railway engines. Hyperinflation, hunger and shortages alienated many different groups from the regime and led to the collapse of the greatest support the regime needed — the army.

You should now have a good picture of the causes of the revolution up to the end of 1916.

THE FIRST WORLD WAR AND THE RUSSIAN REVOLUTION: THE POLITICAL IMPACT

The personal failings of the Tsar were highlighted. Nicholas II's insistence on autocracy had led Russia into a war which demanded the leadership he could not provide. Unwilling to delegate and with a lack of able ministers, Nicholas II floundered. Ministers came and went. He abandoned the capital for the front and failed there. The roles of his German wife and Rasputin were suspected; the *dumas* and *zemstva* were alienated and provided no support. Nicholas II's failure to provide any form of coherent leadership ensured agreement on one issue by 1917 — that he had to go, and his regime along with him. He simply failed to grasp how he could use the latent patriotism of the Russian people and harness its huge energy and forces against the Germans and Austrians. The personal incompetence of the Tsar was a central cause of the revolution.

THE CHRONOLOGY OF THE 1917 REVOLUTIONS

1916	Duma turns against Tsar and his conduct of the war
	The Brusilov offensive fails
	Harsh and repressive Sturmer as prime minister
	Tsar leaves capital to command armies personally
	Growing influence of Tsarina and Rasputin
	Assassination of Rasputin
March 1917	Riots, strikes and military mutinies in Petrograd destabilise Home Front
	Duma ignores demand for dissolution
	Provisional Government set up by Lvov
	Petrograd Soviet starts to undermine military authority
	Abdication of Tsar
April	Lenin returns to Russia
May	Lvov brings Kerensky, Social Revolutionaries and Mensheviks into the government
June/July	New offensive against Austria finally fails
	Army discipline totally collapses
July	Kerensky becomes prime minister
September	Bolsheviks used to defeat Kornilov
	Bolsheviks armed and Trotsky released from prison
October	Bolsheviks dominate soviets
November	Bolshevik seizure of power
	Action endorsed by soviets
December	War ended with Austria and Germany
	Cheka created
January 1918	Constituent Assembly is opened and closed by Bolsheviks

REVOLUTION DURING FEBRUARY AND MARCH 1917

Disasters in the war led to a breakdown in military discipline, riots and strikes at home and what was, in effect, mob rule in many parts of Russia. This in turn led to the intervention of the Duma once it was clear that tsarist rule in Russia had collapsed. The move from tsarism to the Provisional Government was remarkably smooth and showed how far the Tsar's authority had vanished. It was largely non-violent and although it was a revolution constitutionally, it did

Note the speed and ease of the first revolution.

not appear so in terms of upheaval. The central reason why it failed was its inability to develop the radical policies needed to solve Russian problems quickly enough.

THE PROVISIONAL GOVERNMENT

What were the main reasons for the failure of the Provisional Government?

Lvov's leadership of the Provisional Government lasted only until his replacement by Kerensky in July 1917. Consider what chances, if any, the Provisional Government, supported by such groups as the Cadets, stood of dealing with the range of crises affecting Russia in 1917. Could moderate liberalism have provided the solutions? The problems facing the government ranged from peasant land seizures, further military collapse and the Kornilov coup (when a disaffected general tried to overthrow the Provisional Government) to inflation and economic collapse. It is argued that the Provisional Government could have survived with firmer action against Lenin and other radical groups, and a quick end to the war. However, Kerensky failed to realise that the army was a spent force and failed to deal with the ruthless and radical Bolsheviks. Given the huge range of political groups from the left to the right, it is unlikely that any workable consensus could have been achieved. How could democracy suddenly work in such appalling conditions? Consider whether there was any chance for the Provisional Government to succeed.

REVOLUTION DURING OCTOBER AND NOVEMBER 1917

The Bolsheviks were the only group prepared to take a radical initiative.

The Provisional Government's failure to deal with the Bolsheviks and the fact that it allowed them arms to deal with Kornilov were critical to the development of the revolution. Lenin played more of a symbolic role initially. The key individual was Trotsky and the key groups were the soviets, especially in Petrograd where they cleverly seized the means of communication in the railway stations and the post, telephone and telegraph offices. The flight of Kerensky — the head of the government — left a void at the top and only Lenin's Bolsheviks were prepared to fill it quickly. It is the sheer audacity of this tiny minority that is so remarkable.

THE REASONS FOR THE SUCCESS AND SURVIVAL OF THE BOLSHEVIKS IN 1917

You need to consider why the Bolsheviks were successful.

There are several broad areas to consider here. The first is the dire condition of Russia and its people, who were looking for radical solutions and aware of the need for them. The second is the inability of the Provisional Government to solve the problems of Russia and convince the Russian people that it could provide the required leadership. The third is the strengths and skills of the Bolsheviks themselves. Finally, there is the attitude of the main groups of Russian people — the army, the peasants, the urban workers and the (small) middle class. The first factor has already been considered in the causes of the revolution, and the others are outlined below.

THE BOLSHEVIKS

Make sure you have the necessary facts to back up these broad ideas.

The Bolsheviks were a small group inspired by Lenin's leadership and subject to Trotsky's organisational skills. Their ability to be flexible and to communicate a clear and effective message to the masses and the soldiers gave them a strong position. Lenin offered them a clear strategy with his Marxist ideas on the state and the economy, and Trotsky supplied excellent tactics for actually seizing power.

They listened to what the people wanted, and included those wishes in their programme as necessary, especially in the case of the peasants. Boldness, vision, discipline and flexibility combined with all-important communication skills to ensure Bolshevik success.

THE ATTITUDE OF THE RUSSIAN PEOPLE

The population's war weariness was critical to the events of 1916–17. The Bolsheviks were one of the few groups to argue for the need to end the war. The peasant revolt and land seizures were recognised by the Bolsheviks as critical. The Bolsheviks recognised peasant demands in the April Theses, which allowed the peasants to keep the land they had seized. The urban workers, who had spearheaded much of the revolutionary activity, were also integral to Bolshevik success. Finally, the army shared the general population's wish for Russia to leave the war. Key to Bolshevik success is that they ensured that their policies were sufficiently in tune with the demands of these three groups to gain their support, at least initially. How much the Bolsheviks led or simply responded to popular wishes, is open to debate.

The fact that the Bolsheviks agreed with the basic demands of the peasants, the urban workers and the army is vital.

THE FAILURE OF THE PROVISIONAL GOVERNMENT AND OTHER POLITICAL GROUPS

It is much debated whether the problems facing Russia allowed the Provisional Government any chance of survival. Problem after problem emerged — the war, land seizure, Kornilov and the increasingly radical behaviour of the Bolsheviks and the soviets — and Kerensky had no acceptable solutions. The failure of Brusilov's summer offensive is important, and the decision to continue with the war made it clear to a large number of Russians that the Provisional Government had to go. It had no secure power base and its support was profoundly split. A large number of groups, from the liberal Cadets to the radical Social Revolutionaries and Mensheviks, considered replacing Kerensky, but it was the Bolsheviks who stopped talking and acted.

Again, it was the Bolsheviks' willingness to take the initiative which was critical in 1917.

THE RUSSIAN REVOLUTION

The Bolshevik seizure of power should be seen as the first stage in the revolutionary process. You now need to see how the Bolsheviks survived and became established. When considering the causes of the revolution you need to consider the long term up to around 1900, the medium term from 1900 to 1914 and the short term, and to consider at what stage the revolution became likely, then possible and then probable.

Avoid the issue of inevitability.

Key causes of the Russian Revolution

- the war
- the failure of the autocracy to adapt
- the failure of reform
- the personality of the Tsar
- the conservatism of the Tsar
- military disaster
- economic collapse
- the collapse of tsarist government
- the attitude of the army

- the attitude of the peasantry
- the attitude of the urban workers

Key factors behind the success of the Bolsheviks

- the failure of the Provisional Government to deal with the war, the land issue, economic collapse and mass starvation
- the continuation of the war
- Bolshevik boldness
- the leadership of Lenin providing ideas and taking action
- the divisions amongst Bolshevik opponents
- the management of the Kornilov affair, where the Bolsheviks were armed
- the organisation and leadership of Trotsky, particularly with the soviets
- the role of the soviets in providing the assault forces for the revolution
- the backing of the urban proletariat
- good planning
- decisiveness
- flexibility
- war weariness

F Lenin and the establishment of Bolshevik power, 1917–24

Key questions

Why were the communists able to win the Civil War in Russia?

How important was Lenin to Bolshevik victory in the Civil War?

What type of regime did Lenin impose on Russia?

THE CIVIL WAR

You need to remember that Russia is (and was) as much an Asiatic power as it is a European one, and that it has China and the USA for neighbours in the East. During the Civil War it had to maintain military campaigns from Siberia to the Baltic, Poland to Murmansk, the Caucasus to the Volga and the Crimea to Siberia. Its fight on multiple fronts was not supported by an economic infrastructure to match those of its enemies and there was considerable foreign intervention, all on the side of the anti-Bolshevik supporters of the Tsar. The Russian Civil War was not a simple White versus Red issue, however, as the Bolsheviks ended up fighting peasants and other radical groups such as the Social Revolutionaries. There were great atrocities on both sides, terror became an integral part of the Bolshevik methodology and appalling famine resulted.

Note the large number of different participants in the Russian Civil War.

THE CAUSES OF THE CIVIL WAR

The forces of the right wished to restore tsarism, and in this sense the cause of the Russian Civil War was simple. But the picture is complicated by a range of conflicts embracing Red versus White, foreign versus Bolshevik, and the Bolsheviks

The Russian Civil War, like many others, was fought with considerable savagery on all sides.

against the rest of the radical and liberal political groups. Hatred of communism was a major factor in foreign intervention. In addition, the French were prepared to support military leaders such as the White generals Kolchak and Wrangel, because they felt betrayed by Russia leaving the war. The fact that the Bolsheviks had declined to repay French debts was another factor. Within Russia rival groups such as the Mensheviks and the Social Revolutionaries were furious at the Bolshevik domination of power, particularly after they forced the elected Constituent Assembly to close.

THE REASONS FOR BOLSHEVIK VICTORY: THE OPPOSITION

The incompetence of the opposition was a central cause of Bolshevik victory.

The removal of the German threat by the Treaty of Brest-Litovsk in 1918, which the Bolsheviks felt was a short-term concession, enabled them to deal with their internal enemies quickly. White military leadership was poor, they were disunited, they had no agreed policy or plans and — with the assassination of the Tsar in July 1918 — they had little to fight for. A restoration of aristocratic domination had no appeal to many Russians. The White campaign had poor liaison with foreign intervening powers and there was great personal rivalry between the various generals. Foreign intervention was never properly co-ordinated and aroused a nationalist movement in favour of the Bolsheviks. Many Russians were more prepared to accept a Bolshevik victory than a White/foreign victory. The Bolsheviks' opponents were unable to convince the Russian people that they were a viable alternative to either Bolshevism or tsarism.

THE REASONS FOR BOLSHEVIK VICTORY: THE BOLSHEVIKS

Note the strengths of Bolshevik leadership.

Inspired leadership and a willingness to compromise and adapt were key factors, as were Lenin's decisiveness and the achievements of Trotsky in commanding the Red Army and raising a force of over 5 million men. The Bolshevik leadership was aware that the Civil War was for the minds of the people as well as for territory. The propaganda war was well targeted to win support. Bolshevik internal lines of communication enabled their control of the key cities, centres of communication and factories. Lenin's flexibility on policy is shown by the shift from War Communism to the New Economic Policy (NEP), which permitted some capitalism to survive in Russia.

THE IMPACT OF THE CIVIL WAR ON RUSSIA

Consider the implications of the Civil War for the rise of dictatorship in Russia.

One view is that Bolshevik victory in the Civil War meant that the revolution had been attained, while others argue that Bolshevik success ended any chance of a real revolution taking place. Democracy died in 1918. There were changes to Communist Party policy (such as the NEP and not shooting all tsarist officers) and there was a move towards repression and dictatorship. The Cheka (Lenin's secret police) and the terror came out of the war and were to remain the central features of Russian communism. The economics of communism were abandoned and by 1922 the peasants were seen as an enemy by the Bolsheviks. The economic impact of the Civil War was terrible, as millions died through war and famine. Agriculture and industry were badly damaged, to the extent that Russian agriculture never became as efficient as in the West. By 1922 Russia had been more or less destroyed, and what scope there had been for democracy had gone as well. The Cheka replaced the Okhrana (the old tsarist secret police), and Siberian centres for exiles became death camps.

THE BOLSHEVIK POLITICAL REGIME

Some understanding of what Marx predicted is called for, notably the Marxist anticipation that the state would 'wither away' and become irrelevant. Lenin was probably correct in his fear that if the Constituent Assembly were allowed to remain, then tsarism (or something worse) might reappear in Russia as the splits amongst the revolutionaries would never permit a united front against the Whites and interventionist foreign powers. You need to consider the various debates about Bolshevik intentions in the early years. Did they intend to establish the revolution after they had won the Civil War, or did they use the Civil War to secure total control? Was power an end in itself? Was the Bolshevik seizure of power to be the revolution, or was it intended as a first stage?

THE NEW POLITICAL SYSTEM

An obvious feature of the Bolshevik regime is its similarity to what had existed before 1914. The essence of Bolshevism was leadership by a tiny group dominated by one man, which reflected tsarism and did not change much after the Civil War. The powerful Constituent Assembly was banished. The Communist Party and the soviets were kept as fronts, but both were means by which the Bolsheviks exercised power. This exercise of power comprised the use of terror, the banning and destruction of all other political groups and the suppression in 1921 of the Kronstadt rising, which demanded a return to communist values. The NEP showed how quickly idealism disappeared, and the refusal to allow any of the outer peoples — such as the Georgians, Ukrainians and Don Cossacks — their freedom revealed a lack of belief in national self-determination. With the establishment of the Orgburo (party organisation) and Politburo (cabinet), power came from the very top. All else was window-dressing.

SOVIET FOREIGN POLICY UNDER LENIN

Survival and the wish to spread communism were the two main strands in Lenin's foreign policy. The dual aim led to inconsistencies — for example, the terms of Brest-Litovsk and the attitude of the Bolsheviks towards it, as they were determined to repudiate it as soon as they could. Survival dominated the years of the Civil War, but memories of Allied intervention against the Bolsheviks were to colour relations in the interwar years. Lack of foreign recognition and the refusal of Russian entry to the League of Nations aroused antagonism, as did French support for the Poles and the Treaty of Riga where Russian territory was given to Poland. Look carefully at the work of the Comintern (which was designed to spread revolution throughout the world), and the various attempts — even in the early years of Bolshevism — to undermine western democracies such as Britain. Other evidence, such as a trade deal with Britain in 1921, points to a desire for co-existence. Note also Rapallo (the treaty of mutual assistance with Germany in 1922) and how it might link with the 1939 German pact. Is this another example of the Bolsheviks abandoning their ideology and policies to retain power?

ECONOMIC POLICY UNDER LENIN

Much of Marxism was concerned with economics and this raises complex questions about Lenin's economic policy. Was Lenin really a Marxist, or did the desire for power make the need for pragmatism so great that in the end he was no more than a simple dictator? Look at the regime's early relationship with the

Did Lenin aim at dictatorship, or was it a step he had to take to prevent a resurgence of tsarism?

Consider the view that the Bolshevik victory in the Civil War destroyed the chances of revolution in Russia.

Note the two differing strands of foreign policy, i.e. simultaneously opposing and trying to co-operate with the West.

Note how quickly the Bolsheviks abandoned communist principles in order to ensure survival.

peasants, including the Decrees on Land, which allowed the peasants to keep the land they had seized. There was some nationalisation initially — banks and armaments, for example — but state control was not new to Russia and in any case many enterprises were left in private ownership. War Communism caused chaos, alienated the peasants and played a part in the famine of the early 1920s. Arguably it was the biggest mistake made by the Bolsheviks.

ECONOMIC POLICY UNDER LENIN: THE NEP

An analysis of the NEP is critical for any study of Lenin.

A consideration of the New Economic Policy (NEP) prompts questions about the extent to which it mixed socialism and capitalism and how great a compromise it was with Marxist principles. Some argue that the NEP — which allowed capitalist enterprises to exist — represented the abandonment of socialism and that it showed how clearly War Communism had failed. It did not prevent famine and there was a serious financial crisis in 1923. However, it could also be argued that it saved the regime, and gave the Bolsheviks time to plan an advance to socialism later. The split the NEP caused within the Communist Party — between supporters like Bukharin (a key communist thinker, an ally of Lenin and a member of the Politburo) and more left-wing socialists like Trotsky — was to be used by Stalin in his rise to power. Critics of Lenin see the NEP as an abandonment of any pretence at socialism, whereas his defenders see it as a necessary compromise to survive. By 1926 production had returned to 1913 levels and the famine was over, so he must get some credit.

THE NATURE OF LENIN'S ACHIEVEMENT

You need to be able to argue both the merits and demerits of Lenin's achievement.

Lenin played a central role in toppling the centuries-old tsarist system. He got Russia out of the First World War and won a civil war against huge internal and external opposition. His ability to lead and inspire was remarkable, and he got the loyalty and support of able men, most notably Trotsky. On the other hand, Lenin has been criticised for betraying the class he came to power to save, and for abandoning the revolutionary ideals he had preached for so long. By failing to make full provision for his succession he also paved the way for the rise of Stalin. Millions died in the Civil War, and the purges and terror became part of the regime under his orders. Any chance of establishing a liberal and democratic society was lost, and questions about Lenin's responsibility for genocide and totalitarianism are central to an assessment of his role.

Key factors in the Bolshevik victory in the Russian Civil War

- quality of Bolshevik leadership
- geographical factors
- internal lines of communication
- Trotsky and the Red Army
- the flexibility of Lenin
- the divisions amongst opponents
- the war weariness of the intervening powers
- Russian nationalism
- White incompetence and divisions
- effective propaganda
- the use of terror
- autocratic leadership

Key features of the work of Lenin

- his inspirational leadership
- his ideas and communist ideals
- his willingness to compromise to survive
- his ability to choose able subordinates
- his dictatorial methods
- his foreign policy — Brest-Litovsk, Poland and Rapallo
- the constitution
- War Communism
- the New Economic Policy, which permitted capitalism
- the Cheka (the secret police)
- his responsibility for the rise of Stalin and the establishment of dictatorship
- the establishment of a new government and administrative system in Russia
- the creation of Soviet federalism

G Stalin's rise to power

Key questions

Why and how was Stalin able to gain and consolidate power?

How successful were Stalin's industrial and agricultural policies?

What was the impact of Stalin's dictatorship on the Soviet Union?

STALIN'S RISE TO POWER: THE EARLY YEARS

Careful and meticulous planning, the ability to be underestimated and ruthless ambition are the key features of Stalin's rise to power. Never a dominant or particularly senior figure under Lenin, Stalin took on low-profile bureaucratic tasks. There is evidence that Lenin sensed how dangerous Stalin was from critical comments in Lenin's will, which warned communists of Stalin's ambitions. Lenin's fears were soon to be realised, as Stalin overcame this criticism and seized power completely. The idea of a collective leadership from a group as diverse as Trotsky, Rykov, Bukharin and Kamenev was unlikely. However much Lenin may have disliked the idea of a leader, he must have been conscious that his death would leave a void and he had made no proper provision for replacing himself as leader.

> Consider the responsibility of Lenin for the rise of Stalin.

STALIN'S RISE TO POWER: THE MIDDLE YEARS

Stalin became a contender by 1925, by which time he had identified his most serious opponents and was forming alliances with Zinoviev and Kamenev, two key members of the Politburo, to help him destroy Trotsky. He manipulated men and issues to his advantage. Stalin used the NEP to isolate Trotsky further and exploited the 'socialism in one country' versus 'permanent revolution' clash. His management of the Party Congress in 1925 was astute and the isolation of Trotsky continued. Similar techniques were used to ally with Bukharin, another prominent member of the Politburo, and the rightists, in order to defeat the left opposition and get Trotsky and his allies thrown out of the Politburo — and power.

> Note the mixture of planning and opportunism in Stalin's rise to power.

Note the range of
different skills that Stalin
demonstrated in his rise
to power.

Assess the responsibility
of Trotsky and the other
leaders for Stalin's rise to
total power.

STALIN'S RISE TO POWER: THE FINAL YEARS

By 1929 Stalin was the dictator of the Soviet Union (as Russia became called after 1922) and the policies that happened from then on — whether the purges or collectivisation — were his ideas. He appropriated the policies of the left whom he had expelled, and eliminated the rightists, including his former Politburo allies and Bukharin in particular in 1929. The old guard was replaced by the cronies whom Stalin had been grooming for the previous decade. He mixed planning and manipulation with a ruthless opportunism that played on his awareness of strengths and weaknesses among possible opponents. Once in complete power, Stalin was determined to ensure he stayed there.

WHY DIDN'T TROTSKY BECOME THE SOVIET LEADER?

Trotsky had neither the ambition nor the ruthlessness to reach the pinnacle of power and he was identified with failed policies, particularly when European revolution in the early 1920s didn't materialise. He was personally disliked by many of the other leading Bolsheviks, several of whom were anti-Semitic, and he had never matched Stalin's grasp of party detail. Trotsky was one of the many who underestimated Stalin, and his disregard of party infighting led to his political isolation. Though a proven wartime leader, he failed to act quickly in the light of Lenin's damning comment on Stalin in his will. Other potential leaders like Kamenev and Zinoviev also lacked the skills and ruthlessness required, and the absence of an able and determined opponent was a key factor in Stalin's rise to power.

The main reasons for Stalin's take-over of power

- his party base
- control of party membership and Congress
- his ideological flexibility
- his management of Lenin's will
- his ability not to appear a threat
- his ability to appear manageable to his allies
- his ability to seize any opportunity and turn it to his advantage
- his political skills
- his ruthlessness and ability to plan ahead
- driving ambition

H The years of Stalin's domination

Key questions

What was the effect of Stalin's social and economic policies?

What were the causes and outcomes of Stalin's purges?

What were the reasons for the change in Stalin's foreign policy?

You should know the causes, course and results of collectivisation.

STALIN'S DOMESTIC POLICIES: COLLECTIVISATION

Stalin's position was secure in 1929 and his first independent action was to abandon the NEP and start on a programme to create an economy which would enable the Soviet Union to lead the world revolution and compete effectively with the other industrial powers. The NEP had not worked, for an acute food shortage in 1927–28 left no surplus to feed what Stalin had hoped would be a growing urban proletariat. Collectivisation was Stalin's answer, and it devastated the Soviet people to the extent that millions died of starvation. The principle was to use economies of scale to feed a growing population and end the limited self-sufficiency of the small peasant farmers (*kulaks*) who dominated Soviet agriculture. Make sure you know the mechanics of collectivisation, with its amalgamation of many small peasant holdings into larger collective units. What may have appeared a good idea in theory totally failed in practice and many feel that collectivisation caused the greatest (and possibly the only) deliberately created famine in history. The Soviet Union never recovered and — in spite of having some of the richest farming land in the world — Russia still cannot feed itself properly.

STALIN'S DOMESTIC POLICIES: INDUSTRIALISATION

Stalin's industrial policy centred on the Gosplan organisation, which was created to lead the industrialisation of the Soviet Union. The Five-Year Plans and the achievements of the Soviet people in creating a major industrial power between 1930 and 1939 are remarkable. It was the fastest industrial revolution the world has seen and within a decade the Soviet Union had grown into a major industrial power. Industries which had not existed before — such as electrical, oil, truck, tractor and textile industries — were created from scratch with no foreign investment and limited foreign expertise. The price was immeasurable suffering among a people whose only choice was between hardship and squalor and the terror of the Stalinist purges. By 1941 the Soviet Union was able to take on the German *Wehrmacht*. Avoid the propaganda about Stakhanov, the miner who produced more coal than anyone else, but look at how much steel was being produced by 1940 (18.3 million tons, compared with 4.3 million tons in 1928).

One justification for the purges was that terror was the only way to have motivated the Soviet people to tolerate the pains of rapid mass industrialisation.

You need to have an understanding of the possible causes of the purges.

THE CAUSES OF THE STALINIST PURGES

There are many theories about why Stalin embarked on the purges in which millions of people who could not even have been described as potential opponents were murdered. Some argue that Stalin was driven by fears that the Nazis and the West were out to destroy him, while others put the purges down to Stalin's paranoia and murderous personality. Other arguments hold that terror was an integral part of the Leninist system which Stalin merely developed, or that he was so determined that socialism should come to the Soviet Union that the only way to get it was through ideological cleansing. Others suggest that the state-inspired mass murders were the only way to destroy capitalism and achieve a classless society. Defenders of Stalin tend to argue that he only wanted to remove a few key opponents and that over-enthusiastic subordinates got carried away. Given the scope of Stalin's power, that is as unlikely as the case put forward by those who assert that Hitler was ignorant of the Holocaust. The evidence is that Stalin knew what he was doing and that the purges were part of his plan to submit a terrorised nation to his will.

THE COURSE OF THE PURGES

The total number of dead is not known, but it is well into the millions. Archives are still being opened and graves uncovered. All the evidence is that Stalin had been planning the purges for several years and had the required people and the necessary machinery of death camps and informers in place. There was a kind of test run in the early 1930s when some foreign engineers were put on trial and confessed to sabotage. The later show trials destroyed key Bolshevik leaders like Bukharin and established torture and the destruction of the accused's family as the norm. Stalin escalated the purge to include army officers, party officials, biologists, artists and lawyers. No group in Soviet society escaped. A murderous mentality was embedded in Soviet foreign policy when, for example, the NKVD (the replacement for the Cheka) shot the captured Polish officer corps when Poland was invaded in 1939.

THE RESULTS OF THE PURGES

The Soviet Union was traumatised. No nation had ever had to endure such large-scale terror. While Stalin was able to impose his brand of socialism, he weakened his country's defences, as the ease with which Hitler smashed his armies in 1941 showed. Finland proved hard to defeat as well. Initiative was destroyed in all areas of the Soviet Union as fear of failure dominated managers. Productivity was hit as key managers were killed. Butchery was not the way to improve agriculture either. The industrial achievements of the Soviet Union under Stalin happened in spite of, rather than because of, the purges. Stalin also killed the leaders of communist movements in other countries, which hindered the spread of communism and helped the progress of fascism. The purge mentality continued after the Second World War, with many hundreds of thousands murdered when the Soviet Union took over eastern Europe and the Baltic states. Even Soviet soldiers who had been captured by the Germans were sent to the death camps when freed.

THE SOCIAL IMPACT OF STALINISM

In many respects Stalin was the opposite of what a good Bolshevik should have been. Equality was abandoned and the party élite became the new aristocracy. The armed services were as hierarchical as before, and stress was placed on the family unit. The morality of the 1930s was very similar to that preached by the tsars and their Church. Women were exploited even more, and were seen both as child bearers and as cheap manual labourers.

EDUCATION UNDER STALIN

Education was an area where the tsars had spent money. By and large, the quality of education for the masses improved under Stalin due to the growing focus on producing the skilled workers demanded by the Five-Year Plans. Stalinist Russia was more of a meritocracy than earlier Russian society, and industrialisation created greater scope for those whose talents were in demand.

CULTURE UNDER STALIN

As in Nazi Germany, there was a comprehensive attempt to dominate the whole cultural and artistic life of a nation. Culture was to serve the state (and Stalin) and there were centralised definitions of art, music and drama. Stalin laid down

---

Note the creation of a huge machinery of death and terror, similar to that created by Hitler.

The psychological impact of the purges on the Soviet Union is still evident today.

Like Hitler, Stalin had no coherent social policy.

Educational advances were a definite gain for poorer Soviet people.

Note the wish of a dictator to dominate the whole life of a nation.

what should be in poems, nursery rhymes and even folk songs. Socialist realism was the dominant form and censorship was the order of the day.

THE NATURE OF STALINIST GOVERNMENT

In practice, Soviet government from 1929 onwards was simple: Stalin ruled with even more power than the tsars. In theory, the Soviet Union was a democratic and federal system under a central ruling party, but after the purges the party was reduced to a limited role similar to that of the Nazi Party in Germany. You need to look at the 1936 constitution in some detail, as theoretically it made the Soviet Union into a genuinely socialist state, which apparently had no place for a dictator like Stalin. Although Congress still met, it had no role but to applaud Stalin and register his decisions. Though the old administrative and party organisations remained, they exercised no real power.

FOREIGN POLICY UNDER STALIN: THE EARLY YEARS

During the struggle for power, Stalin had limited interest in foreign policy, and the background to those years was increasing recognition by the West and a continuation of the Treaty of Rapallo of 1922. Stalin's assumption was that capitalism would collapse — which it nearly did in the Great Depression of 1929 — and that world revolution would follow. He failed to see Hitler as a threat initially and, in his refusal to allow German communists to work with the SPD (the German socialist and anti-Nazi party), he played a role in the rise of Hitler. He did not make that error later, as Soviet support of Spanish and French communists showed.

FOREIGN POLICY UNDER STALIN: THE THREAT FROM GERMANY

By the mid-1930s Stalin appreciated the German threat and Hitler's intentions. He tried to contain the spread of fascism via treaties with France and Czechoslovakia and by attempts to deal with the British. The Soviet Union joined the League of Nations, and for a while Stalin was one of the most ardent supporters of collective security. He was worried, but not worried enough to prevent the majority of his senior officers being killed in the purges. Meanwhile, he became alarmed at the Nazis' progress as Hitler breached the Treaty of Versailles with German rearmament and then moved eastwards with the *Anschluss* and the invasion of Czechoslovakia. Stalin's suspicions about the West's intentions over Nazism were fuelled by British and French anti-communism in the Spanish Civil War and the Anti-Comintern Pact (the treaty between Germany, Italy and Japan directed against communism). Suspicion intensified to fear after Munich and the West's failure to involve him in negotiations. The combination of these factors make Stalin's deal with Hitler in 1939 comprehensible.

FOREIGN POLICY UNDER STALIN, 1939–41

The Nazi–Soviet Pact of 1939 was a devastating blow to loyal communists in many countries who could not see how a communist could deal with Hitler. Some argue that, having executed most of his general staff, Stalin needed to buy the time to rebuild the Red Army. And the Soviet Union benefited from the pact, gaining the Baltic republics, parts of the Ukraine and a free hand in Finland. The evidence suggests that Stalin, pleased with territorial gains, thought he had prevented war and helped turn Hitler's attention westward. This begs the question of whether or not Stalin was wholly misled by Hitler.

Note how Stalin went to great lengths to disguise his absolute power.

Note Stalin's rapid realisation that he had made a considerable mistake over the rise of Hitler.

Consider the idea that Stalin viewed Britain and France, with their capitalist systems, as just as much of a threat to the Soviet Union as Germany.

Try to see the 1939 pact from Stalin's point of view.

Key features of Stalin's reign
- the purges
- collectivisation
- industrialisation
- the Five-Year Plans
- social change
- educational change
- propaganda
- cultural control
- indoctrination
- the cult of the personality
- the constitution of 1936

Key factors in Soviet foreign policy under Stalin
- the role in the rise of Hitler
- joining the League of Nations
- the desire for collective security
- the impact of the purges on the military
- the Spanish Civil War
- the attempt at an alliance with the West
- Stalin's suspicions of the West
- Stalin's reaction to Munich and the invasion of Czechoslovakia
- the Nazi–Soviet Pact
- the annexation of the Baltic republics
- the invasion of Finland
- the German invasion
- the decision by Japan not to fight the Soviet Union in 1941

The last days of Stalin

Key questions

Were there any signs of change in the final years of Stalin?

Was there any continuity with the 1930s?

SOVIET FOREIGN POLICY, 1945–52

After the Second World War, a distrust of the West and a desire to build a defensive barrier against further aggression were the dominant features of Soviet foreign policy. Make sure that you have the full details of Yalta and Potsdam, the treaties with the USA and Britain which reorganised Germany and eastern europe in 1945, and that you have some mastery of the highly divisive Polish issue. The Soviet Union lost Yugoslavia and failed to gain Iran, but eastern Europe and Czechoslovakia were colonised and subjected to a policy of Russification. As the years progressed, the Cold War and the espionage war developed and Cominform and the Warsaw Pact came to rival the Marshall Plan and NATO. Though Stalin gave some help to Mao, his policy towards fellow communists in China was devious.

What was Stalin's responsibility in causing the Cold War?

SOCIAL AND ECONOMIC POLICY: THE FINAL YEARS

Given the human and material damage done by the Second World War, the Soviet recovery was remarkable. Grand plans such as the Volga–Don Canal were still the order of the day. Education and health care were improved and major efforts were made to increase the birth-rate. Consumer goods and housing were neglected and living standards in 1952 were lower than in 1940. Heavy industry and defence projects were given priority as the Soviet Union built its first atom bomb and put a man in space before the Americans. Agriculture remained a failure and food supplies were increasingly dependent on the wheat fields of the American Midwest.

In many ways, the Soviet people had to endure once again the privations of the 1930s.

THE POLITICS OF THE LAST YEARS

Intolerance was the order of the day, the slave camps flourished and the Doctor's Plot and the Zhdanov/Leningrad affairs, where a key Politburo member was purged to warn others, showed that the age of the purge was not dead. It is estimated that well over a million were butchered in the purges of the Baltic States and the Ukraine alone, most organised by a rising star called Khrushchev. More purges were planned when Stalin died in 1952, though he might have lived longer had his servants not been so terrified of touching him after he suffered a stroke.

The only major contrast with the 1930s was that the purges in the Soviet Union were less dreadful.

Key points to note in Stalin's final years
- the development of the Cold War
- the continued aggression and expansion
- the undermining of the United Nations, in Korea for example
- the recovery of the Soviet Union after the devastation of the war
- the continuation of the terror and the cult of personality
- the failure to provide for the consumer needs of the Soviet people
- the continued failure of Soviet agriculture

UNIT France

A The causes of the French Revolution

Key questions

What were the main causes of the French Revolution?
What were the economic and social causes of the French Revolution?
What were the political causes of the French Revolution?

Even though this part of the course starts in 1789, an understanding of earlier causes is required.

THE DEEP-ROOTED PROBLEMS OF THE *ANCIEN RÉGIME*

Many historians argue that the roots of the French Revolution lie far back in French history. The crown had never solved its financial problems or brought in an efficient and fair system of taxation. Nobles and clergy were free from most taxes, and taxation fell on those least able to pay. There was no system of representation in France, so no effective outlet for grievances. Deeply conservative attitudes were held by most of the governing classes. The country was regularly involved in expensive wars, which it usually lost and which, by the eighteenth century, it could not afford. The need for efficiency and professionalism in government clashed with the right to inherit and buy official posts, and attempts by the crown to reform were always bitterly opposed as despotism.

Social division is traditionally cited as the central cause of the French Revolution, though recent historians are challenging this view.

THE SOCIAL PROBLEMS OF THE *ANCIEN RÉGIME*

Taxes largely fell on the rural and urban working classes who formed 85% of the population. In addition to the basic tax, the *taille*, they had to pay taxes on necessities such as salt, undergo compulsory service such as road building and pay a tax (the tithe) to the clergy. The nobility exploited their tenants, while not having to pay much tax or put up with compulsory military service. The middle class was able to purchase a way into the noble class, and therefore was also able to avoid taxation. Within the clergy — who were exempt from taxes and military service and other burdens which fell on commoners — there was a gulf between the rich and poor, the latter wanting less control by their aristocratic bishops.

Economic problems — and their interaction with political problems — are now seen as very much the central cause of the French Revolution.

THE ECONOMIC PROBLEMS OF THE *ANCIEN RÉGIME*

Inefficient taxation, rather than a lack of wealth in the country, was central to a state which needed high taxes to maintain a luxurious court at Versailles and to wage expensive wars. Office holders responsible for assessing and collecting taxes could inherit or buy their offices, and so incompetence could not be weeded out. There was a lack of investment in production or agriculture, and internal customs barriers made commerce difficult. The nobility did not get involved in trade because wealth creation was not seen as a worthwhile occupation. By 1789 there was a national deficit of 112 million *livres* and in the late 1780s bad harvests led to rising food prices. With real wages falling in the towns and a rising population, there was hunger amongst the peasantry.

The causes of the French Revolution

While the Enlightenment is not now seen as a vital cause of revolution, it formed an intellectual backdrop that made it possible.

THE IMPACT OF ENLIGHTENMENT IDEAS ON FRANCE

There was ferment among French intellectuals who, while they did not advocate a programme for reform, raised real doubts about the *ancien régime*. Enlightenment writers challenged doctrines such as the divine right of kings, Rousseau attacked organised religion, Montesquieu criticised despotism and the Physiocrats challenged many traditional ideas such as protection and privilege.

Events in America were an influence, albeit an indirect one.

THE IMPACT OF THE AMERICAN REVOLUTION AND WAR OF INDEPENDENCE

Ideas behind the American Revolution of the 1770s — no taxation without representation, and the overthrow of autocracy and despotism — had broad appeal to a French population ruled by the *ancien régime*. Those who had fought with the French armies and navy in America in the late 1770s were exposed to democratic American ideas, and returned home fired up with radicalism. The French government's authority was further undermined by debts incurred in helping the Americans in their struggle against the British.

If a central trigger is looked for, then it is probably taxation.

FINANCIAL PROBLEMS OF THE CROWN

Financial difficulties were a fundamental cause of the French Revolution. Not only was the crown deeply in debt and having to pay out insupportable amounts in interest, but it was also seen as likely not to pay its debts and so had difficulties in raising any more money. The hopelessly corrupt tax system could offer no support, and the inequality and incompetence of the system drove many to believe that only a radical solution would work.

While political difficulties were central to the causes of revolution, their overall importance is hotly debated.

POLITICAL PROBLEMS OF THE CROWN

The bulk of the peasants were alienated from an *ancien régime* which left them hungry and exploited. There was a growing and educated middle class which was so deprived of political power that it had no desire or need to support the crown either. Most of the nobility had a vested interest in resisting change and in any case there were no representative institutions to put forward protest peacefully and warn the King of the need to change. There was simply no base around which royal support could gather.

It is important to remember the limitations of French absolutism when arguing about the role of individuals in the French Revolution.

THE DEFECTS OF ABSOLUTIST MONARCHY

The monarchy was expensive, uncaring and determined to resist change. In an absolutist system where one rules all, if the ruler is defective the system will not work well. There was no scope for public debate, and dissent could be seen as treason. Such limits as there were on royal power tended to be ones which stopped the monarch from making much-needed changes to the financial system.

THE INFLUENCE OF LOUIS XVI

Louis XVI, who was King from 1774 to 1793, was known as an honest and God-fearing family man. However, he lacked self-confidence, had no drive or determination, was weak and evasive and was ignorant about the real state of France, and his passivity prevented any chance of serious reform. His wife, Marie Antoinette of Austria, was hated and much of her advice to him was positively dangerous. His predecessor, Louis XV, had done little more than prop up a decaying system that had been causing serious problems since the early seventeenth century. No French monarch was prepared to tackle the problems of finance in France, and economic catastrophe had been predicted for decades.

THE FAILURE OF THE REFORM ATTEMPTS BY TURGOT, CALONNE AND NECKER

There were three attempts at financial reform in the 1770s and 1780s led by Jacques Turgot, Charles Calonne and Jacques Necker, successive comptroller-generals of finance. Turgot had tried to reform trade and taxation, but was dismissed by the King. Necker followed him but got no backing either and was forced to borrow to pay for the war in America because the crown could not and would not pay for it out of taxation. The last serious attempt to reform the crown's finances and stave off a major crisis was undertaken by Calonne from 1783 onwards. He tried to stop the tax exemptions of the rich and free up internal trade, but again got no royal backing and was sacked in 1787.

THE DECISION TO CALL THE ESTATES GENERAL

After Calonne's failure to reform and the failure of the Assembly of Notables and the Paris Parliament, it was clear that there was limited support for the monarchy anywhere in France. The problems were compounded by imminent bankruptcy and the revolt of the nobility in 1788 against any royal reforms. In the same year, the decision was taken to call the Estates General — the nearest France had to a national representative institution — to help solve the economic and political crisis. This has always been seen as the start of the French Revolution.

Key factors behind the French Revolution
- the archaic nature of the *ancien régime*
- autocracy
- the closed aristocratic caste
- the position of the clergy
- taxation
- the impact of constant wars
- hunger
- Enlightenment ideas
- involvement in the American War of Independence
- national bankruptcy
- lack of any representative system
- the personal failings of the monarchy
- the failure of reform
- the mismanagement of the Assembly of Notables and the Estates General

Perhaps a central weakness of French absolutism in the eighteenth century was that it was aware of its weaknesses, but was not absolute enough to do much about them.

There is real doubt as to whether any financial reform could have worked given the fundamental nature of the social and economic crisis in France.

Factors other than calling the Estates General would have sparked off the crisis.

B Development of the revolution, 1789–92

Key questions

What was the nature of the French Revolution between 1789 and 1792?

Why did the French Revolution become more radical after 1789?

Why did the constitutional experiments up to 1792 ultimately fail?

How important was the crowd in the revolution up to 1792?

It is vital for all candidates to know these events in detail.

THE MAIN EVENTS BETWEEN 1788 AND 1792

1788 Bad harvests

1789 The recall of Necker, which it was hoped would lead to reform
The meeting of the Estates General
Third Estate declares itself to be the National Assembly
Tennis Court Oath
Union of the three Estates
Dismissal of Necker
Bastille taken

1790 Festival of the Champs de Mars
Louis XVI accepts the Constitution

1791 The flight to Varennes
Declaration of Pilnitz
Constitution passed by the National Assembly — limited monarchy in France
Legislative Assembly meets in Paris

1792 Girondins form government
France declares war on Austria
Revolutionary commune in Paris
Massacre at the Tuileries
National Convention meets
Republic proclaimed
Jacobins in power and King put on trial
Religious orders abolished

1793 Execution of King Louis XVI

THE MEETING OF THE ESTATES GENERAL

The Estates General had not met since 1614. Reconvened at the end of the eighteenth century, all three Estates — aristocracy, clergy and commons — were hostile to absolutism. Even the aristocracy had revolted in the crisis of 1787–88. There was considerable suspicion amongst the Third Estate (the commons) against the other two, which they suspected of being likely to support the King. With the failure of the King to offer any programme of reform, the Third Estate formed itself into a National Assembly.

The National Assembly has to be seen as the key trigger to subsequent events. The crown had no idea how to manage it.

These events are vital to note as the first sign of a radical attack on royal power.

THE TENNIS COURT OATH

The Tennis Court Oath was a public promise made by the Third Estate (the commons) not to disperse until the King had agreed to a constitution and a limitation on his absolute powers. It was called the Tennis Court oath because it was taken in the royal tennis court at Versailles. In the background was the threat of royal armies assembling near Paris, the dismissal of Necker by the King, and the revolt of the Parisians culminating in the fall of the Bastille. There was also hunger in France and the first flight of the nobility abroad.

The storming of the Bastille was the first real sign of the potential power of the working class and radical forces in France.

THE STORMING OF THE BASTILLE

The storming of the Bastille was the symbolic start of the French Revolution. Real hunger combined with the dismissal of Necker and news that the King had assembled around 30,000 troops near Paris to inflame the Parisians. First to act were middle-class citizens looking for arms and ammunition in Les Invalides and the Bastille. Then the movement became dominated by a more working-class element, the *sans-culottes*. The soldiers who were in Paris stood aside and when de Launay, the governor of the Bastille, tried to resist, he and his garrison were massacred. Royal power vanished and political power was now with the more radical elements of the Parisian population. The Bastille's fall inspired further outbreaks across France, both in towns and in the countryside.

The attitude to the clergy and to religion signalled a growing split between the radical and conservative revolutionary forces.

DISBENEFIT OF THE CLERGY

The main privileges of the clergy were abolished in 1789 when they lost their right to the tithe and their exemption from taxation. In line with the democratic ideas elsewhere, the Civil Constitution tried to make the clergy elective and to reduce the number of bishops. This was rejected by the Papacy and caused a real split among French Catholics.

The 1791 Constitution was the main legacy of the French Revolution.

THE CONSTITUTION OF 1791

The 1791 Constitution's stipulation of a limited monarchy was reluctantly accepted by Louis XVI in 1791. The Constitution also introduced locally elected councils, fairer taxes, free trade, poor relief and judicial reforms. It amounted to a major revolution, particularly when coupled with the Civil Constitution of 1790.

Given the personalities of the King and his wife, consider the inevitably of their execution.

THE OVERTHROW OF THE MONARCHY

Given the reluctance of the King to accept change and reform, it could be argued that his overthrow was inevitable. Bringing troops to Paris in 1790 and the dismissal of Necker were seen as provocative actions. After Louis XVI's flight to Varennes in 1791 there was no trust left and the King was taken prisoner. The demand for a republic was staved off in 1792 when the National Guard broke the radicals at the Champs de Mars, but war with Austria and Prussia and the treasonable behaviour of Marie Antoinette, the King's wife, in encouraging an Austrian invasion of France made the execution of the King highly likely.

The importance of rioting and popular action is a central topic for all examination boards.

THE SIGNIFICANCE OF RIOTS AND POPULAR ACTION IN 1789–92

Middle-class and working-class unrest — the former over the conduct of the King in 1789 and the latter over hunger — led to the storming of the Bastille. This inspired the National Assembly and the Paris Commune into radical action and was to prove fatal to royal power from then on. A collapse of royal authority in other towns followed, with the middle class assuming power. Rioting and direct action precipitated the collapse of aristocratic authority in the countryside, the flight of the Intendants (agents of the crown in the provinces) and the sacking of both noble and Church property in the search for food. This inspired the Assembly to abolish feudalism with the August Decrees. Inflation and hunger in 1790–91 further inflamed the poor and encouraged them to support even more radical political action.

THE REVOLUTIONARY CLUBS

Revolutionary clubs formed soon after the meeting of the Estates General. One of the major ones was that of the Jacobins, who began as liberal constitutional monarchists and became more radical under Robespierre. The Cordeliers were originally more radical. Both soon spread throughout France and were to form a focus for political activities.

THE FLIGHT TO VARENNES

The flight to Varennes was one of many unwise moves made by Louis XVI. He hated his forced acceptance of the Civil Constitution of the Clergy and hoped that flight might enable him to renegotiate the deal, along with other parts of the Constitution. It stimulated a strong move towards republicanism and an irrevocable loss of public trust.

THE MASSACRE AT THE CHAMPS DE MARS

The radicals, led by the Cordeliers revolutionary club, wanted the King removed after Varennes. Others wished to compromise. The differences were made more obvious in July 1791 when thousands met in the Champs de Mars to celebrate the fall of the Bastille and were fired on by the National Guard. It was the first open clash between moderates and more radical revolutionary forces, and demonstrated that the French were by no means united in revolutionary ideas.

THE OVERALL SIGNIFICANCE OF 1789–92

Many would argue that 1789–92 were the most important years until the return of the monarchy in 1815. The old feudalistic and absolutist monarchy had gone and the Declaration of the Rights of Man was now built into French life. The basic ideas of liberty, equality and fraternity had been taken on by the French and they would not ultimately be given up.

Key factors in the growth of radicalism in France
- royal mismanagement of the Estates General
- pressure from the crowd
- fear of royal armies/the mob
- the storming of the Bastille setting the tone
- the flight and resulting mistrust of Louis XVI
- the total collapse of royal authority in France
- war with Austria and Prussia
- the acceptance of radical ideas by middle-class leaders of the Assembly

Key factors in the nature of the French Revolution to 1792
- the clash between the Third and the other two Estates

Revolutionary clubs became the engine room of the French Revolution.

The flight to Varennes was a key stage in Louis' self-destruction.

The massacre was an important sign of the internally divisive forces which would ultimately destroy the French Revolution.

Note that the greatest changes were made in the first part of the revolution.

- crowd pressure
- the role of the army
- the flight of the aristocracy
- the sudden collapse of royal authority
- the popularity of the reforms of 1789–92
- the attitude of the monarchy
- the pressure caused by the war
- the growth of the radical clubs

C Development of the revolution, 1792–97

Key questions

Why did the nature of the French Revolution change so radically after 1792?

What was the role of the Jacobins and the *sans-culottes*?

What was the impact of war, economic crisis and religious divisions?

THE MAIN EVENTS BETWEEN 1792 AND 1797

1792 The first terror
       The September Massacres
       The Battle of Valmy
1793 Execution of the King
       France declares war on Britain and Holland
       Royalist revolt in the Vendée
       Committee of Public Safety under Danton
       Overthrow of Girondins and Terror starts
       New Constitution
       Abolition of Christianity
       Execution of Marie Antoinette
1794 Commune abolished and Robespierre executed
       Invasion of Holland and Spain
       Coalition formed against France
1795 Peace made with Prussia and Austria
       Third Constitution and creation of Directory
1796 Napoleon in command of army in Italy
1797 Napoleon defeats Austrians at Rivoli

THE DEATH OF THE KING

Given the King's refusal to compromise, his death was inevitable.

All were deeply suspicious of Louis XVI and Marie Antoinette, his Austrian wife — and war accelerated their execution. The initial defeat of the French armies by Prussia and Austria led to a growth of radical republicanism in Paris. This culminated in an attack on the royal residence at the Tuileries in 1792, the massacre of the King's Swiss Guard, the rejection of the National Assembly, and the new Convention, whose first act in September 1792 was the abolition of the monarchy. Tension heightened further after the September Massacres in Paris, when a mixture of nobles and criminals in the Paris gaols were butchered. The Jacobins, fearful of the threat Louis XVI posed to the new republic and pushed on by the *sans-culottes*, demanded the King's death.

THE CAUSES OF THE TERROR

A period of terror is a process that many revolutions go through.

There were three elements in the Terror, in which about 50,000 people died. The first element was political and centred on the Committee of Public Safety in Paris and the Revolutionary Tribunal, which were both set up in May 1793; Marie Antoinette, many aristocrats and the Girondins (one of the major radical political groups in the Assembly) suffered under this terror. The second was the imposition by Paris of its will on areas which refused to accept its authority, and it was particularly savage in the Vendée. And, thirdly, there were the local terrors. The violence was partly to counter the anger caused by conscription and taxation needed for the war. One of the key figures was Robespierre, who was backed by the *sans-culottes*. The likelihood of foreign invasion in 1793 by Austria and Prussia heightened tension.

THE IMPLICATIONS OF THE TERROR

Although the Terror is perhaps one of the best-known aspects of the revolution, consider its actual importance to the whole revolutionary process.

The religion of the state changed as part of the revolutionary process. A new calendar came in and by December 1793 there was a virtual dictatorship. A new Constitution was also introduced, which meant almost a return to the *ancien régime*. There was a purge of *sans-culottes*. When the first terror ended in 1794, Robespierre had killed the Hebertists, some of his political rivals, and all other opponents such as Danton. The Terror then intensified when the Law of Prairial was passed, which meant that total power had now gone to an individual: Robespierre. The great terror of 1794 sickened the population and — with the war against Austria and Prussia won — it no longer seemed necessary.

THE IMPORTANCE OF ROBESPIERRE

How central a figure was Robespierre to the revolutionary process?

Robespierre (1758–94) was central to the radicalisation of the revolution after 1792 as he was largely responsible for the Revolutionary Tribunal, the Committee of Public Safety, the Law of Prairial, and the Journée of June 1793. Robespierre was the strangest bundle of contradictions: he was a poor speaker, lacked charisma and yet was widely popular for a while; he was seen both as a moderate and as a radical, a champion of popular liberty and a mass murderer. These contradictions echo through to modern assessments of Robespierre's role and historians are still divided about his importance. Was he the great revolutionary or did he end the revolution?

THE THERMIDORIAN REACTION AGAINST ROBESPIERRE

Think carefully about what type of reaction this actually was.

Plots against Robespierre (known as the Thermidorian Reaction) began to multiply when he turned on supporters such as Carnot and Fouché. Although a democrat, he did little to advance the condition of the people and he lost the support of the Parisian left when the Commune turned against him. The *sans-culottes* were broken as a major force now and the White Terror attacked those who had gained from the revolution. The new Constitution of Year III was vital in ensuring that the early gains of the revolution were embedded in France. There was no dictatorship. The rich ruled through the property qualification for voting and participation. A system of checks and balances was set up to ensure that power was dispersed. The Directory now ruled.

WAR AND ITS IMPACT, 1792–94

The decision to go to war had a profound effect on the direction of the revolution.

Foreign wars against Prussia, Austria and then Britain played an important part in intensifying the revolutionary processes in France; they led to the overthrow of the revolution itself and the arrival of dictatorship. The initial disasters in 1792 and the desertion of Lafayette fuelled the Terror and made the execution of the King more likely. Later success against Prussia and Austria at Valmy and Jemappes made the revolution much more secure. They gave the revolutionary regimes popularity, particularly once foreign territory on the Rhine was gained. The arrival of Britain and Austria led to French military defeats in 1793, which encouraged a royalist backlash. The cost of the war and conscription, coupled with the Civil Constitution of the Clergy, led to major revolts such as that in the Vendée. Troops had to be taken from the front to deal with them. The printing of *assignats* to fund the war led to inflation and tension which — with further defections such as that of Dumouriez (a revolutionary general) — fuelled the Terror in France.

THE WAR, 1794–99

Consider the reasons for extending and continuing with the war.

With victory at Fleurus against the Prussians and Austrians in 1794, the revolutionary regime seemed well established and it gained further credibility with the occupation of Belgium, Holland and the Rhineland. Austria and Prussia were humiliated and there was also a French attack on Spain. The most remarkable success was by Bonaparte in Italy in battles at Lodi and Rivoli. Bonaparte went on to organise his own foreign policy by dictating terms at Campo Formio without consulting his fellow Directors. The British navy's destruction of the Spanish and Dutch fleets prevented total French victory. The British in Egypt put a halt to French expansion in North Africa.

THE ECONOMY OF REVOLUTIONARY FRANCE

Note that the economic impact of the revolution was much more limited than its social and political impact.

A more efficient, fairer and more centralised tax system was one of the main legacies of the revolution. While the military campaigns caused foreign trade to decline, they also stimulated domestic output. Beyond these factors, the impact of the revolution on the economy was surprisingly limited. Perhaps the main change was in the move from feudalism to capitalism, though it is argued that in the short term the economy was actually set back.

THE CIVIL CONSTITUTION AND THE DIRECTORY

Note the increasing authoritarianism of the methods by which France was governed.

The middle-class men of property were in power. The Civil Constitution under which the Directory (a small executive chosen by the Assembly) governed codified the gains of the revolution by abolishing privilege and autocracy, and by setting up elections and freedom for individuals. With annual elections and a separation of the executive from the legislature, the Directory was perhaps too idealistic to work for long. However, it survived until 1799 because it was keen on law and order, had few effective opponents and had the backing of the army. The Directory became more authoritarian after an attempted coup in 1797, when many deputies were arrested.

The Directory's failure was a major reason for the rise of a dictatorship.

Why did the Directory fail?

A reliance on the army and a dependence on war for much of its popularity meant that the Directory had inbuilt weaknesses. Annual elections made it complex to organise and its purge of the Councils (another attack on elected deputies) in 1797–98 lost it popularity, as did the high taxes which war demanded. The Directory never gained a feel of legitimacy and, with too few friends and too many critics, it fell easily under the pressure of Bonaparte in his *coup d'état* of 1799.

A major social, economic and educational force was radically changed.

The impact on the clergy

The clergy's wealth, privileges and monopoly of education had gone. The clergy was badly divided over the Civil Constitution and diminished as a social and political force from then on. Many of the clergy were killed — especially its aristocratic leadership — and the relationship between church and state was to remain a divisive issue well into the twentieth century.

The demise of the nobility was one of the greatest consequences of the revolution.

The impact on the nobility

Having led the revolution in its very early days, the nobility was largely destroyed by it. The nobles lost much of their wealth, and their traditional social domination disappeared. The aristocracy's right to office went for good, as some aristocrats fled the country and others died under the guillotine. However, those who did survive combined with the wealthier bourgeoisie to form the Notables, a group which went on to provide political and social leadership well into the nineteenth century.

The impact on the middle class

Middle-class French enfranchisement had huge consequences in the nineteenth century.

The revolution was initially seen as belonging to the new middle class, but they did not gain much materially, especially the merchants and industrialists. The middle class provided the main revolutionary leaders, such as Robespierre and Danton, and it was the main electorate from then on. Most officials and elected posts were middle class and much of the aristocratic and Church land which came on the market fell into their hands. The middle class became the dominant political force in France.

Although the working class may well have been a driving force in the revolutionary process, many gained little from it.

The impact on the working class

The urban working class played a vital part in the revolutionary process, but made few if any immediate gains. Though to the forefront in the assaults of Germinal and Prairial, they never got the vote and — with no more charity from an emasculated Church — hunger, inflation and underemployment were their lot. The rural peasantry, which made up the bulk of the French population, gained from a reduction in taxation, while inflation eased their debt problems. The *seigniorial* system had gone, and justice in the localities was not so biased to the rich proprietors. However, rent increases and conscription were unpopular and the changing role of the Church also led to much dissent. On balance, the gains of the French peasants outweighed their losses.

The most important gains had been put in place by 1792.

The impact of the revolution on France up to 1799

The monarchy had gone — temporarily — and when it returned in 1815 its power was always to be limited. The principle of elections was embedded and the old rigidities of institutionalised class privilege had gone for good, as had the old

system of taxation, bought offices and tithes. The power of the church and nobility diminished and there were new administrative areas, a new legal system and career progression that was open to talent.

Key factors in the nature of change after 1792

- the death of the King
- the Terror
- royalist revolt
- the work of the Revolutionary Tribunals
- the new state
- new religion and calendar
- the rise of Robespierre
- the depth of the Thermidorian reaction
- the new Constitution
- the Directory
- the rise of authoritarianism after the death of the King

Key factors in the impact of the war on revolutionary France

- the Terror
- the economic impact — especially inflation
- the pressure on internal politics
- the cost
- conscription
- the rise of Napoleon

D Napoleon Bonaparte, 1799–1815

Key questions

Why did Napoleon rise to power?

What was Napoleon's impact on France and Europe?

Was Napoleon a dictator, an enlightened despot or the true heir to the French Revolution?

Why was Napoleon initially so successful militarily?

Why was Napoleon finally defeated?

NAPOLEON'S BACKGROUND

Napoleon Bonaparte exploited the revolutionary ideal of opening careers to the talented. As a young Corsican artillery officer, he was immensely hardworking and had a great belief in his own ability. Military success in Italy gave Napoleon a national reputation and fuelled his ambition. With the failure of the Directory before 1799 to provide political stability, and with the army playing an increasingly important role in politics, the scene was set for Napoleon's rise to power.

Note the mix of opportunity and ambition.

THE SEIZURE OF POWER

Consider how difficult it was for Napoleon to seize power.

Plotting with the Abbé Sieyès (always a radical in spite of being a clergyman) and with the help of his brother Lucien, Napoleon took a central role in the coup of Brumaire which overthrew the Directory. From this point on, it was clear that Napoleon intended to gain total power. The times were difficult due to the costs of war and to property owners' fear of threats from both left and right. Napoleon was popular with the army, which liked his success and willingness to pay his soldiers. With key plotters in high places, a general air of apathy towards the Directory, widespread fear of a breakdown of law and order, and the war not going well at that moment, Napoleon's initial task of seizing power was not too difficult. His key problem was how to become established in power.

NAPOLEON AS A DICTATOR

Consider the type of dictatorship Napoleon created in France.

Napoleon wanted supreme power, but he also wished to be popular. His technique of using plebiscites (usually rigged) and his insistence on having superficially representative institutions such as the Tribunate, the Legislative and the Senate gave an appearance of democracy. However, even the Consulate was seen as a dictatorship by liberals.

THE USE OF THE PLEBISCITE

Note Napoleon's wish to gain endorsement.

In the early years after 1799 Napoleon frequently used the plebiscite (a referendum) to gain public endorsement for additions to his power, such as his life consulship and appointing himself emperor on a hereditary basis. The plebiscites were managed by Napoleon's brother, Lucien.

THE ESTABLISHMENT OF SUPPORT

Napoleon was always conscious of the need to gain popular support for his regime.

Both military success and the provision of law and order were vital ingredients of Napoleon's power base. He was careful always to support the property owners and used honours and patronage — the Legion d'honneur and the Marshals — to bolster his standing. He created a new (and loyal) nobility by granting over 3,500 titles. Where this didn't forge allegiances, he resorted to bribery or repression. All this was leavened with skilful propaganda and the recipe ensured support — or at least limited opposition.

THE MEANS OF REPRESSION

Note the system of repression.

The system of prefects underpinned a centralised and authoritarian administration which had real powers, including arrest. Tight control of judges and the legal process was also part of the repressive system. At the same time Joseph Fouché, his police chief, built a centralised police force — backed by a spy network — and took responsibility for public order. An active censorship system bolstered the legal framework.

THE REFORM OF THE LEGAL SYSTEM: THE CIVIL CODE

In some respects, the Civil Code was a move on from the *ancien régime*, but it is not always seen as an improvement.

The paradox of Napoleonic legal reform is that it can be seen as partly liberal and partly repressive. The Civil Code of 1804 ended all traces of feudalism, but was far from being a liberal system. It favoured property owners and was authoritarian in its tough criminal law and harsh penalties. A major part of the Bonaparte legacy, the Civil Code's clarity was much influenced by Roman law.

Propaganda was important to Napoleon's regime — spin doctors are not twenty-first-century inventions.

CENSORSHIP AND PROPAGANDA

Napoleon took great care to enhance existing support by using censorship and propaganda. He controlled the press tightly, had *Moniteur* as his own official government newspaper and employed artists to boost the image of the regime. Books, plays and lectures were all censored, as were priests' sermons. The similarity with later dictators is strong.

Napoleon laid as much stress on education as the twentieth-century dictators.

THE CHANGES TO EDUCATION

As with other dictators, Napoleon moulded education to his purposes. The *lycées* were formed as a centralised system which has endured to this day. His aim was to ensure a loyal and educated élite, and particularly to create a high-quality caste of army officers. Women and the working class were neglected.

It could be argued that Napoleon's dictatorship was based on popular consent.

WAS NAPOLEON A MILITARY DICTATOR?

Though popular with the army, Napoleon did not use it in political matters, as had happened under the Directory. His was not a military government or a police state. A distance was kept between the civil and military authorities which, however, met up in the person of Napoleon. He worked within the law, but controlled it tightly through a much-expanded and efficient police force.

NAPOLEON AND FINANCE

Well aware of the *ancien régime's* financial failings, Napoleon played a major role in creating the Bank of France and reorganising the French treasury. An efficient and well-controlled system was established via tax registries and full control over the Ministry of Finance. With a stable currency and taxation seen as fair, Napoleon did not lose support here. He realised how high taxation would damage his popularity and started to borrow heavily after 1806. Thereafter France fell into deficit financing, which ultimately proved damaging.

Note Napoleon's unwillingness to alienate support after 1806.

NAPOLEON AND RELIGION

Napoleon knew the Catholic Church would be safer as an ally than as an enemy, and that religion had been a major divisive force in the decade before his seizure of power. He saw the Church's recognition of him as a route to legitimacy and respectability, and he viewed religion as a social cement. The Concordat of 1801 gave the Church the security it had lacked in the earlier revolutionary days, and the deal strengthened the regime by guaranteeing the social peace that many longed for. The Church also became an agent of the state in that the pulpit was turned into a useful propaganda tool to preach civil obedience and aid the development of the cult of the Emperor. Napoleon was tolerant of both Jews and Protestants, as long as they supported him.

Napoleon compromised with the Church in return for its support.

NAPOLEON'S MILITARY SUCCESS TO 1801

Much Napoleonic military history is obscured by propaganda and the creation of the Napoleonic legend. In his early days he was an inspiring leader who took over a seasoned army in 1795 and destroyed the ill-led Austrians in Italy at Lodi and Rivoli. Napoleon's bold tactics, the old-fashioned methods of his enemies, his inspiring leadership and a willingness to gamble were all vital. His Italian successes are remembered, but the defeats at sea and on land in Egypt are downplayed.

A major factor in Napoleon's early victories was the incompetence of his opponents and the experience of the French army.

NAPOLEON'S EARLY MILITARY ORGANISATION

Napoleon's organisational skills were good before and during a battle. His military approach was to travel light to gain the speed and mobility necessary to surprise the enemy. On the whole, the logistic system backing French troops was efficient, and had centralised control, the resources of a rich nation and an absence of patronage and sinecures in the supply system. Napoleon ensured unity of command, was flexible when fighting and harnessed the *élan* of the French troops. He could also be totally ruthless, particularly when it came to killing after the battle was won.

> The competence of the French contrasted strongly with the incompetence of the Austrians.

NAPOLEON'S WEAKNESSES AS A GENERAL

Napoleon never understood naval matters, as frequent disasters such as the battles of the Nile and Trafalgar show. He was reluctant to experiment with new weapons and to delegate or share ideas. This latter failing was a disadvantage with large armies or when fighting on more than one front. There were times later in his career when his whole supply system broke down and morale could fall as the care for his men was poor.

> Note the flaws in Napoleon's military skills.

OTHER FACTORS WHICH HELPED NAPOLEON'S INITIAL SUCCESS

Allied disunity was always a useful aid to Napoleon. His enemies had different priorities: Russia, Austria and Prussia were always suspicious of each other over Poland; Russia already feared revolution; and the British were keen on colonies and the protection of Belgium. The number of separate peace treaties that Napoleon helped negotiate was considerable, and they divided his opponents. Three foreign coalitions against him collapsed and the fourth and final one which culminated in his defeat at Waterloo took a lot of hard work to keep going. Napoleon could be astute, and the way in which he weaned Prussia away from the Third Coalition with the offer of Hanover is an example.

> Note the non-military factors which helped Napoleon.

THE MILITARY SUCCESSES

European history from the late eighteenth century to 1810 is little more than a list of Napoleon's victories: Marengo against Austria in 1800; Hohenlinden in Bavaria in 1800; Ulm in Austria again in 1805; Austerlitz against Russia and Austria in 1805; Jena in Prussia in 1806; Auerstadt against Prussia in 1807; and Eylau and Friedland in Russia in 1807. Napoleon defeated major power after major power and extended his empire to Spain, Italy, Belgium, Holland and parts of Germany. He humbled Prussia, Austria and Russia. He was the master of Europe. Defeat by the British at the Battle of Trafalgar in 1805 prevented success overseas.

> The sheer consistency of Napoleon's military successes is remarkable.

THE REASONS FOR NAPOLEON'S FAILURE

Napoleon's career hit its high point in 1807. He had Russia as an ally, Britain was isolated and the continental system was developing. However, his mass attacks were leading to huge casualties, as at Wagram against Austria in 1809. Napoleon lost many experienced men and officers, and military tactics changed as armies grew bigger. He increasingly relied on foreign mercenaries, and the armies of his opponents improved. There were major military errors in campaigns against Spain (see below) and Russia, and he did not think through the full implications of the Berlin Decrees, as they antagonised potential allies.

> Though there were military victories after 1807, France no longer held total military sway.

THE SPANISH CAMPAIGN

The Duke of Wellington's victories at Vitoria and Salamanca destroyed the French reputation for invincibility, and the actions of the Spanish guerrillas inspired others to rise against France. Though Napoleon was not in Spain and he ceded command to generals unused to such levels of independence, his reputation suffered. His men suffered even more — the French lost over 300,000 men to what Napoleon referred to as 'the Spanish ulcer', and it tied down many more.

RUSSIA

Napoleon's advance into Russia in 1812 did irreparable harm to the Empire and cost it 500,000 men. It boosted Russian, Prussian and Austrian determination, and the French support in satellite states such as Poland dropped away. Napoleon would still not delegate and he could no longer rely on the incompetence of his enemies. By the end of the campaign it was clear that he had lost touch with reality.

THE FOURTH COALITION

Until the Russian campaign, Napoleon had been able to rely on Allied disunity. All that changed with the Fourth Coalition (1813–15) which started with the deal between Russia and Prussia, and had Britain and then Austria joining later on. Though the Coalition had to contain the differing territorial agendas of its participants, the battle at Leipzig in 1813 (known as the Battle of the Nations) showed its strength and, in consequence, French weakness. The satellites continued to desert France — particularly in Germany — and the Fourth Coalition's ability to present a common front put a stop to French expansionism.

THE TREATIES OF PARIS AND VIENNA

The first Paris Treaty in 1814 was lenient to France in terms of border agreements. These were in contrast to the second Paris Treaty after Waterloo in 1815, which revised frontiers to those of 1790 and introduced reparations and an army of occupation. The Treaty of Vienna of 1815, in which France was allowed to participate, established the buffer principle and restored the old monarchies. The fact that Talleyrand, the French foreign secretary, was involved at Vienna was sensible, and on the whole France did not feel it had been too vindictively treated. However, many territorial and colonial gains accrued to Prussia, Russia, Austria and Britain. It is worth noting the similarity between the victors' territorial expansion and Napoleon's.

NAPOLEON'S IMPACT ON EUROPE

In an empire ranging from Italy and Spain to the Baltic, the occupied states were treated very differently. Some countries, like Belgium, were simply absorbed into France and subjected to French law and social values. In the satellite states, such as those in Italy and Germany, there was heavier taxation, though the limited time of occupation reduced its impact. Feudalism remained strong in most, and the restoration to the old order was easy after 1815.

THE CONTINENTAL SYSTEM

The continental system, which tried to damage Britain's export trade to Europe, was set up by the Berlin Decrees. There is debate about the extent to which it

The message of Spain to Europe was as important as the actual defeats of the French armies.

Failure in Russia was critical to France and the rest of Europe.

The continued agreement and co-operation of the participants in the Fourth Coalition was decisive in the defeat of Napoleon.

The precise details of all three treaties need careful analysis.

Generally, the impact on invaded territory was marginal, though probably damaging to the economies of conquered countries.

benefited or damaged Europe. Within France itself there were benefits to manufacturing, but the system does seem to have damaged agriculture. In the other territories, the consensus is that it harmed most aspects of their economies, primarily as the system was intended to favour France and damage Britain.

NAPOLEON'S MOTIVES FOR EXPANSION

Napoleon was a good propagandist and assessment of his motives has been coloured by the legend that he and his hagiographers developed after 1815. His defenders argued that he was out to spread the revolutionary ideals or that he was a French patriot anxious to gain an empire and ensure security. But aggressive nationalism, a desire to be another Charlemagne and the love of battle and glory have to be put into the equation. At times, personal anger played a part, as happened in the invasion of Russia in 1812 against what he saw as a betrayal by the Tsar. There is no simple answer to the question of what motivated Napoleon, but personal aggrandisement is an important factor.

NAPOLEON'S IMPACT ON FRANCE

In the end Napoleon had less impact internally than might be imagined. There were many similarities between Napoleon and the monarchy, notably a shared love of hereditary ideas and grandeur. While feudalism and the privileged position of the nobility disappeared for ever, the extent to which ideals of equality were embraced is still much debated. Napoleon played a part in embedding the reforms of 1789–94 but, whereas the middle class benefited, the poor did not. There was limited liberty and, with the growth in indirect taxation, the poor were hard hit. The impact of a million young men dying in battle also needs consideration.

THE IMPACT OF NAPOLEON ON FRENCH GOVERNMENT

The authoritarianism which predated Napoleon survived his departure. Indeed, a more efficient civil service, police and local government system enhanced authoritarianism. However, equality before the law remained as a principle of law, as did a better educational system and the Concordat with the Papacy.

Key factors in Napoleon Bonaparte's rise

- his military ability
- his self-confidence
- his military successes in Italy
- public apathy towards the Directory
- the desire for stability and order
- his promise of prestige and glory for France
- the timing and organisation of the coup of Brumaire

Key factors in Napoleon's impact on France

- the nature of the dictatorship
- plebiscites
- his appeal to property owners
- his honours
- the system of repression
- his legal reforms

Remember the diplomatic damage that the Berlin Decrees were to do to France, as well as the economic implications.

There are many reasons put forward for Napoleon's expansionism.

Note the difference between myth and reality.

Consider the point that Napoleon's overall legacy to France was actually quite small.

- his educational reforms
- his police system
- taxation
- his relationship with the Catholic Church
- his administrative system

Key factors in Napoleon's military success
- the incompetence of his enemies
- his military organisation
- the experience gained by his armies in the revolutionary wars
- his early logistics
- his boldness and unconventionality
- his divided enemies
- his generalship
- the loyalty of his soldiers

Key factors in Napoleon's decline and defeat
- the skill of opponents such as Generals Wellington, Bagration and Blücher
- naval weakness
- his conservatism over weaponry and tactics
- his reluctance to delegate
- poor logistics later
- the sheer number of his enemies
- the size of empire to maintain
- the Berlin Decrees, which antagonised many European powers
- Spain
- Russia
- the Fourth Coalition
- lack of men and resources

E France, 1815–30

Key questions

What was the impact of the Peace of Paris and the Treaty of Vienna on France?

How successfully were the Bourbons restored?

What were the causes of the crises of 1829–30?

What were the reasons for the overthrow of Charles X?

THE IMPACT OF THE PEACE OF PARIS AND THE TREATY OF VIENNA

The first Treaty of Paris, before Napoleon's return in the 100 Days, had been lenient towards France. The second Treaty of Paris, after the return of Napoleon, was much harsher. Those who had supported the Bourbons were promoted; those who had returned to Napoleon, like Marshall Ney, were shot. An army of occupation was imposed until 1818, along with a heavy but not impossible indemnity. Territory such as Savoy and forts in the north were lost and the Bourbon

monarchy — although seen as dependent on the Allies — was restored. At the Treaty of Vienna of 1815, the Allies involved the French in the restructuring of Europe and did not alienate the vanquished. However, in general terms the settlement did damage Bourbon credibility.

THE KEY PROBLEMS FACING LOUIS XVIII

Louis XVIII's main difficulty was dealing with a republican tradition — a problem exacerbated by his inevitable association with the *ancien régime*. In addition, the Orleanists were rival royalist claimants who jostled for influence along with remnants of the radical left and the Bonapartists. There were too many alternative governments for his comfort. With a million dead and the inevitable dislocation of war, there were serious social and economic problems. There was also a sense of humiliation, which the French felt keenly after their former glories and for which they were bound to blame the leaders.

LOUIS XVIII'S PERSONALITY

In contrast to Napoleon, Louis XVIII was fat, dull and uninspiring. He believed in the divine right of kings and generally appeared too close in spirit to the *ancien régime* that most of France had been pleased to leave behind. Though reluctant to accept limits to his power, he was prepared to compromise.

THE KEY POLICIES OF LOUIS XVIII

The Charter of 1814 accepted the key gains of the revolution and the Civil Code's liberal features. Equality and freedom were there to stay and royal power was to be shared with property owners. It was a constitutional monarchy, though much stronger than the British one. Louis XVIII's abrupt flight on the return of Napoleon after Elba did not impress many; nor did his acceptance of the second Treaty of Paris and the Treaty of Vienna. But he had no choice. He made no major errors and had an able prime minister in Elie Decazes whose financial management was sound and meant that the reparations were paid by 1818.

LOUIS XVIII'S CONTRIBUTION TO THE SUCCESS AND FAILURE OF THE RESTORATION

Louis XVIII was associated with the peace and perhaps failed to capitalise on the economic strength of France after 1815. He benefited from the absence of social tension. Given the desire for peace in France, the potential for the middle class and the absence of a really punitive peace settlement, the Bourbons should perhaps have got better established. Louis made the 1814 Charter work and convinced people of his belief in it. After an initial attempt at press censorship in 1815, he tolerated a free press. However, this could be a savage critic of the regime. He initially undermined the Ultras (the right-wing pro-monarchist party), but must take some responsibility for their later growth as a political force. The appointment of Joseph Villèle as prime minister in 1822 was also an error, as he was a strong Ultra.

SOCIAL AND ECONOMIC ISSUES, 1815–30

Feudalism and the worst social features of the *ancien régime* had gone, but France was still strongly divided by class. The economy was heavily regulated by government when compared with Britain, and the bulk of investment was still in land

---

The full terms of both Paris settlements and the Treaty of Vienna need to be studied carefully.

It is vital to know the nature of the task which faced the restored monarchy.

It was unfortunate for the future of the monarchy that it had such a poor Bourbon candidate.

There are grounds for arguing that Louis XVIII was competent and that many of the problems which faced France were beyond his control.

There is the basis of a reasonable case both for and against Louis XVIII.

rather than industry. Small-scale agriculture grew throughout the period, but output remained low. Overall, growth was about 2% a year and there was equally slow population growth. However, the country was socially and economically stable. The agricultural population grew throughout this period and traditional labour-intensive methods were used. Imports and exports were limited and there was a serious economic dip from 1826 to 1828, which led to hunger in the cities and fuelled a political crisis in 1829–30.

CHARLES X AND A SLIDE TO THE RIGHT

Initially popular, Charles X was old when he came to power in 1824 and was distrusted by the enfranchised, who tended to favour the gains of the revolution. Charles's deep conservatism was seen in his coronation at Rheims, where the excess of pageantry resurrected the worst of the *ancien régime*. It was tactless, as was his concern for the *émigrés*. Given the strong anti-clericalism amongst many of the electorate, the suspicion that Charles favoured restoring the clergy's power caused major concern.

THE BACKGROUND TO THE 1830 CRISIS

A critical press and deep concern over the future of the Church fed a crisis which was intensified by a Chamber of Deputies which was difficult to manage. Charles X's principal minister, Villèle, was an Ultra who led a minority party in the Chamber. With fundamental political and constitutional differences between left, centre and right, no consensus was possible. The election of 1827 resulted in 40% for the centre/government, 40% for the liberal/left and 20% for the Ultras. The King's favourite, Polignac, was an Ultra. Ultras were strong royalists, opposed to any liberalisation of the system of government or extensions of popular rights.

THE FAILURE OF THE BOURBONS

Against a background of hunger and strong press criticism, Charles X called an election in 1830 to help Polignac gain support. When this was seen as likely to fail, Charles used his emergency powers to impose the four Ordinances of 25 July which dissolved the Chamber, restricted the franchise, imposed press censorship and called for new elections. This was viewed in Paris as an attempted coup by Charles X and the right. With no troops available and a reluctance to arrest potential leaders of a coup against him, the 73-year-old Charles X fled. The rioting and barricades of Paris terrified him and he overestimated both loyalty to the regime and the strength of the opposition.

Key factors causing the failure of the Bourbon restoration

- the depth of republican feeling
- the humiliation of the Paris Treaties
- the personalities of Louis XVIII and Charles X
- the flight during the 100 Days — giving in to Napoleon's return from Elba
- the growth of the Ultras
- the free press
- low economic growth
- the conservatism of Charles
- the insensitivity of Charles

A sound economy with little turbulence should have helped the monarchy to get re-established.

The political insensitivity of Charles X was a major factor in his downfall.

Charles X failed to understand the need to manage the Chamber effectively.

Consider whether the Bourbons had a serious chance of success.

* the problem of the Church
* the appointment of the Ultra Polignac
* the mismanagement of events in 1830

F France, 1830–48

Key questions

What were the key social and economic developments in this period?

How successful was the rule of Louis Philippe?

Why was Louis Philippe overthrown?

WHY DID LOUIS PHILIPPE BECOME RULER OF FRANCE?

How good a basis did
Louis Philippe have for
successful rule?

Louis Philippe was head of a major family which, despite having royal blood, had supported the revolution. Although only supported by a small group in 1830, Louis Philippe was the lesser of several evils open to the divided opponents of the Bourbons. The powerful middle class was none too content with republicanism and preferred stability over democracy. Louis Philippe — at the time aged 56 and set in his ways — seemed their best option.

THE SKILLS AND FAILINGS OF LOUIS PHILIPPE

Note both the early
strengths and the
early weaknesses.

Louis Philippe was intelligent and hard working, and genuinely wanted to be popular. He got on well with everyone, and was determined, serious and well educated. Having been in exile when younger, he had no wish to be seen as uncompromising and to suffer any of the fates of his predecessors. He never managed to overcome the fact that he was essentially an elective monarch, in power at the behest of the middle class. He had no friends among the hard right and failed to cope with a frequently savage press.

LOUIS PHILIPPE'S DOMESTIC POLICIES

Consider the basis of
Louis Philippe's power.

Louis Philippe ensured the partial disestablishment of the Church and reduced its impact on education. The franchise remained restrictive and power continued to be held by the upper bourgeoisie. Many old Bourbon supporters were sacked and noble power declined. Louis Philippe managed the middle class and its National Guard well, and the economy's improvement in the 1830s caused a rising standard of living and brought acceptance of his regime.

LOUIS PHILIPPE'S FOREIGN POLICY

Sensible policies did not
gain support among a
population that recalled
Napoleonic glory.

Public opinion wanted glory and gain, but Louis Philippe felt otherwise. He was aware that France was still seen as a dangerous and potentially expansive force in Europe and wanted peace and allies. He co-operated with Britain over the Belgian Crisis of 1830, and would not allow his son to be King of Belgium. He refused to get involved in Spain either, and worked well with Palmerston to defuse tension there. Although France had backed Mehmet Ali against his Turkish master in the 1820s, he was forced to accept Britain and Russia's decision to reduce his power in 1840–41. Public opinion saw this as a second climbdown and was further enraged by co-operation with Aberdeen and Palmerston over

Tahiti. The lack of glory did not gain Louis Philippe supporters, and successes in areas like Algeria were ignored.

A lack of basic support became evident when Louis Philippe was challenged.

THE BACKGROUND TO LOUIS PHILIPPE'S FALL

Louis Philippe's appointment was a useful compromise until something better could be found, but his regime lacked legitimacy. He had outlived his purpose by 1848, by which time republicanism had been embraced by the working class and by the middle class as well. Legitimists (who wanted a return to the Bourbon line) gained ground in his reign, as did the Bonapartists. Aged 70 in 1848, he was too old and too conservative to adapt. His favourite minister, Guizot, was politically out of tune and the vital middle-class National Guard was being neglected. The death of his popular heir in 1842 did not help his regime either.

Note the role that economics and hunger again play in French politics.

ECONOMIC FACTORS BEHIND THE CRISIS OF 1848

There had been slow but steady growth in the economy in the 1830s, and a railway boom in the early 1840s. But the pace of industrialisation was slow amidst a growth of poverty, underemployment and a move to the towns in the 1840s. A Europe-wide depression starting in 1846 led to a drop in shares and layoffs in all areas, and then crop failures led to high food prices in 1847. With middle-class investors losing money and the government seen as too middle class by a hungry and underemployed working class (and with ministerial corruption in the background), there were many grounds for limited support for the regime, if not outright hostility to it.

Contrast Louis Philippe's fall with the falls of Louis XVIII and Charles X.

THE FINAL COLLAPSE OF LOUIS PHILIPPE

The absence of a strong domestic or foreign policy had led to apathy towards the regime. Louis Philippe would not extend the limited franchise, and his policy of laissez faire did not appeal to a France used to greater government intervention. He was uninterested in a moderate reform to tackle poverty, and his support for Guizot lost him considerable political ground. His eventual dismissal of Guizot let the radicals in and made Louis Philippe seem even more indecisive. When he declared the meetings of February 1848 illegal, the barricades went up in Paris. A neglected National Guard meant that he could not (or would not) use force as he had in the attempted coups of 1831 and 1834, and he simply abdicated. The government was not overthrown; it allowed itself to fall. The attempt at a constitutional monarchy had failed.

Key elements in Louis Philippe's reign

- the press
- the Church
- the National Guard
- the conservative work of Guizot
- the seemingly ineffective foreign policy in Spain and the Middle East
- the absence of a strong foreign or domestic policy
- limited economic and social change

Key factors in the fall of Louis Philippe

- he was only the lesser of evils in 1830
- his age

- his indecisiveness
- the basis of his regime was popular support
- the National Guard
- his foreign policy
- the unpopularity of his minister, Guizot
- the death of his heir
- economic depression and hunger
- mismanagement of events in 1848

G France, 1848–52

Key questions

Why was a republic created in France in 1848?

Why did republicanism fail to survive in France between 1848 and 1852?

Why was the Second Empire established in 1852?

THE ESTABLISHMENT OF THE REPUBLIC

There were major differences between the opponents of Louis Philippe.

The monarchy was not re-established, as the republicans dominated the Assembly and acted quickly. Working-class Parisian radicals dominated republicanism and a radical and free Parisian press set the tone. Divisions between those who overthrew Louis Philippe were immediately seen. Left wingers, such as Alexandre Ledru-Rollin, wanted radical social and political change, an anti-poverty programme, the right to work, higher taxes and a much wider franchise. The middle-class republicans had other ideas: they wanted to preserve their property and their money, and were genuinely frightened of the mob. A Provisional Government was quickly established.

THE PROVISIONAL GOVERNMENT

The radical nature of the Provisional Government angered French property owners.

The Provisional Government brought in one man, one vote and agreed to a right to work. High taxes were needed to pay for this, but the National Workshops which were to provide it failed economically and politically, and aroused fears amongst both peasants and the bourgeoisie that their property was at risk.

THE CONSTITUENT ASSEMBLY

There was now no chance of a move to the left.

Elections produced an Assembly dominated by badly divided monarchists and a few left-wing radicals. With the bourgeoisie very much in charge, they ended the reforms of the Provisional Government, such as the National Workshops, and started to conscript the unemployed or send them back to the provinces. This led to the June Days and barricades, which were brutally suppressed by General Cavagnac. The left and the radicals were destroyed as a force in France. Cavagnac remained loyal to the republic and ensured that no dictatorship occurred.

THE CONSTITUTION OF 1848

The new Constitution divided power between a directly elected president and the single-chamber Assembly. The widened franchise produced another Napoleon,

Louis-Napoleon Bonaparte (the nephew of the former Emperor, later to become Napoleon III) as president. His opponents were Lamartine (who was too poetic to succeed), Ledru-Rollin (who was too radical) and Cavagnac (who was loathed). The new Constitution was probably too idealistic for a France unused to democracy and accustomed to strong central government.

It was perhaps a regime doomed to failure from the start.

THE RISE OF NAPOLEON: FROM PRESIDENT TO EMPEROR

France and the rest of Europe had been hostile to Napoleon's ambition in the early 1840s. His earlier attempts at trying to seize power had failed and he was gaoled between 1840 and 1846. Like Hitler, he used a prison sentence to refine his political plans, and he aimed to give France status and glory, strong leadership and a sense of direction and purpose. His Bonapartist ideas were liked, he had a great name and he was backed by the centre and the Church. He also showed an awareness of the need to care for the poor, was not involved in the June Days and avoided the hatred which accrued to Cavagnac. He was seen to be prepared to operate within a democratic framework, and manoeuvred himself into a position to win the support of a newly enfranchised electorate.

Consider what alternatives, if any, there were to Napoleon.

NAPOLEON AS PRESIDENT, 1848–52

Napoleon left most actions to Assembly politicians and travelled widely in France to gain support, exploit his powers of patronage and generally ensure the retention of power. He repressed radicalism, supported the Papacy, helped the Church return to educational dominance in the *Loi Falloux* and built up power in the Assembly.

Note the preparations that Napoleon made for the eventual seizure of power.

WHY WAS PRESIDENT NAPOLEON ABLE TO SEIZE POWER IN 1851–52?

The Constitution of 1848 stated that presidents could only remain in power for one term. Napoleon could not get the required support to change the Constitution, so he decided to seize power by arresting his opponents, closing the press and deploying the military. The Parisian barricades were smashed and a well-organised plebiscite endorsed this action in 1851. After that a new constitutional system was created giving him a 10-year presidency, and a further plebiscite agreed to convert the republic into an empire under Napoleon in December 1852.

Note the combination of the legal and the illegal, the careful planning and the concern for popular support.

WHY DID THE REPUBLIC FAIL?

Many Frenchmen, particularly those of property, viewed the republic as a radical system imposed by Paris on the rest of France. They craved a monarchy, but the disagreements between the Bourbons and Orleanists weakened the cause. Few really backed the republic, and Napoleon — with his political skills — was felt to be a better alternative.

Yet another French ruler seems to have been the compromise candidate.

Key factors in the failure of the republic and the rise of Napoleon
- the destruction of the left by the army
- the radicalism of the left
- middle-class fears for their property
- the divisions within the Assembly
- the 1848 Constitution
- the skill of Napoleon

- the French preference for authoritarianism
- support for Napoleon from the Church and the centre
- the effective campaigning of Napoleon
- the lack of any clear alternative

H France and the Second Empire

Key questions

How liberal a ruler was Napoleon III?

What were the main achievements of Napoleon III?

What were the main social and economic developments in France during the Second Empire?

Why was the Second Empire overthrown?

Questions about Napoleon III concentrate on his strengths and weaknesses.

THE PERSONALITY OF NAPOLEON III

Napoleon III's abilities were matched by many failings. He had a great sense of mission, liked power and was ambitious for France as well as himself. He had some good ideas as far as domestic policy was concerned and sensed what the French people, in their very different ways, wanted. However, he was neither a good analyst nor strategist. Frequently out of his depth in foreign affairs, he managed to damage French prestige by his incompetence.

There was an appearance of democracy and consultation.

THE GOVERNMENT OF THE SECOND EMPIRE

Initially the government was quite authoritarian. The 1852 Constitution gave considerable power to the President, who operated with two legislative houses. However, the Upper House was appointed by the Emperor and elections to the Lower House were by a limited franchise, which tended to favour men of property. Ministers were tightly controlled by the Emperor and he worked hard to eliminate political parties. Generally, the government was modelled very much on that of his uncle. Measures were seen as more important than men, and thus Napoleon III had the pragmatism to employ those who had worked for previous regimes, provided they remained loyal.

Contrast this authoritarianism with the republican system which followed.

AUTHORITARIAN FEATURES OF NAPOLEON III'S REGIME

Napoleon III took action against those who might oppose him with arrests, imprisonment and exile. Tough press censorship was introduced and remained. Opposition parties were banned and political meetings tightly monitored. Napoleon rewarded officials for loyalty and ensured that he had support of the Church.

If Napoleon III was a dictator, then it was with the acceptance of the people.

LIBERAL FEATURES OF NAPOLEON III'S REGIME

Napoleon III encountered little opposition for the simple reason that he provided the leadership, law and order which the majority of French people wanted. Provided there was loyalty to the regime, careers were open to talent. There is

an argument that he saw repression as temporary, that he was not vindictive; his leniency towards Orsini — who had tried to assassinate him in 1858 over his Italian policy — is a good example to back up this viewpoint.

THE SECOND EMPIRE'S MAIN CHANGES TO GOVERNMENT

> There were genuine moves by Napoleon III towards a democratic and liberal state.

There were three main changes to the method of government, all relaxing the authoritarian system of 1852. The first in 1860 gave more influence to the Corps Legislative, the Lower House, which gained the right to be consulted. The second in 1867–68 eased the press laws and gave the Lower House the right to question ministers. The final changes came in 1869–70, and marked a shift to a constitutional emperor with power being devolved to the two chambers. These moves were supported by a plebiscite in 1870 and led to power-sharing with Emile Ollivier as prime minister.

THE REASONS FOR THE EMPEROR'S REDUCTION IN POWER

> Note the division of opinion about Napoleon III's motives.

The Constitution of 1870 left considerable power with the Emperor. Some historians argue that Napoleon III was just buying off a growing opposition; others see it as genuine liberalism. His government had been losing support at elections, so concessions had to be made. The diminution of power was the result of both common sense on Napoleon's part and pressure from below.

NAPOLEON III'S FOREIGN POLICY

> Arguably, Napoleon III's greatest failings lay in foreign policy.

Given Napoleon's name and family background, there were great expectations from the French, and fears from foreign countries. Much influenced by public opinion, he sensed that the French wanted prestige yet also favoured peace, and so he set out to achieve status and glory without war. He wished France to be a major power in Europe, to revise the hated Vienna settlement and to break up the unity of Russia, Prussia and Austria. He supported nationalism in Poland and Italy, but this policy was contradicted by his desire to gain Catholic support. Priorities could change, for sometimes he appeared aggressive and expansionist, and at other times peaceful and conciliatory. Though he saw himself as the arbiter of Europe's destiny and a major force in European diplomacy, other powers did not. He was too much of a gambler in foreign affairs and lacked the diplomatic skills of Bismarck and Palmerston.

THE CRIMEAN WAR

> The Crimean War, like most of Napoleon III's foreign adventures, brought him no credit, and France few gains.

The Crimean War is an example of Napoleon III's foreign policy at its worst. He was inexperienced in the early 1850s. The idea behind the invasion of Russia was misconceived and the whole issue should have been sorted out by diplomacy. He was manipulated by the Turks into supporting them against Russia, and his wish to appear as protector of the Christian holy places was absurd. There was little popular support in France for the war, particularly as it dragged on. However, peace was finally made in Paris, so some prestige may have come from it.

ITALY

> Italy provides a vivid example of Napoleon III's weakness in foreign policy.

The reasons for France's Italian campaigns were various and always muddled, since Napoleon III's simultaneous support of nationalism and the Catholic Church led to contradictions. He wanted to undermine Vienna and Austria, and perhaps repeat his uncle's great victories. He was also keen to get Nice and Savoy, and was manipulated into greater involvement than he intended by Cavour and later by the Italian revolutionary leader Garibaldi. He gained limited support in Italy by abandoning Cavour at Villafranca, but alienated the Papacy and thus Catholic support, and infuriated Austria. The heavy casualties suffered by his armies at Magenta and Solferino alienated his own people, and Prussia moved closer to Austria as well. Overall his Italian involvement must be seen as a failure, as he was manipulated and lost friends and public support. He was a poor planner and analyst, and showed indecisiveness and a lack of determination.

MEXICO: THE REASONS FOR INVOLVEMENT

Napoleon III's reasons for Mexican involvement were highly suspect.

The story of drift and manipulation continues in a line from Crimea and Italy through to a Mexican adventure which did considerable harm to Napoleon III and his regime. The government of Juarez in Mexico — hostile to the Catholic Church and payment of debts to France — aroused the antagonism and ambition of Napoleon, and possibly his wife Eugenie. The neutrality of Britain and the involvement of the USA in its civil war gave France a chance of intervening to get its debts paid, save the Church and gain prestige and possibly empire. Napoleon calculated that as the USA had taken huge amounts of Mexican territory, so too could France — a judgement that was seriously called into question by his involvement.

MEXICO: THE REASONS FOR FAILURE

The Mexican campaign was a catalogue of disasters.

After Napoleon had imposed the Austrian Maximilian on the throne of Mexico, the Mexicans fought furiously against foreign intervention and 40,000 French troops proved no match for a united Mexico's deployment of troops using guerrilla techniques. After a 3-year war, Maximilian was captured and shot, and France's unrealistic dream ended in humiliation. Napoleon III simply had not thought out the implications of the process; nor did he have the ability or resources to follow it through.

THE FRANCO~PRUSSIAN WAR: THE CAUSES

Note the way in which Napoleon was completely outmanoeuvred by Bismarck.

The rise of Bismarck in Germany led to the marginalisation of France as a major European power. Bismarck was aware that France lacked allies and had alienated Russia over Poland in 1863 and the British over Belgium. Bismarck ignored France when he took over Denmark in the early 1860s, and he misled Napoleon III over both Austria and Luxembourg. Meanwhile, Italy was still upset with France over unification issues. War was foolishly threatened by France over the Hohenzollern candidature for Spain. Bismarckian diplomacy reached its height over the Ems telegram, and France was provoked into declaring war on Prussia. The idea of war was hugely popular with the French public and this was a major factor in the outbreak of the Franco–Prussian War, as was Napoleon III's lack of awareness about the weakness of his forces.

THE FRANCO~PRUSSIAN WAR

Foreign policy was Napoleon III's greatest weakness.

With no allies and no serious spending on defence, France was in a hopeless position. The army was committed to the offensive; so much so that it had maps of Germany but not of France. In 1870 the French army was destroyed within weeks at Metz and Sedan, and Paris was surrounded. Napoleon III was completely humiliated.

UNIT 3

France

ECONOMIC DEVELOPMENTS UNDER THE SECOND EMPIRE

Napoleon III had few original ideas. He was concerned for the poor, though this was partly defensive as he knew that hungry mobs could overturn regimes. He was always anxious to ensure cheap credit, and the new *Credit Mobilier* helped capital creation and the railway boom, which had established a national network by 1870. Overall there was little other economic change. Agriculture remained a dominant force in the French economy, the small farm and the small firm prevailed and there was little large-scale entrepreneurship. The free trade ideas that Napoleon advocated were probably unsuited to France in the second part of the nineteenth century. Part of the liberalisation programme of the 1860s was the legalisation of trade unions.

SOCIAL CHANGE

The Second Empire was the age of the bourgeoisie, but — given the huge ideological and religious differences which divided the middle class — there were no clear-cut class politics. A few very rich aristocratic families dominated society and had huge landholdings populated by a profoundly conservative peasantry. The growth of an urban proletariat was to come much later.

WHY DID THE SECOND EMPIRE FAIL?

Napoleon III's political support gradually dwindled, but he was tolerated until he proved his incompetence in the wars against Mexico and Prussia. By the end of his rule, he was old and ill and at odds with ministers who would not support his political and constitutional reforms. The aristocracy felt that he did too much to help the *nouveaux riches*, industry did not like his free trade ideas, the urban poor felt neglected and he had taken few steps to combat a growing opposition. He was long past his sell-by date and the disastrous military defeat at Sedan showed it.

Key factors in Napoleon III's reign

- domestic policy
- methods of government
- attitude to political parties and opposition
- authoritarianism
- the support of the Church
- the gradual liberalisation of the regime
- cheap credit
- absence of social and economic change
- the Crimean War
- Italian intervention
- Mexico
- the lack of foreign allies

Key factors in Napoleon III's fall

- his foreign policy
- the Franco–Prussian War
- his failure as a diplomat
- Bismarck

There were no significant economic changes — and none was particularly wanted by the French people.

There was little major social change.

Military failure led to the failure of the Second Empire.

94

- the defeat by Prussia at Sedan
- the lack of support amongst the middle class
- the lack of support from the working class

France, 1870–1914

Key questions

How and why was the Third Republic established by 1875?

What problems faced France in the early years of the Third Republic and how did it overcome them?

How was the Third Republic able to overcome the crises it faced after 1875?

How successful was the Third Republic up to 1914?

What were the main social and economic developments between 1871 and 1914?

Why did France become involved in the First World War?

PROBLEMS FACING FRANCE IN 1870

Key French problems after the Second Republic were the defeat by the Prussians and the occupation of France by a hostile army; the resistance of Paris to both the Germans and the Assembly; the rise of a militant left under Blanqui; the need to create a new system of government after the collapse of the Second Empire; and the need to get the Prussian army out of France.

THE COMMUNE

The Commune demonstrated the divisions between Paris and the rest of France.

The Commune was the Paris-led revolt against the Assembly led by Louis Thiers, who was elected to head the executive of the new Third Republic in 1871. It represented the most radical forces in France. Strong amongst the urban workers and the lower middle class, the Communards' left-wing ideas were not favoured by the rest of France. The Commune wanted control by local areas of tax and education; it was strongly anti-clerical, and held anti-capitalist ideas on pay and conditions.

WHY DID THE COMMUNE FAIL?

The Commune attracted limited support in the provinces, which viewed it as a dangerous Marxist force which pitted Paris against the rest of the country. There was no support from the rich and powerful, and the Communards lacked any real organisation. With the Prussians allowing the Assembly under Thiers to use the French army against the Communards, the latter were bloodily smashed. The changes made by Prefect Haussmann to Paris made the traditional barricades of old Paris difficult to sustain and Thiers' army was quickly victorious. At least 20,000 Communards and their sympathisers died in the Parisian fighting.

The Commune was the end of the radical left as a major force in French politics.

THE PEACE WITH GERMANY

After the defeats at Metz and Sedan and the humiliation of the Hall of Mirrors — when the French were made to surrender in their own Palace of Versailles —

The 1871 peace was a central cause of the First World War.

Note the vote in the 1871 election and the rival monarchist claimants.

Note the splits within the republican camp.

Thiers is vital to the establishment of the Third Republic.

French politics was dominated by an old struggle for power.

Note the fragility of the early republic and its limited support.

the French were in no position to do anything but give in. The final settlement was agreed by Thiers at Frankfurt in 1871. Alsace-Lorraine was lost and a large, though not impossible, indemnity had to be paid. It was seen as a humiliation for France, and both foreign and military policy from then on were directed towards revenge.

ESTABLISHMENT OF THE THIRD REPUBLIC: THE MONARCHISTS

The Assembly of 1871 produced a majority for the monarchists, who were split between three rival claimants: the Comte de Paris; the legitimist Comte de Chambord; and the Bonapartist Prince Imperial. There was no possibility of compromise between them, and this effectively ensured that a republic would survive.

THE REPUBLICANS

Republicans were a minority in the 1871 Assembly, but formed a larger group than any single one of the three monarchist factions. Republicans, naturally, agreed on a republic, though beyond that their ranks were divided between a strong left-wing group led by Gambetta (who had been supporters of the Commune) and a more centrist group led by Rivet. Unlike the monarchists, they each had a coherent set of policies.

THE WORK OF THIERS

Louis Thiers was the dominant figure of the early years of the Third Republic. He provided desperately needed leadership after the collapse of Napoleon III and took the key decisions about the Commune and the peace. Though he preferred a constitutional monarchy, he realised that a republic was the only workable option for France given the monarchists' divisions and the way some of their views shaded into right-wing extremism. He became the Third Republic's first president, but was voted out of office in 1873 after failing to please the Assembly's many factions.

THE FAILURE OF THE MONARCHISTS

The years 1871–75 were dominated by the struggle between republicans and monarchists over the type of government for France. The republicans were ultimately to win, but it was never a foregone conclusion. The key reasons for the eventual victory were the monarchists' ineptitude and divisions.

THE PRESIDENCY OF MACMAHON

President Patrice MacMahon had a reputation as the destroyer of the Commune and was put into office by the monarchists to pave the way for Henry V and the defeat of the radical left. By 1875, however, monarchist blundering had led to an Assembly decision formally and permanently to adopt a republican constitution. It passed by a single vote and elections from then on confirmed a decline in monarchist support. This — together with MacMahon's reluctance to take power illegally — ensured the future France as a republic.

THE 1875 CONSTITUTION

The 1875 Constitution was a series of separate laws rather than a single document. The original intention was to give some succour to the monarchist

cause. The result was the opposite, for the new Constitution established a presidency elected by the Senate and the Chamber of Deputies for 7 years. The president could appoint ministers (who were responsible to deputies) and dissolve the Chamber. Political initiatives were now expected to come from the deputies and ministers. The lack of a dominant authority was a major contrast to the past.

WHY DID THE REPUBLICANS WIN?

The republican cause benefited considerably from monarchist division and the inept leadership of MacMahon. MacMahon, refusing to consider a coup, tried to use his power and patronage, but neither electoral manipulation nor monarchist ministers and civil servants could help. Elections constantly boosted republicanism and the able leadership of republicans such as Gambetta and Grévy proved difficult to overcome. Republicans grew to be the dominant force in both the Senate and the Chamber of Deputies, and in 1879 MacMahon resigned. This demonstrated that the republic was there to stay.

REPUBLICAN IMPACT ON FRANCE, 1879–85

Pushed by the left and opposed by the right, the new President Jules Grévy saw republicanism implement its ideas in France. These ranged from amnesty for the Communards to the establishment of trade unions and co-operative societies. Attacks on the Church recommenced, with Jules Ferry, the minister of education, reducing its influence on all parts of education. This was bitterly opposed by the right. Public worship became unrestricted, press censorship was removed and local elections were made more democratic. The Senate was made a totally elective body and this further strengthened republicanism.

THE INSTABILITY OF 1885–89

Divisions within the republican movement and the possibility of a coup by General Boulanger (a senior and popular soldier) caused political instability from 1885 to 1889. Republicanism split over demands of the left for higher taxation of the rich, the total separation of Church and state, and further reforms to benefit the working class. With attacks from the right opposed to the anti-clerical laws, and President Grévy linked with sleaze concerning his son-in-law, the moderate centre was under siege.

THE BOULANGER CRISIS

General Boulanger was a soldier and politician who was intensely ambitious and had a flair for self-publicity. The radical right hoped that Boulanger might push out more moderate republicans and — in the absence of a monarchical candidate — he became a figurehead who promised a return to authoritarian rule. He could have seized power, but hesitated and then fled. The left realised how great a threat to the republic he had been and worked with the moderate republicans to ensure an end to Boulangerism. The elections of 1889 confirmed republican domination in politics.

OPPORTUNISTS IN POWER, 1889–98

The last decade of the nineteenth century was one of political stability in France. Both left and right accepted the moderate republican leadership of Ferry and

Note the shift downwards in decision-making.

The central reason for the republican victory was the lack of a credible alternative to a republic.

The years between 1879 and 1885 were critical for the establishment of the republic and the growth of public acceptance.

Consider the nature of the threats to the republic.

The actual nature of the threat needs to be carefully analysed.

Make sure you know the main social reforms of the opportunist period, especially the welfare changes.

Leon Gambetta. Apart from the Panama and Dreyfus scandals (see below), domestic politics were quiet, with modest social reform, a truce with the Church and the *Ralliement* (a move by both Royalists and Catholics to support the Republic) rallying to the Republic.

THE PANAMA SCANDAL

After the Panama Canal Company, led by the builder of Suez, de Lesseps, collapsed in 1892, its losses had to be borne by thousands of French citizens. The project was too ambitious and unrealistic, and when the financial details emerged it was felt that too many of those in office had profited unduly. Unlike the Boulanger affair, the Panama scandal did not affect the constitution, but the sleaze did harm the political process and lessen support for the republic.

THE DREYFUS AFFAIR

Falsely accused of spying, the Jewish officer Alfred Dreyfus was convicted and sentenced to imprisonment on Devil's Island. The issue divided France. The Dreyfusards saw the sentence as a violation of rights which showed a corrupt republic. The anti-Dreyfusards used it to rally the right against the Jews, the left and everything that they felt was wrong with the republic. The gap between left and right widened and the eventual victory of the Dreyfusards paved the way for the left's electoral success after 1900.

THE RADICALS IN POWER

The leftist governments led by Waldeck-Rousseau, Clemenceau, Briand and Caillaux put through a great deal of reforming legislation, but had run out of steam, in the face of revolutionary socialism, by 1914. The Laws of Association and the Law of Separation had a big impact on the Church and its relationship with the state, social reform dealt with unemployment, working hours and public health, and tax reform tried to pay for it all.

SYNDICALISM AND SOCIALISM

Syndicalist government by trade unions was never a major possibility, as its support was largely confined to the urban proletariat. The peasantry, who formed the majority of the electorate, ignored it. The radical Georges Sorel wished to use general strikes as a political weapon to change the republic, but after 1906–07 the radicals lost support to the far left and were pushed towards the more moderate republican camp.

FOREIGN POLICY UP TO 1905

Always determined to avenge the 1871 Treaty of Frankfurt, French military policy and diplomacy had been focused on hostility to Germany. France's alliance with Russia (which entailed major French investment) and its *entente* with Britain had this more in mind than considerations about national security. Britain was not always close, as the Fashoda incident (a quarrel between Britain and France over Sudan) showed. But the Moroccan crisis (a quarrel with Germany) helped to repair good relations with Britain, and detailed planning was undertaken with the British army and navy. France had comprehensive conscription and participated in the colonial scramble.

What, if any, was the nature of the threat to the republic?

Consider whether the results of the Dreyfus affair were more important than the affair itself.

Note the major social changes in this period.

While it is not necessary to have in-depth knowledge of the conflicting ideas, it is necessary to know that radicalism was defeated.

French foreign and military policy was very clear.

The flaws in French military planning and diplomatic procedures during 1914 played a major part in starting the war and in initial French defeats.

THE BUILD-UP TO WAR

The government of René Viviani was inexperienced in foreign affairs. Although France had played a part in restraining Russia against Germany in 1908, it was not in a position to do so in 1914. The growth of French military power was not seen as a deterrent by the Germans, but created the need for a pre-emptive strike through Belgium into France. France showed restraint in the initial weeks of the crisis of 1914 between Austria, Russia, Serbia and then Germany, but harmed its chances of obtaining military advantage by keeping its troops well back from the frontiers until it was too late to stop the Schlieffen steamroller. The Schlieffen Plan was the only German war plan, and was designed to start with the invasion of Belgium and the destruction of France.

Key factors in establishing a French republic

- the divisions amongst the monarchists
- the failure of Napoleon
- the ability of Thiers
- the Commune
- swift adaptation to middle-class demands

Key factors during the Third Republic up to 1914

- the divisions within the monarchists
- the work of Thiers
- the 1875 Constitution
- the presidency of MacMahon
- the growth of the democratic process
- the work of Gambetta and Grévy
- the relationship between Church and state
- changes to education
- Boulanger
- the Panama affair
- the Dreyfus affair
- the role of Clemenceau in providing policies and stability
- the growth of unions
- the development of co-operative movements
- social reforms such as pensions and the growth of a welfare state
- industrialisation
- the dominance of agriculture

A The unification of Italy

Key questions

What were the main obstacles to Italian unification between 1830 and 1849?

Why did the revolutions of 1848–49 fail to unite Italy?

What were the main factors in the establishment of the Kingdom of Italy up to 1861?

How important were the individual contributions of Cavour, Mazzini and Garibaldi to Italian unification?

How important were foreign intervention and foreign circumstances to Italian unification?

How divided and how united was Italy between 1861 and 1870?

THE BACKGROUND TO 1830

This historical background is fundamental to the whole study of this topic.

Napoleon Bonaparte's legacy to the many differing states of Italy was to awaken liberal and nationalist ideas. Austria was determined to stamp these out. The Vienna settlement of 1815 restored old monarchies, installed reactionary systems and returned the Papacy as a major political force. The autocratic role of Austria, especially in the north of Italy, was central.

THE REVOLUTIONS OF 1820

The 1820 rebellions were important as forerunners to the later revolutions and as part of the learning process for Italian nationalists.

Hostility to the Vienna settlement started with attacks on the restored systems in Naples, Sicily and Piedmont. The rebels had different aims: the Sicilians did not like unity with Naples; the Neapolitans were reacting against the corruption and poverty in southern Italy; the Piedmontese (perhaps most influenced by Napoleon) were mainly concerned with getting a constitutional and limited monarchy. These separate movements were led by a middle class who often belonged to secret societies such as the Masons and the Carbonari. All were savagely repressed by the Austrians.

THE REVOLUTIONS OF 1831

It took the Italians a long time to learn the lessons needed for victory.

The 1831 revolutions were inspired by the French revolution of 1830 and had much the same story and fate as the revolutions in 1820. Loyal troops and the ever-present Austrians smashed insurrection in Modena, Parma and the Papal states where constitutional and limited monarchy was the objective. The Italian actions were localised and unco-ordinated, had conflicting aims and were largely led by the middle class with no serious working-class support.

CAUSES OF THE 1848 REVOLUTIONS

These revolutions need to be seen as part of the wider European movement at the time.

By the middle of the nineteenth century, the demands were more uniform across Italy. There was a consistently liberal theme with demands for administrative reform, individual freedom, a united Italy and independence from foreign control and influence. The bad harvest of 1846–47 fuelled working-class support, but co-ordination remained difficult in a fragmented political landscape where regional interests often prevailed over the emerging liberalism.

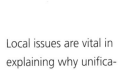

Local issues are vital in explaining why unification took so long.

THE REVOLUTION IN SICILY AND NAPLES

The 1848 revolutions started with conflict between Sicily and Naples in the form of a Sicilian reaction against the Neapolitans' barbaric rule. Hunger and cholera were also factors, but it seems that the separation of Sicily from Naples was more important than liberalism or Italian unity. Bitter fighting against Bourbon rule spread to Naples, but although concessions to liberalism were initially granted, the Bourbons were eventually victorious and an even more damaging repression fell on both Sicily and Naples.

REVOLUTIONS IN THE REST OF ITALY

The implications of the revolution in Piedmont for Italian unification are important.

Revolt spread northwards throughout the Papal States and into Austrian-held territory in the north. The Austrians, masters of much of northern Italy, had to withdraw into the Quadrilateral and their fortresses in the north. Biding his time, Radetzky, the Austrian military commander, returned soon enough to smash the Piedmontese at Custozza and then pick off Venetia and Tuscany. When the Piedmontese tried again, they were smashed at Novara, and Charles Albert, King of Piedmont, abdicated in favour of Victor Emmanuel, his son.

ROME AND THE PAPACY IN 1848

Note the importance of the repressive role of the French.

The Pope provided no lead to the reform movement, and would not confront Austria at all. He withdrew backing for liberalism and fled to the reactionary Naples. Mazzini (the radical nationalist thinker), Garibaldi (who was to become the military leader of Italian unification) and the radicals declared a republic in Rome, but that was smashed by the French army. Again, outside forces played a large role in Italian history.

RESULTS OF THE 1848 REVOLUTIONS

Knowledge of the impact of 1848 is vital for this topic.

What seemed outright defeat proved an educative experience for those involved. The need for a centralised leadership and the establishment of common aims became clear, as did the need to deal with the Austrians and the French. The Pope was seen as an obstacle rather than a possible leader, and there was a growing sense that Piedmont was now in a position to provide the leadership.

WHY DID THE REVOLUTIONS FAIL?

Do the chances for Italian unification look better or worse after 1848?

Piedmont was led by a monarch, Charles Albert, who would not work with others and insisted on loyalty to himself, not the wider cause. The liberals still believed that the way forward lay with constitutionalism, while the radicals who did most of the fighting wanted republicanism. There was no leadership, and all the contenders — ranging from Mazzini to the Pope to Charles Albert — were badly flawed. The various governments set up in 1848 were all different and inexperienced. There was virtually no working-class support, for social reform was not really on the liberal middle-class agenda. Foreign hostility was strong.

THE DEVELOPMENT OF PIEDMONT IN THE 1840S

Consider whether there was any chance of unification and independence without Piedmont.

Piedmont was key to the unification and independence of Italy. Initially reactionary, Piedmont made important economic and political developments in the 1840s, culminating in the establishment of a liberal and constitutional monarchy of a British type. This acted as a source of inspiration for the rest of Italy. Piedmont could also act as a safe haven for those on the run from the governments of the other Italian states. For a time Piedmont was the only place that could provide leadership for Italian unification and independence, and the rule of Victor Emmanuel provided an example which many Italians wished to follow.

THE ROLE OF CAVOUR

Camillo di Cavour came from Piedmont, was highly educated and widely travelled, and belonged to an aristocratic family with a long history of serving the state. He played a large part in the modernisation of Piedmont into an effective, liberal state. He had been influenced by his travels in Europe, especially in Britain, and returned home to found the Risorgimento with its liberal, nationalistic and non-revolutionary ideals. As the Piedmont prime minister from 1852 to 1861, he shared with Garibaldi the claim of being the founder of Italian unity.

CRIMEAN INVOLVEMENT

It is much debated whether involvement in the Crimean War helped or hindered unification, and historians disagree over Italian motives for involvement. The traditional view held that Cavour went in willingly to gain friends and to influence European opinion on Italy. More recent historians argue that Cavour was pressurised by British and French demands for allies and troops, and even that he was encouraged by the Austrians, who were anxious to divert Piedmontese soldiers away from Italy. Though there were no immediate successful outcomes for Italy in the Crimea, the involvement helped develop useful contacts with France and Britain, both of which were to prove useful later.

CAVOUR AND NAPOLEON III AT PLOMBIÈRES

The Pact of Plombières was a secret agreement in 1858 between Cavour and Napoleon III to join forces against the Austrians. The aim was to drive the Austrians out of northern Italy and expand Piedmont. Seen by many as a vital part of the unification process, Plombières was instigated by Napoleon, with the purpose of gaining Nice and Savoy and weakening the Austrians. Napoleon insisted that war had to be provoked against the Austrians, and Cavour — though aware that Napoleon was not the ideal ally — took the best option he had at the time.

CAVOUR AND THE WAR OF 1859

As required by the terms set at Plombières, Austria was provoked into a war. This proved short, and the two main battles of Magenta and Solferino were marked by carnage. A shocked Napoleon withdrew from the war without consulting Cavour. The threat of Prussia helping the Austrians encouraged the decision. Napoleon also feared alienating his own Catholic and conservative constituency by supporting Italian radicalism that might spread into the Papal States. However, Piedmont gained Lombardy and was confirmed in power in a plebiscite. Nice and Savoy went to France. Elsewhere the establishment of legitimate rulers in states like Tuscany failed, but independence was several steps closer and a date seemed set for Austrian departure. It was a crucial stage in the unification of Italy.

THE ROLE OF POPE PIUS IX

Pope Pius IX held office from 1846 to 1878. Seen initially as a liberal supporter of Italian unification and independence, he started by freeing political prisoners, limiting censorship and introducing educational and legal reforms. He allowed

Cavour's contribution to unification needs to be contrasted with those of others, especially Garibaldi (see below).

Consider whether Crimean involvement was a significant part of the Risorgimento.

Plombières is vital for questions on the importance of foreign intervention to unification.

There was now a real momentum behind unification.

Consider whether Pius IX was more of a negative than a positive factor in the unification process.

political meetings and some elected, consultative, bodies in the Papal States, but he would not lead against the Austrians in 1848 and fled to reactionary Naples. He withdrew his backing for liberalism, thus fuelling anti-clericalism amongst opponents of the status quo.

THE ROLE OF MAZZINI

Giuseppe Mazzini, who came from an educated middle-class background, was a romantic revolutionary nationalist who argued and wrote for the unity and independence of Italy. He took part in the revolts of 1848, carried the flag in the dark days and founded Young Italy. He was a dreamer and an idealist, and at times there was an element of farce in what he did, as he lacked much sense of the practical. He was too radical and revolutionary for the times, but he was a source of inspiration to many Italians.

> Perhaps Mazzini's contribution to Italian unification is the most difficult to assess. How do you compare ideas with actions?

GARIBALDI'S ROLE

Many historians are fascinated by the contrasting characters of Garibaldi and Cavour. Giuseppe Garibaldi came from Nice, was a radical guerrilla fighter who had fought in South American wars and in the 1848 revolutions, and fled to the USA after the defeat of the Roman republic. He was strongly influenced by Mazzini and had a deep hatred of Austria, and his charismatic leadership was vital in the final stages of unification when he was prepared to invade Sicily and the Papal States. Garibaldi accepted Piedmontese leadership and constitutional monarchy and did not divide the movement by being too republican or too revolutionary. Though aware of the limitations of French help, he fought in the wars of 1859.

> The contribution of the man of action needs comparing with those of Cavour the politician and Mazzini the romantic idealist.

THE DEBATE ABOUT THE DIFFERING AIMS OF CAVOUR AND GARIBALDI

There is much debate about the relative importance of Cavour's and Garibaldi's influence, but both were indispensable to Italian unification. They had a difficult working relationship. Cavour was much more of an opportunist and less of a committed Italian nationalist. Garibaldi was less of a realist than Cavour, but much more ambitious. Cavour gave a respectability to the work of Garibaldi. Without Garibaldi's success in Sicily and Naples, Cavour would never have invaded the Papal States, though it could be argued that Cavour acted more in fear of what the radical Garibaldi might do rather than finally to unite Italy.

> Consider whether Italian unification could have occurred without the work of both men.

THE ROLE OF VICTOR EMMANUEL II

Victor Emmanuel was the first King of Italy, who took the throne of Sardinia and Piedmont in 1849 after his father, Charles Albert, abdicated. He appointed Cavour as his first minister in 1852 and was prepared to keep the constitutional settlement that he inherited from his father, if only because the alternative might have been a more radical republic. He was content for Piedmont to become the focal point for anti-Austrian and unification ideas, and he supported a free press. The idea of leading all Italy had appeal for him, though he was more a figurehead than a real leader. Cavour was the dominant force.

> Is Victor Emmanuel a neglected figure? He did, after all, support Cavour.

THE CAUSES AND OUTCOMES OF GARIBALDI'S INVASION OF SICILY

The invasion of Sicily in 1860 was one of the most dramatic parts of the Risorgimento movement. Taking advantage of a local revolt in Sicily, Garibaldi

> Consider whether Sicily was the start of the final phase of Italian unification.

sailed to the island with his immortal 'one thousand heroes' and, with the support of the Sicilian landowners, became dictator of Sicily. He crossed the sea to Naples with British assistance, took Naples and was heading north for Rome when pre-empted by Cavour, who invaded Rome from the north. He was later involved in the disasters in Rome in 1862–67, when there were attempts to drive out the Pope. Rome eventually became part of the Italian state in 1870.

THE IMPACT OF GARIBALDI

Garibaldi was certainly the most popular and best known of the Italian leaders. Was he the most important?

Garibaldi's dramatic leadership forced the pace of events in 1860. He was an experienced fighter who provided charismatic and flexible leadership both in politics and in war. His inspirational ideals were matched by a remarkably persistent approach.

THE ROLE OF THE FRENCH

Questions on the role of both Austria and France are likely.

Napoleon Bonaparte's liberal and nationalist ideas provided the original inspiration for Italian unification, but it is the later French actions that were arguably as important as the work of Cavour and Garibaldi. On the plus side was France's involvement with Italy in the Crimean War and the Peace of Paris, the encouragement of Plombières and the role the French played in 1859. On the negative side there was the French intervention in Rome in 1848 and the support of the Papacy until 1870. Perhaps the French were keener on Nice and Savoy and retaining support of French Catholic opinion than on Italian unification?

THE FINAL STAGES OF UNIFICATION

Consider the key reasons why Italian unification took so long.

Unification was not finalised until 1870 when Church and state were separated in Italy, and Rome became the national capital. This was 8 years after the death of Cavour. Venetia was gained in 1866, but even then Austria needed to be defeated by Prussia first. Battles with the Austrians, such as at Custozza in 1848, showed the ability of the Austrians to fight in order to retain their Italian territory. With France defeated by Prussia in 1870, the support for the Papal States had gone. Perhaps more was owed to Prussian military ability than is often noted.

THE CONDITION OF ITALY, 1861–70

The initial unification was quite superficial and there were still many problems for Italy to solve.

Unification did not see the end of Italy's problems. The north and south were divided socially, culturally, politically and economically, and the divisions persisted. Piedmontese views gradually dominated in legal, administrative and educational matters, and a single army was finally formed. A constitutional monarchy along the lines of the Statuto (the Piedmontese Constitution of 1849) was embedded into a system where the logic of geography and language also played their parts.

Key obstacles to Italian unity
- the geography of Italy
- the Austrians
- the legacy of 1815
- the Papacy
- the differing aims of the supporters of liberalism and national unity
- the predominance of local interests

- the failure of the radicals to co-operate
- the poor quality of radical leadership
- the lack of working-class support

Key reasons for Italian unification
- the ideas of Mazzini
- the decline of Austrian power
- the support of Napoleon and France
- the incompetence of reactionary leadership
- the decline of papal power
- the rise of Piedmont
- the work of Cavour
- the work of Garibaldi
- the work of Victor Emmanuel
- the Crimean involvement
- the war of 1859

B Mussolini's rise to power

Key questions

What were the reasons for and the consequences of Italy entering the First World War?

Why did fascism develop in Italy after the First World War?

Why was Mussolini able to consolidate his power between 1922 and 1928?

THE CHRONOLOGY OF THE RISE OF ITALIAN FASCISM

1915 Entry into the First World War
Mussolini supports the war
Mussolini sets up Il Popolo d'Italia

1919 Humiliation at Versailles
Mussolini sets up Fascist Movement
Mussolini tries to enter Parliament

1920 Development of fascist activities nationally, including use of force against the left

1921 Formation of Fascist Party, with parliamentary power as its aim
The Fascists win 35 seats in Parliament

1922 Preparation for the march on Rome
King Victor Emmanuel III refuses to declare martial law
Threat of the march on Rome
Mussolini accepts the King's offer of the premiership
The march on Rome

WEAKNESSES OF THE LIBERAL STATE

Not all sections of Italy had welcomed unification. The Papacy was still fundamentally opposed and refused to recognise the new state. The north versus south

The failure of the state to rule Italy effectively is seen as an important factor in the rise of fascism.

Consider the issue of whether democracy was likely to survive in Italy.

The First World War was fundamental to the collapse of democracy in Italy.

Consider the reasons why the First World War hit Italy harder than other countries.

The loss of faith by many Italians in the ability of democracy to solve problems is crucial.

split remained and there were still strong class divisions and no real economic strength. Many sectors of the new nation state were reluctant to think of themselves as Italian. Power tended to lie with an educated élite. The lack of political and economic success meant little affection for a state which had not embedded itself deeply and was not seen by all as legitimate. The quality of the leadership was never strong.

POLITICAL PROBLEMS BEFORE 1914
There was a proportional representation electoral system and frequent coalitions with 22 governments between 1860 and 1900. Democracy did not establish deep roots and was not seen to be solving Italy's problems. Politicians were viewed as self-seeking and the system did not arouse much faith or enthusiasm.

POLITICAL CONSEQUENCES OF THE FIRST WORLD WAR
The decision to enter the war against Germany in 1915 proved divisive and was a negative factor in Italian political development. Key prewar politicians such as Giovanni Giolitti opposed it and would not co-operate with war leaders like Vittorio Orlando. Disunity inevitably led to low morale, which was worsened by defeats such as Caporetto. Parliamentary government did not deal well with problems caused by the war.

SOCIAL AND ECONOMIC CONSEQUENCES OF THE WAR
Inflation, unemployment, budget deficits and a badly damaged industrial structure were the main outcomes. War left Italy with a vast debt, which entailed borrowing because a weakened government was reluctant to tax highly. Government had few powers to remedy the situation and no knowledge of how to use even those. There was a huge balance of payments deficit. Frequent governments did not help either. The war also caused class conflict — both urban and rural working-class people were desperate to avoid worsening living standards, while the industrialists of the north and the landowners of the south and centre feared higher taxes.

THE IMMEDIATE POLITICAL IMPACT OF THE WAR
The First World War exacerbated the instability caused by the old difficulties of frequently changing governments, coalitions and an inability to solve problems. In fact, the problems grew and the issues were more divisive. There was an increasing number of political parties hostile to the state itself, on both the left and the right, as well as the Catholic Party, making any form of consensus virtually impossible. The inability of democratic governments to act was harmful to the re-establishment of democratic processes after the war.

THE POSTWAR SETTLEMENT
Initially Italy had been an ally of Germany and Austria, but it had remained neutral in 1914. It was wooed into the war by the desperate France and Britain, with the promise of great gains at the Treaty of London. These were not forthcoming at Versailles, largely because the Italians' dismal military performance had deflected Allied resources away from the Western Front and had not encouraged support from the other victors. The ideals of President Wilson

also contrasted with Italian determination to return from war with loot in the form of territory. The 'mutilated peace' was a stick with which Italian governments were beaten during 1919–22, and was a major reason for the rise of a fascist alternative.

CONTEMPORARY DEFINITIONS OF FASCISM

Dino Grandi was Mussolini's theorist and he tried to concoct a coherent ideology from the turmoil of events. His definitions of fascism included: a) nationalistic fascism, with an assertive foreign policy and dictatorial political system; b) conservative fascism with its retention of the monarchy and co-operation with the Catholic church; c) technocratic fascism with its attempts to revive and develop Italian industry; d) rural fascism (a contradiction of the technocratic strand) which was pro-peasantry and anti-urban; e) national syndicalism and the corporate state. Inevitably Grandi had problems trying to reconcile the many inherent differences in his definitions.

WHO SUPPORTED FASCISM?

Fascism had a diverse appeal which relied on a host of negative reactions. Support ranged from industrialists who disliked unions and socialism, to landowners who backed fascist attacks on peasant co-operatives. At the same time, some of the peasants approved of the small land grants that fascist policies offered to individuals. The Catholic Church liked fascism's anti-communism and authoritarianism, and the military liked its aggressiveness. Meanwhile, the lower middle class was looking for a middle way between capitalism and socialism. War veterans hated the peace and were inspired by D'Annunzio's seizure of Fiume, a port on the Adriatic which had not been given to Italy at the end of the war. The aristocracy liked fascism's commitment to law and order, and the political establishment began to see an authoritarian movement as the only viable alternative.

MUSSOLINI'S ROLE IN THE RISE OF FASCISM

Was Mussolini in the right place at the right time or was he the key factor in the seizure of power? Benito Mussolini founded Il Popolo d'Italia in 1915 and organised the *fascisti* as militant nationalists to defeat socialism. From the start he gave people the feeling that he could solve problems and provide a co-ordinating role. In the 1921 elections he led his Fascist Party to a taste of formal power with 7% of the vote and 35 seats. He then set about making fascism a national movement as well as a national party. He used whatever opportunities came his way and played on the existing weaknesses of the political system. Mussolini provided the ideas which appealed and his sheer flexibility and adaptability were vital. No Mussolini would probably have meant no fascism, but he needed the instability of the war and the incompetence of his opponents as well.

THE MARCH ON ROME

During the March on Rome, Mussolini did not actually try to seize power personally, but stayed in the north ready to flee abroad if his coup failed. Nobody knows why King Victor Emmanuel III refused to give the army the power to shoot the few fascist rebels who did march to Rome but instead summoned Mussolini and made him prime minister. Mussolini travelled to Rome by train.

Versailles had a great impact on Italian politics. Compare this with its effect on Germany.

Given that Italians had problems in defining fascism at the time, you are not expected to define it now.

The vagueness of fascism, and its ability to fit in with the wishes of many people, was one of its strengths.

The extent of Mussolini's influence is an interesting debate.

The reasons for the King giving Mussolini the premiership are not known.

Do not see the King's offer before the March on Rome as the establishment of a dictatorship.

A key factor in Mussolini's acceptance by so many Italians was the minimal use of force.

You need to consider how absolute a dictator Mussolini was.

HOW DID MUSSOLINI ESTABLISH HIMSELF IN POWER?

Mussolini's initial position was not strong. He had to make himself a dictator. Initially he had only 7% of seats in Parliament and four out of ten of the Cabinet were fascist. He had no strong or loyal national following and he had no effective organisation nationally either.

THE CHANGES TO THE ITALIAN CONSTITUTION

Once in power, Mussolini forced through the Acerbo Electoral Law to ensure a parliamentary majority. Note the use of legal means — later copied by Hitler — which gave Mussolini the ability to change the constitution. He then banned other political parties. The Aventine secession after the Matteotti murder — when the opposition who had walked out in protest at Matteotti's death were simply banned from returning to Parliament — is an example of Mussolini's quasi-legal and non-violent methods. He then ensured that all parliamentary candidates were selected by the Grand Council.

THE CREATION OF THE DICTATORSHIP

Mussolini used the Matteotti crisis to purge fascists who were not totally loyal, and he set up the Fascist Grand Council to give the party a semblance of involvement and power. The Fundamental Law removed his responsibility to the legislature and in 1926 he got the power to govern by decree, which he used more or less permanently from then on. Mussolini also took on responsibility for eight key ministries himself. Like Hitler, he used the divide and rule principle by creating divisions between the old system of prefectures and the local fascist bosses. He created a political vacuum which could only be filled by himself. Add to this the cult of *Il Duce* and Mussolini was in a strong position by 1928.

Key factors in the rise of Mussolini
- the failings of the Italian political system
- democracy and unity were new in Italy
- the impact of the war
- economic hardship
- the failure of democratic governments
- Versailles and the 'mutilated peace'
- coalitions
- the growth of anti-democratic parties
- the actions of the King
- Mussolini's skills
- the rejection of the democratic process by élites

Key reasons for the support of fascism
- its flexibility
- the attitude of the Catholic Church
- the attitude of industry
- the attitude of the aristocracy
- the support of the army
- the support of the landowners
- the attitude of the peasants
- the attitude of the war veterans

Key reasons for Mussolini's establishment of a dictatorship
- his use of legal methods
- the Acerbo Law
- constitutional changes
- the Fundamental Law, which extended Mussolini's power
- the banning of parties
- the endorsement by the élites — especially the army and the Papacy

C Mussolini's domestic policy

Key questions

How successful were Mussolini's domestic policies?

How totalitarian was the state created by Mussolini?

The relationship with the Church is important to an understanding of Mussolini's dictatorship.

THE RELATIONSHIP WITH THE ROMAN CATHOLIC CHURCH

Although an atheist, Mussolini knew the value of support from the authoritarian and conservative Catholic Church. The Concordat and the Lateran agreements of 1929 gave the Church financial compensation for its earlier losses, a recognised status in Italy and control of education and morality. In return, Mussolini got the Pope's endorsement of his regime and his foreign policy. The Papacy's strong anti-communism was also useful to Mussolini. There were disadvantages, in that he was tolerating a potentially rival body and he could not use education for indoctrination to the extent that he wished. Catholicism eventually became part of the opposition to Mussolini.

Mussolini's economic strategy reveals much about his brand of fascism.

MUSSOLINI'S ECONOMIC POLICIES

Mussolini's economic strategy was a mixture of free enterprise and state control. The former pacified his industrial backers and the latter enabled him to fulfil many of his promises. The corporate state ideas started with the Rocco Laws of 1926 with their seven branches of economic activity, such as agriculture and transport. It was an interesting idea in theory, but probably unworkable in practice, particularly with the erratic leadership and interest of Mussolini.

MUSSOLINI'S FINANCIAL POLICIES

Finance was an area where Mussolini did real harm to Italy.

Mussolini's initial financial success was largely the work of De Stefani, the finance minister whom he inherited when he took power. When Mussolini took a more active role in reflating the lira, the combination of machismo and nationalism worsened the depression of the early 1930s and hit exports. Retaining strong controls in the late 1930s helped prevent some of the worst economic damage that hit other countries, but that was more by accident than by design.

MUSSOLINI'S INDUSTRIAL POLICIES

On attaining power, Mussolini began by appeasing his backers and thus favoured heavy rather than light industry, and private enterprise rather than state control. He had shifted to more state intervention by the 1930s, and economic depression plus the needs of an ambitious foreign policy led to his founding the Institute for the Reconstruction of Industry (IRI) in 1933. From then on the state took more and more control in areas like iron, steel and shipping. Industry outstripped agriculture as the main employer and Italy became more self-sufficient. Mussolini electrified the rail network and (yes) the trains did run on time. However, the north/south divide remained and Italian industry was unable to cope with the demands of war.

MUSSOLINI'S AGRICULTURAL POLICIES

Mussolini's agricultural policies were hurried, ill thought out and reactive. The idea of self-sufficiency appealed, but there was no analysis of its practicality. Mussolini initiated the Battle for Grain, which increased grain production, but severely limited the output of other productive (and exported) crops like olive oil. The amount of arable land increased, and the Pontine Marshes were drained after a major investment that could have been more productively used on less prestigious projects.

MUSSOLINI'S POPULATION POLICY

There was concern about Italy's declining population. Mussolini felt that Italy needed a growing population for his wars and expanding empire. Though incentives were given to marriage and childbirth — and disincentives to the single and childless — the policy did not work and the decline in the birth-rate continued. A failure of the Battle for Births was probably to the benefit of Italy.

MUSSOLINI'S POLICIES TOWARDS WOMEN

Italy under Mussolini remained a totally male-orientated society. Women lost out as their childbearing role was emphasised and their employment opportunities were restricted. The fascists' relationship with the Church ensured that no advances were made in areas like contraception and divorce.

THE WORKING CLASS

There were few gains for either rural or urban workers. Real wages fell in the 1930s and rural poverty grew, especially in the south. Attempts were made to keep the peasants on the land, but many fled to industrial squalor. In the cities, urban workers fared badly. Unemployment was high in the 1930s, unions were banned and real wages fell.

THE MIDDLE CLASS

On the whole, those in industry and the professions lost out through falling salaries and restrictions on private enterprise. Depression and war did not help either. The only ones to gain were the senior bureaucrats who had to cope with the chaos of Mussolini's administration. A tradition of inefficiency, overlapping jurisdictions and plain corruption became endemic in government.

THE UPPER CLASS

Perhaps the upper class — a tiny percentage of the population who owned nearly half the land — was the only sector of Italian society to make significant gains under Mussolini. The landed aristocracy benefited from the subsidies granted during the Battle for Grain and from government restrictions on the peasants.

Industrial policy eventually proved another of Mussolini's weak points.

Agricultural policies are a further example of Mussolini's failings.

Yet another example of a Mussolini error.

Again, the thinking seems to have been reactive and disorganised.

There is little evidence of any benefits to the Italian working class.

It becomes increasingly evident that it may have been the lack of any alternative that was the main reason for Mussolini staying in power for so long.

When the upper class turned against Mussolini, he was out of power within days.

Major industrialists also did well, due to their close involvement with government and the fact that government restrictions fell on labour but not on management. On the downside, industry suffered from greater interference, the weakness of the lira and ultimately from war.

POSSIBLE GAINS FROM MUSSOLINI'S DOMESTIC POLICIES

Mussolini brought enough stability to ensure a consensus in his favour. Major industrialists and the landed aristocracy gained, as did the Church and Roman Catholicism generally. Some social groups gained in status and prestige. There was some better welfare and medical care for the working class, pensions and unemployment benefits improved and infant mortality dropped. The big killers such as TB began to decline and there was a greater acceptance that the state had a duty to care for its citizens.

MUSSOLINI'S RACIAL POLICIES

Initially Mussolini was tolerant enough to be critical of the Nazi obsession with anti-Semitism. But after the alliance with Germany, Mussolini copied Nazi jargon and began talking of such things as the master race. In the 'Manifesto on Race' in 1938 and in decrees of the same year, anti-Semitism became Italian state policy. In general, it was not as horrific in practice as Nazism, partly through incompetence and partly through a reluctance of many Italians to implement it fully. However, Italian treatment of other races in Ethiopia, North Africa and the Balkans was as barbaric as anything perpetrated by the Germans.

MUSSOLINI AS A TOTALITARIAN DICTATOR: THE IDEAS

Although *Il Duce* may not necessarily have set out to establish himself as dictator, he was happy to develop the cult of personality. In this he predated both Stalin and Hitler. Absolute power probably mattered less to Mussolini than it did to Hitler or Stalin, and he was careful not to offend many powerful élites.

MUSSOLINI AS A TOTALITARIAN DICTATOR: THE METHODS

As with the cult of personality, other twentieth-century dictators copied Mussolini's methods. He had his secret police, the OVRA, exploited his ability to overrule the normal legal channels and denied opponents basic rights. He tried to dominate Italian culture and took complete media control. Youth groups were set up with the aim of indoctrination, and education — as far as the Catholic Church would allow — was strictly controlled and again used for indoctrination.

MUSSOLINI AS A TOTALITARIAN DICTATOR: THE LIMITATIONS

Mussolini was never as determined as Stalin or Hitler to secure total power and as a result his system cannot really be called totalitarian. Rather, inefficiency, laziness and a lack of will on the part of both the ruler and his agents led to limited totalitarianism. Cultural control was limited, and both the Church and the universities resisted his educational demands. Large numbers of boys and girls avoided Mussolini's youth groups or only turned up for the football and missed the indoctrination. The press was so badly managed that most Italians simply disbelieved anything they read or heard. The military was fairly obedient, but never totally tamed, and — with the monarchy and the Papacy remaining — it formed a powerful institution around which opposition could focus.

The regime could point to some achievements.

Italian atrocities in the Balkans and Africa reveal a racism at the heart of Italian fascism.

You need to think whether Mussolini considered dictatorship a means to an end, or an end in itself.

Mussolini's opponents were dealt with far less viciously than in most other twentieth-century dictatorships.

Consider the nature of Mussolini's dictatorship.

Key factors in Mussolini's domestic policies
- the relationship with the Catholic Church
- the Concordat
- the corporate state
- the failure of his economic policies
- his ideas about self-sufficiency
- the failure of his industrial policy
- the Battle for Grain
- the Battle for Births
- his social policy — especially towards women
- the increased hardship of the working class
- the impact on the rich and the middle class

Key factors in Mussolini's dictatorship
- his racial ideas
- the cult of personality
- the OVRA
- his youth movements
- his indoctrination programme
- his education policies
- censorship
- his treatment of opponents
- the reduction of the power of the parties
- the power of the Catholic Church and the retention of the monarchy

D Foreign policy under Mussolini

Key questions
How successful was Mussolini's foreign policy?

What was the effect of Mussolini's foreign policy on Italy?

MUSSOLINI'S AMBITIONS, 1922–30
Aware that failure at Versailles was a significant factor in the hostility to governments before 1922, Mussolini knew he had to make an impact in foreign affairs. He wanted to make Italy 'great, respected and feared'. Initially he varied between sensible diplomacy and flamboyant attention-seeking, aggression and simple trouble-making, and he seized whatever opportunity came along to gain political kudos.

MUSSOLINI'S POLICIES, 1922–30
The results of Mussolini's early opportunism in foreign policy included the aggression shown over Corfu and Fiume (where he was prepared to use force), the diplomacy shown at Locarno (where a peaceful solution to the problem of German

There was no consistent pattern to Mussolini's foreign policy.

Ensure you have examples to illustrate Mussolini's different policies.

borders was attempted), and his attitude to collective security. His trouble-making side emerged in attempts to undermine the French and their policies in the Balkans and eastern Europe, and his approach to Albania, where he was simply out to gain territory for Italy.

INITIAL FOREIGN POLICY SUCCESS TO 1930

Are there signs of success and sense here?

Italy had gained in international respect by 1930. The Treaty of Locarno was partly responsible for this, but whether the boost it gave to German revisionism was a good idea is arguable. The French were still the major force in the Balkans, and Italy made no serious progress there. Versailles still stood as far as Italy was concerned, and Mussolini was conscious that Italy was neither great nor feared. Italy remained at peace, and was uncommitted to possibly aggressive alliances.

MUSSOLINI'S AMBITIONS, 1930–39

Note the fundamental shift in policy after 1930.

Mussolini abandoned his moderate policy because of a lack of progress in concrete terms and, from 1936 or so, because of anxiety about German expansionism. After the killing of Dolfuss, which he saw as German interference in 'his' area, and the Stresa Front, when he joined with Britain and France to try to stop German aggression, Mussolini moved into open aggression against Abyssinia and Spain, and then formed an alliance with Hitler that culminated in Mussolini's humiliation and death.

MUSSOLINI'S POLICIES, 1930–34

Pressure on Mussolini to gain prestige abroad came from the domestic front.

Though under some pressure from public opinion, Mussolini did not immediately abandon his pragmatic approach of the 1920s. Instead he played a mediator's role between Germany on the one side and France and Britain on the other. This led to the negotiations with France in 1934 to try and get a good working relationship, and then to the Stresa Front with Britain and France.

REASONS FOR INVADING ABYSSINIA

Abyssinia is an excellent example of Mussolini at his worst.

The invasion of Abyssinia was a turning point for Italy and Mussolini, and for international relations in general. Motives for the invasion ranged from an Italian desire for empire and status to a need to show a military resolve that might persuade Hitler to keep out of Austria. The regime — suffering from economic depression — welcomed the distraction of a foreign campaign, and the inactivity of the League of Nations did not put any brake on a lurch towards another world war.

THE COURSE AND RESULTS OF WAR IN ABYSSINIA

The war was conducted with brutality by an Italian military which used poison gas against unarmed civilians. Limited action was taken by the League of Nations and Britain and France. However, the Hoare–Laval Pact — when the British and French foreign secretaries effectively endorsed Mussolini's aggression — inspired Hitler to occupy the Rhineland. German support of Italy in Abyssinia brought the Second World War significantly nearer.

Abyssinia had major implications for both Italy and international relations in the 1930s.

MUSSOLINI AND SPAIN

The Spanish Civil War was fought between a legitimate left-wing government and the rebellious right, and it gave Mussolini a chance of making trouble for

Britain and France. It also offered an opportunity for territorial expansion in Africa, and Mussolini hoped to gain an ally in Spain's General Franco. The Italian contribution to Franco's victory was significant in terms of money and resources, and yet Italy emerged with no apparent gain. Italian involvement in Spain helped spur Britain towards rearmament, and Italy was to suffer as a result. Italy backed the winner, but lost a great deal, and the Spanish Civil War was another key stage in the build-up to the Second World War.

Backing Franco in Spain did Mussolini's regime a lot of harm.

ITALY AND GERMANY

An alliance between Italy and Germany was sealed by the Rome–Berlin Axis in 1936, with the Anti-Comintern Pact and the Pact of Steel following. Having overcome his dislike of Hitler's Austrian ambitions, Mussolini became a subservient agent of Hitler. The 'brutal friendship' benefited neither party. By the time of Munich, Hitler's contempt for Mussolini meant that the Italian leader was not informed about such decisions as the German invasion of the remainder of Czechoslovakia in 1939. With Mussolini prone to fight wars which created demands for German assistance, Hitler would arguably have been better off with Italy as an enemy, or at least neutral.

Some would argue that the Rome–Berlin Axis worked against the interests of both the signatories.

MUSSOLINI AND THE SECOND WORLD WAR

Although initially successful in invading Albania, Mussolini needed to be rescued by the Germans after botched campaigns in Greece and North Africa. This had disastrous consequences for Hitler. Allied invasion of Sicily and then Italy followed, and led to Mussolini's overthrow by the Italian élite whom he had failed to crush. Hitler rescued Mussolini from his captors in 1943, and Mussolini was retained as a puppet until his execution by Italians in 1945. Italy suffered major losses in the war, and was badly damaged in the fighting of 1943–45.

The Italian war record was one of failure and consistent humiliation.

Key factors in Italian foreign policy, 1922–30

- Versailles — the 'mutilated' peace
- Fiume — the attempt to seize territory in the Adriatic
- Corfu — the confrontation with the Greeks
- Mussolini's Balkan ambitions
- the distrust of France and the Little Entente (France's attempt to gain allies in eastern Europe and the Balkans)
- Locarno — Mussolini's bid for respectability and the status of honest broker
- the dual policy as both arbiter and troublemaker

Key factors in Italian foreign policy, 1930–43

- the influence of domestic policy on foreign policy
- the lack of prestige
- the murder of Dolfuss — part of the German attempt to take over Austria
- the Watch on the Brenner — Mussolini's determination to gain part of Austria
- the Stresa Front — the attempt by the Italians, British and French to stop Nazi advances
- the invasion of Abyssinia
- the Hoare–Laval Pact, when Britain and France allowed Mussolini's take-over of Abyssinia
- Libya and North Africa

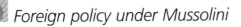

Foreign policy under Mussolini

- the Spanish Civil War
- the Rome–Berlin Axis
- the Anti-Comintern Pact
- the Pact of Steel
- the Munich negotiations between Hitler and the British and French over Czechoslovakia
- the declaration of war
- the disasters in Greece and North Africa
- the Allied invasion of Sicily and Italy

A The revolutions of 1848

Key questions

What was the role of Metternich in causing and containing the revolutions?

Why did revolutions break out in Europe in 1848?

Why did the revolutions fail and what was their impact?

Middle-class discontent was a fundamental cause of the revolutions of 1848.

SOCIAL AND ECONOMIC CAUSES: THE MIDDLE CLASS

A bourgeois revolt against aristocratic domination was a key stimulus of the revolutions in mid-nineteenth-century Europe. The *ancien régimes* had not adapted to the new forces of liberalism and nationalism, and the repression of middle-class demands enraged educated and relatively rich people who felt that careers should be open to talent. There were no revolutions in Britain and Belgium because their middle classes had already achieved considerable power.

Contrary to popular belief, the working class played a limited part in the revolutions.

SOCIAL AND ECONOMIC CAUSES: THE WORKING CLASS

Working-class grievances were not the major cause of the 1848 revolutions in France, Germany and Italy. There was certainly industrial unrest in 1848, and that was fed by poor pay and conditions helping to politicise the working class. However, the working class was weakened by splits between the skilled and unskilled, and the most industrialised nations with the most deprived working class were Belgium and Britain, and they had no revolutions.

Consider whether the revolutions would have happened without widespread hunger.

HUNGER AND POVERTY

There was a major food crisis in Europe between 1845 and 1847, with a series of bad harvests and crop failures. The Irish potato famine was not an isolated incident. Population growth placed a strain on existing resources, prices soared and the lack of any welfare system exacerbated widespread hunger. Note also that in Germany and the Habsburg lands there was a strong reaction by a peasantry opposed to the landowners' feudalistic rule.

Leadership must be seen as a central cause, and also a reason why the revolutions were to have such an immediate impact.

FAILURE OF POLITICAL LEADERSHIP

Without exception, the quality of leadership in countries which revolted was poor. Look at the incompetence of Louis Philippe in France, the blind reaction in Naples, the repression in Rome and the reaction which characterised Metternich's regime. The *ancien régime* tendencies of élites such as the Magyars and the *Junkers* (the Prussian aristocracy) must also be seen as central causes, as were the implications of the Carlsbad Decrees, which led to widespread political repression.

The end of autocracy was a fundamental demand of the middle-class revolutionaries.

LIBERALISM

Running through all the revolutions was a common liberal theme. The educated middle class wanted an end to autocracy and the aristocratic domination of society and government. Criticisms of censorship and Church power, and demands for free trade and parliamentary government, ran through all revolutionary events. Do not see this as a democratic movement though, for universal suffrage rarely

formed part of their demands. The middle class wanted to share power with the old élites, not extend it to the working class.

RADICAL DEMOCRACY

Given the advance of industrialisation and the spread of the ideas of Robert Owen (the British socialist), it is surprising that radical or socialist ideas played a small part in 1848. Only in France — with the ideas of Blanc and Blanqui — were there signs of a radical working-class movement and they (quite literally) were quickly gunned down. There are one or two cases of socialist ideas being debated at a local level in Italy, but they were not a major factor there either. (Remember that the *Communist Manifesto* was published after 1848, so Marxism played no part.)

NATIONALISM

The nationalist influence of Napoleon is supposed to have been strong, especially in Germany and Italy. Certainly anti-Austrian feeling was a key factor in Germany, Italy and the Habsburg lands, but that was not always the same as nationalism. The Croats, Romanians and Magyars all wanted freedom from Habsburg domination and the Czechs also pressed for independence. But the Frankfurt Parliament in Germany revealed the weakness of nationalism as a motivating revolutionary force.

ITALY

Look at Unit 4 for details and note the features which were unique to Italy — the colonial presence of the Habsburgs, the existence of the Papal States and the highly fragmented nature of Italy. The first revolts took place here, fed by all the ingredients of nationalism, liberalism and underlying social and economic changes. Harvests had failed, and Habsburg taxation and conscription demands had worsened. The ambition of Piedmont is vital, and when it came to incompetence and repression the Neapolitan government had few rivals. Note the middle-class leaderships of Manin and Mazzini, and also the middle-class hostility to both nobles and the working class.

FRANCE

This is covered in depth in Unit 3. Look closely at the roles of Louis Philippe and Guizot. France had a unique revolutionary tradition, a smaller aristocracy and a ruler who was hardly a tyrant in the mould of Metternich. Look at the importance of the National Guard and the financial collapse. The immediate results of the February revolution are important, and the emergence of some left-wing ideas, but once you look at the results of the elections of April 1848, the June Days and the work of General Cavagnac, it is arguable whether the events in France warrant the title 'revolution' at all. France was to go from a moderately authoritarian system to a very authoritarian one under another Bonaparte.

GERMANY

Various German examples provide different reasons for the 1848 revolts. The Lola Montez affair in Bavaria, which damaged the monarchy in a serious scandal, is one, and the deep hatred of feudalism in East Prussia another. Middle-class demands for liberalisation were a force, as was illiberal nationalism. There are many examples of incompetent leadership and Frederick of Prussia is a good

---

Note how little radicalism or left-wing ideology appeared in 1848.

Nationalism was a revolutionary factor in Austria, but the jury is very much out on its place in the list of key causes.

Italy offers many examples of all the main revolutionary motives.

Although it had a strong revolutionary tradition, France was to end up with a more authoritarian government than it had before.

A pattern of complex causation emerged in the Germany of 1848.

one. There was high urban unemployment and real hunger, especially in Cologne. As in France, middle-class fear of working-class radicalism is a major factor in the limited nature of many of the demands, and in the speed with which order was restored. Financial collapse in many areas had hit the middle class hard, and encouraged them to challenge governments which failed to protect their interests.

THE AUSTRIAN EMPIRE

Make sure that some of your examples are drawn from the Habsburg empire.

Look at a political map of mid-nineteenth-century Europe for a picture of the Austrian empire's size and the number of differing peoples it contained. They lived under the most feudalistic of all the systems and had no outlet for their many grievances beyond revolt. There were strong liberal and nationalist movements in Poland, and in other cases — such as the Magyars — there was an equally strong illiberal nationalism. Loathing of Metternich was uniform and the ruling élites simply collapsed in a demonstration of fear and incompetence. Firmer handling by rulers would have changed events but, though it was used to ruling by brute force, the Austrian empire had allowed the army to shrink.

WHY DID THE REVOLUTIONS FAIL?

Once you look at the reasons above, the limited survival period of revolutionary forces is unsurprising.

Brute force was the main reason for the failure of the 1848 revolutions, which, in the main, were finished when professional armies butchered the opposition. Social division — in particular, middle-class hostility to working-class aspiration — also weakened the opponents of government. Huge divisions within the nationalist groups — especially in the Habsburg lands — was another weakening factor. Finally, it is hard to spot a talented leader amongst the revolutionaries.

THE RESULTS OF THE REVOLUTIONS OF 1848

Consider the argument that the 1848 revolutions had marginal impact.

Overall, the 1848 revolutions had a limited impact. The regimes in France, Austria and Prussia were in most cases more authoritarian after 1848 than before and, arguably, revolution delayed Italian unity and independence. Illiberal and aggressive nationalism grew in force, and major economic changes also came much later. Meanwhile the old élites returned, shaken and — in Prussia, France and Italy — wise enough to take a less authoritarian and illiberal stance.

Key factors in the causes of revolution in 1848
- hunger
- poverty
- middle-class grievances
- the survival of feudalism
- the failure of leadership
- the lack of representative assemblies
- the growth of education
- reactionary governments
- the repressive policies of Metternich
- liberal and enlightened ideas
- nationalism

Key factors in the failure of the revolutions of 1848
- the successful use of force
- the negative role of Russia and Britain

- social divisions among the revolutionaries
- poor leadership
- fear of radical forces
- lack of co-ordination

B The causes and results of the First World War

Key questions

To what extent should Germany be held responsible for the First World War?

What was the impact of the First World War?

How fair was the Treaty of Versailles?

Many important factors in the causes of the First World War lie well back in the nineteenth century.

THE LONG-TERM CHRONOLOGY

You need a working knowledge of international history from at least the Congress of Berlin in 1878 onwards. Bismarck's foreign policy, the early growth of the alliance systems and the terms that Bismarck imposed on France in 1871 are important. So too were the early colonial rivalries, particularly in Africa and the Far East. Russia's and Austria's Balkan ambitions were crucial, as was the collapse of the Turkish empire.

The Bosnian crisis of 1908 is seen very much as the turning-point in international relations.

THE BALKANS

The Congress of Berlin failed to solve Balkan tensions, with the Bulgarian crisis of 1885 and its international repercussions showing the extent of the failure. Key events in the Balkans were the Austro–Russian agreement of 1897; the growing Austrian involvement in the region; the dynastic changes in Serbia in 1903; the Bosnian annexation; and the Balkan Wars of 1912 and 1913.

The domestic politics as well as the foreign policies of the major powers need studying.

THE MEDIUM-TERM CAUSES

Look carefully at all the major countries involved in the build-up to the war between 1900 and 1914, and the minor players as well, such as Turkey, Italy and Japan. Note all the alliances and *ententes*, such as the Franco–British. Make sure you know who was allied to whom and precisely what the agreements were. How binding were they? What was the effect on their rivals? The key areas to focus on in this period are, of course, the Balkans and Morocco, but you also need to look carefully at what was happening to public opinion in the various countries and also at the growing arms races.

THE SHORT-TERM CHRONOLOGY

The assassination of the Austrian heir in Sarajevo was followed by the sequence of events below:

- the Kaiser's favourable response to the Austrian request for support
- the Austrian ultimatum to Serbia — in effect, a declaration of war

- the Serbian reaction, which was in effect accepting the war
- Russian mobilisation, which was designed to threaten Austria
- Germany's response to Russian mobilisation
- the implementation of the Schlieffen Plan
- the German moves against France and Belgium
- British declaration of war against Germany
- Austrian declaration of war against Russia
- Italian neutrality

BRITISH RESPONSIBILITY

> Britain must take some responsibility for starting the First World War — but the responsibility is less easy to quantify than with other countries.

British public opinion had been strongly anti-German since the Boer War. However, it was not in Britain's interests to become involved in a continental war and there was an over-reaction to German naval expansion and German colonisation. Links with both France and Russia had tied Britain to continental commitments that probably went beyond national self-interest. Given those commitments, Earl Grey, the British foreign secretary, might have clarified Britain's position earlier, and this might well have deterred the Germans from invading Belgium.

FRENCH RESPONSIBILITY

> France must be seen to have a major responsibility for starting the First World War.

Memories of French military defeat by the Prussian army in 1871 were strong, and *revanche* was a major factor in French policy. Germany was seen as the enemy, and war was seen as likely by both public and politicians. The French alliance with Russia was directed deliberately against Germany and became a major contributor to both the medium- and short-term causes of the war. A major part of French policy after 1911 was to commit Russia to invading Germany in the event of a war, and French support of the Russians in the Balkans did much to encourage the creaking Russian war machine to be more assertive against Germany and Austria. France put pressure on Russia to mobilise in 1914, and this was critical to the outbreak of Europe-wide warfare.

RUSSIAN RESPONSIBILITY

> Russia, and the Tsar in particular, must be held substantially responsible for the outbreak of the First World War.

Russian foreign policy was irresponsible and aggressive. Its involvement in the Balkans and its attitude to pan-Slavism were catastrophic, and its failure to understand the attitudes of both the Turks and the Austrians was a major cause of the war. The Tsar abandoned the realistic and pacific policies of Stolypin and listened much more to the aggressive Sazanov and the military. The Tsar seemed unaware of the strength of Germany and the weakness of his own armies. Russia's blind support of Serbia and its lack of awareness of military and diplomatic reality were crucial in the outbreak of the war.

AUSTRIA-HUNGARY

> Austria-Hungary must be seen as a major cause in the long to medium and short term. Perhaps it is because the issues surrounding it are so complex that the Austrian stance has often been overlooked.

Austria-Hungary should also take considerable responsibility for the First World War. Its Balkan policy provided the key. The Austrian Emperor ignored the advice of those, such as Tisza, his key minister, who wanted a diplomatic solution to the assassination crisis and listened to those who wanted a military solution to end the Serbian issue once and for all. Austrian leaders were frightened that Serbian success would further weaken the empire, and they might have been less aggressive if German support for them had not incited the Russian support of Serbia. Their Serbian obsession led to a deliberately provocative ultimatum which

demanded unrealistic terms of the Serbs in July 1914. This must be seen as a major short-term cause of war.

THE CASE AGAINST GERMAN RESPONSIBILITY

Both the German acceptance of the blame — which was written into the Treaty of Versailles in 1919 — and then its prime role in causing the Second World War have coloured judgements. But there is a case for the defence. Germany saw itself surrounded by hostile powers as Britain, France and Russia forged military and diplomatic links. French, Russian and British rearmament was directed specifically against Germany, and Germany was being deliberately excluded from the colonial acquisitions which other powers were happily engaged in. The Russians and French made attempts to undermine German commercial interests, especially in Turkey. With unreliable allies such as Austria and Italy — plus a full awareness of the military intentions of Russia and France and a quite legitimate fear of an attack on two fronts — Germany's belligerent attitude is at least understandable.

THE LONG-TERM CASE FOR GERMAN RESPONSIBILITY

Long-term German responsibility for the war goes back to the work of Bismarck with his alliances, the terms imposed on France and the rearmament agreement. This prompts questions about the German role in stimulating the gradual division of Europe into rival armed camps. Note also the colonial rivalry, the military spending and issues such as the Kiel Canal (which enabled German warships to go from the North Sea to the Baltic) and the Berlin–Baghdad railway. And there was other unnecessary provocation, such as the Kruger telegram which inflamed the British in the Boer War, and involvement in Morocco which infuriated the French.

THE SHORT-TERM CASE FOR GERMAN RESPONSIBILITY

The Schlieffen Plan (the German war plan which required the invasion of Belgium) was a major factor in causing the war in 1914. It brought Britain into the war against Germany. The military thinking behind it is understandable, but the failure to think out the diplomatic implications is frightening. Too many in Germany saw conflict as inevitable, and too many saw the idea of a pre-emptive strike as a good one. The support for Austria over Serbia is key, and the ultimatum to Russia is also a central part of the case against Germany. The willingness to allow military solutions to problems is a central cause.

WHAT WAS THE IMPACT OF THE FIRST WORLD WAR?

The difficulty with this question is knowing where to start. First consider the 13 million dead. Then there were the financial costs, the destroyed political systems, the revolutions and the eventual dictatorships. The war helped the emancipation of women and created the League of Nations, but the peace terms arguably led directly to the next great war.

THE IMPACT ON RUSSIA

The First World War brought horrendous casualties, was a direct cause of the Russian Revolution and thus gave rise to the first major communist system. Without the war there would have been no Lenin and no Stalin. There was to be a long and bloody civil war and a famine which caused further catastrophe and

Consider the case that Germany was more sinned against than sinning.

German actions were highly provocative.

Simply blaming Germany does not work, so try and consider the degree of responsibility Germany should take. There is no simple answer to what caused the First World War — and you are not expected to produce one. It is awareness of the many sides of the issue that is needed.

No other war had ever had such an impact.

influenced the course of a revolution which has profoundly affected the whole course of world history ever since. Note also the effect of the Treaty of Brest-Litovsk in 1917, when Russia lost a huge amount of territory.

THE IMPACT ON GERMANY

Germany lost 2 million dead and then had to contend with defeat, blockade, humiliation, starvation, economic collapse and the destruction of its ruling class. It was further devastated by influenza and — in theory — crippled by reparations. However, social and economic recovery did not take long and Germany got full employment long before its former opponents. Arguably the rise of Hitler can be blamed on the war, but perhaps it was just one authoritarian system replacing another.

THE IMPACT ON AUSTRIA-HUNGARY

The Austro-Hungarian empire was split up into new countries — Austria, Hungary, Romania, Czechoslovakia, Poland — and an empire which stretched back to Charles V disintegrated. This created non-viable states and destroyed a power bloc which had dominated central and eastern Europe for over four centuries. The whole European balance of power altered, with Russia and Germany facing each other across a series of small states.

THE IMPACT ON FRANCE

The First World War was fought largely on French territory. The nation was traumatised by horrendous casualties and damage to infrastructure, which combined to have a destabilising effect on French society. France sought revenge — both for the recent war and for the terms imposed in 1871.

BENEFICIAL CHANGES

Democracy and national self-determination emerged as the repressive Austro-Hungarian empire came to an end. Parliaments and their electorates prevailed over monarchical and aristocratic influence, and egalitarianism flourished. Many women found a new freedom. The League of Nations also resulted and formed a blueprint — albeit one that failed and needed much amendment — for the international institutions necessary for diplomacy in a nuclear age. One could also argue that the demands of war stimulated advances in technology and medical care that were of general benefit.

CRITICISMS OF THE 'WAR AS A LIBERATOR' IDEA

Democracy did not last long in most of the countries which gained it. Colonies were not given freedom, and mandates to govern overseas territories seemed little more than spoils awarded to the victors. New and terrible ideologies emerged from the economic instability caused by war debts and reparations. A desire to alter the peace treaties, together with bitter resentment, was a dominant theme. Homes were not built for heroes, the USA retreated back into its shell and the effects of war seemed to have had no influence on countries like Japan.

THE TREATY OF VERSAILLES

The Allies brought conflicting aims to the Treaty of Versailles. Britain wanted an independent Poland; France did not. The French wanted a weaker and partitioned

Perhaps Russia is the best example of the First World War's devastating and far-reaching impact.

Contrast Germany with Russia when considering the impact of the war.

Austria-Hungary suffered the greatest territorial losses in Europe.

The social, economic and above all psychological consequences in France were greater than the political ones.

One of the greatest gains in terms of international relations, the League of Nations, was to end in failure.

The strong pacifist movements in the 1920s had their roots in the failure of the war to achieve any real objectives.

It proved impossible at Versailles to reconcile the conflicting interests of the victors.

B *The causes and results of the First World War*

Germany, plus the return of Alsace-Lorraine. The British wanted Germany's colonies and an end to the German navy. The British views on colonies, navies and free trade were in conflict with the ideas of others. The US President Woodrow Wilson had the clearest aims with his Fourteen Points. But Wilson failed to recognise that eastern Europe would not fit into neat national units. The peace didn't account (and perhaps never could have) for the varied forces of public opinion in its neatly parcelled solutions. Future German needs were almost disregarded. Besides loss of territory in Prussia, Silesia, Saar, Schleswig, Alsace-Lorraine and Danzig, there were military clauses which affected the army, navy, airforce and the Rhineland. Add to these the war guilt clauses, the loss of the merchant marine and the reparations, and it is clear why German grievances were bound to demand some sort of an expression.

THE OTHER TREATIES

> Some of the minor treaties were more successful over the long term than Versailles, though another political map of Europe had to be drawn after the Second World War.

While the Treaty of Versailles — and the way it affected Germany — has had the most attention, there were other important international agreements. The Treaty of St German affected Austria by redrawing the map of central Europe. The Treaty of Neuilly dealt with countries in the eastern Balkans, such as Bulgaria, and the Treaty of Trianon rationalised the Hungarian situation after the failed revolution of Bela Kun. The Treaties of Sèvres and Lausanne dealt with Turkey and the Middle East.

THE MERITS AND DEMERITS OF THE EASTERN EUROPEAN TREATIES

> Given the fact that the Austro-Hungarian empire collapsed, what alternatives could have been found?

President Wilson's basic idea in the Fourteen Points was that the new eastern European states needed sound economic bases to underpin their political viability. This was easier said than done because economics often played a minor role in new states, whose many ethnic and national differences were free to flare up in the absence of the suppressing hand of the vanished Austro-Hungarian empire. There were non-Slav groups in the new Slav countries, Germans in Czechoslovakia and an age-old dispute between Serbs and Croats. Democracy went to countries which had never experienced it and, though it worked in some cases, it led to dictatorship in others. Criticisms are also made of the way in which the economic resources were divided up with, for example, a huge percentage of Austria-Hungary's heavy industry going to the new Czechoslovakia.

THE CASE FOR VERSAILLES

> It is vital that you understand the atmosphere of 1918–19.

Given German expansionism over the half century prior to 1918, it could be argued that it had to be forcibly restrained. As for war reparations, the war in the west had been fought in France and Belgium, and Germany had escaped any fighting on its own territory, so it was only fair that it should help to rebuild France and Belgium. Remember, Germany had imposed reparations on France in 1871. A good case can be made out for Germany bearing the prime responsibility for the First World War and — if that line of argument is accepted — then the Commission on War Guilt's attribution of blame was natural justice.

> The Treaty of Versailles is easy to criticise but, given the atmosphere of the times, it is difficult to imagine an alternative which might have worked.

THE CASE AGAINST VERSAILLES

To exclude Germany from all discussion was foolish. Arguably, either the Allies should have been harsher and pushed forward to occupy Germany and impose a policy of divide and rule, or they should have ignored the whole issue of blame and punishment and concentrated on avoiding future wars. Instead there was an unworkable compromise with a lack of German self-determination, the gift of German colonies to the victors, economic provisions which failed to create viable economies and, above all, the resentment stoked up by ludicrous demands for reparations to repair war damage.

Long-term causes of the First World War

- the work of Bismarck
- the early alliance system
- French attitudes to Germany after 1871
- colonial rivalry
- growing commercial rivalry
- Balkan nationalism
- the decline of the Turkish and Austro-Hungarian empires
- the rise of pan-Slavism

Immediate causes of the First World War

- military planning on both sides
- the lack of political control over military planning
- the lack of will by politicians and leaders to prevent war
- public opinion
- alliances and military agreements
- colonial and commercial rivalry
- the role of the Balkans
- the arms race
- the atmosphere of fear and suspicion in Europe
- the absence of any forum for solving disputes

C International relations, 1919–39

Key questions

Why were there no major conflicts in the 1920s?

How successful was the League of Nations?

What were the main causes of the Second World War?

This topic should be revised by using other parts of this book. Look at section B of this unit on the First World War for the Versailles Treaties, and at the units on Russia, Germany, Italy and the USA. All have separate foreign policy sections. France, Spain and Britain are dealt with here.

EUROPE IN 1919–23

In the immediate postwar period, few countries paid much attention to the League of Nations and their main interest was directed to recovery and re-establishing

You always need to go back to Versailles for any study of international relations during the interwar years.

national interests. The focus in these years was on the immediate effects of Versailles and the growth of revisionism in Germany and Italy. The intervention by many foreign powers in the Russian Civil War had a profound long-term influence and Rapallo, the treaty between Russia and Germany in 1922, was a precursor to the 1939 Nazi–Soviet Pact. Meanwhile, Britain was involved in the Middle East, France invaded the Ruhr and trouble brewed in Italy.

1923–29: ATTEMPTS AT PEACE

Note the important role of the Americans as peacemakers as well as bankers.

The Dawes and Young Plans (the two American attempts to help ease German reparations) and American investment in Germany stabilised the country, but the economic foundations were too flawed to guarantee a Germany which could find an equilibrium with its neighbours. However, Dawes got the French out of the Ruhr and Young ended Allied occupation, and the reparations burden on Germany became more reasonable.

COLLECTIVE SECURITY

Make sure you know the implications of Locarno.

The best example of collective security was the Treaty of Locarno between Britain, France and Germany in 1925. The treaty set the boundary terms to the east of Germany and the role allocated to the League of Nations. It led to the entry of Germany into the League and then to the Kellogg–Briand Pact of 1928, by which all the nations who signed it renounced war. Hopes for a peaceful resolution of disputes were raised by this and subsequent disarmament talks. However, Locarno could also be seen to have encouraged German revisionism (i.e. the wish to revise the terms of Versailles) and it was fundamentally flawed by its lack of guarantees for eastern European boundaries.

THE LEAGUE OF NATIONS

You will need to consider the role of the League of Nations in both the maintenance of peace and the causes of war.

The League, an idea of President Wilson, was created at Versailles and designed to prevent further war. It was flawed in excluding Russia and Germany initially, and the absence of the USA was a major weakness. The lack of any means of enforcing its decisions, or preventing aggression, was also a serious error. The League was a marvellous ideal and Wilson deserves real credit for it, but perhaps it took too generous a view of nations' attitudes to their own interests. Most of its successful features were copied when the United Nations was created.

THE PEACE OF THE 1920S

Consider whether the First World War had settled any issues.

Exhaustion and a genuine desire to avoid another horrific war are the key reasons for peace during the 1920s. The League of Nations had its successes, such as Corfu, and received considerable support from Ramsay MacDonald, the British prime minister. However, the USA and the Soviet Union were still not in the League and much of the practical work towards peace — Dawes, Young and Kellogg, for example — was not carried out under its auspices. Meanwhile, there were warning signs that the peace was tenuous. German and Italian revisionism was evident.

A CHANGED ATMOSPHERE, 1929–33

The collapse of the world economy threatened peace by destabilising Germany and Italy and allowing aggressive nationalism to replace internationalism. Disarmament talks in Geneva collapsed in 1933 and American attempts to limit arms and naval power foundered after the Washington Conference. The Japanese invasion of Manchuria was a significant departure from 1920s' idealism, and the League of Nation's reaction to Chinese requests for help (along with American and Soviet attitudes) demonstrated that the League could achieve little and that armed aggression worked.

ITALY

Mussolini emerged to disrupt any League of Nations consensus with his seizure of Abyssinia. Blatant Italian aggression spread to the Balkans and North Africa, and was a central cause of the problems in the 1930s. Italian intervention in Spain further heightened tension, as did Mussolini's attitude towards Hitler and Germany. At the time of the assassination of Dolfuss and the Stresa Front, Mussolini seemed to be anti-German, but following the Pact of Steel and the Anti-Comintern Pact, Mussolini became Hitler's ally.

THE SOVIET UNION

Though the Soviet Union was initially excluded from the League of Nations, it lent support to the idea of collective security. When admitted to the League, self-interest led to the hope that collective security would work. The Soviets made attempts to co-operate with Britain and France to contain the Nazi menace, but Stalin never managed to allay the West's hatred of communism, and his aggression in Finland and the Baltic republics further alienated support. The Nazi–Soviet Pact had huge implications, but was perhaps predictable after the Soviet Union had been ignored at Munich.

FRANCE

French desire for revenge and reparations was a major cause of instability during the 1920s and is context enough for the invasion of the Ruhr in 1923. Another destabilising factor was that constantly changing governments were able to produce little by way of a coherent foreign policy. France promoted the Little Entente, forming alliances with new nation states in Poland, Czechoslovakia and Yugoslavia. By 1930, French support for collective security and disarmament had gone, and it started to pin greater hopes on the Maginot Line and its treaty with the Soviet Union in 1935. As its alliance system started to fall apart in the 1930s, France was forced to rely more on Britain and yet was unhappy with the Baldwin/Chamberlain ideas on appeasement. The inability of France and Britain to work well together was a crucial factor in the build-up to the war, and French responsibility for the collapse of collective security needs to be considered.

BRITAIN

Look at the British attitudes towards both disarmament and interventionism from 1929 onwards. The ideas and policies of MacDonald on collective security, rearmament and disarmament need careful study. Do not see all British foreign policy between the wars as the work of Chamberlain alone — he was not involved until 1937. Look at its policies of non-involvement towards Manchuria and the League in particular. Did that set a vital precedent? Britain's work on Stresa, in trying to contain Hitler, is important, but look also at the Anglo–German Naval Agreement, which made major concessions to his rearmament. The Hoare–Laval Pact is seen by many as a significant piece of appeasement, and perhaps as

---

Consider the role of Manchuria in the decline of collective security and the abandonment of the ideals behind the League.

How responsible was Mussolini for the drift to war?

Consider the responsibility of Stalin for the drift to war.

How important was the passivity of France in the rise of Nazi aggression?

Try and look at the role of Britain in the 1930s from an international standpoint.

important as Munich. British sympathy for German revisionism was always strong, going back to Keynes in 1919. Should a firm line have been taken over German rearmament and conscription? Should firmer action have been taken over the Rhineland with France? Consider British policy over the *Anschluss* and Czechoslovakia — should a firmer line have been taken, or was appeasement the only viable policy? Should a stronger line have been taken over Spain, or a greater attempt made to work with the Soviet Union?

THE IMPACT OF THE SPANISH CIVIL WAR

Spain had a major impact on international relations in the 1930s.

The Spanish Civil War was a definite move towards the Second World War. The realignment of Italy and its move into the Nazi camp began in Spain, and the Rome–Berlin Axis was soon to follow. The League of Nation's non-intervention committee was revealed as weak and was ignored quickly by Germany and the Soviet Union as well as by Italy. The Spanish Civil War shaped much of later German policy, because Hitler saw France and Britain's reluctance to intervene. The *Anschluss* followed shortly afterwards. Collective security was now dead, the mediation capacity of the League had clearly gone, and Britain and France travelled further down the appeasement route. Spain proved a good testing ground for the German military, but perhaps Mussolini should have noted that Italy was not a strong military power. The bombing of Guernica was to have an important effect on appeasement as well as on military thinking.

GERMANY: NAZI AGGRESSION

Don't let hindsight play too large a part. We know there were horrors to come, but politicians were desperate to prevent another Somme or another Guernica.

There is a huge debate about the degree of Nazi responsibility for causing the war — and about Hitler's responsibility for causing Nazism. Hitler's *Mein Kampf* is a vital, if poisonous, document, though it doesn't answer questions about whether he was a planner or simply reacted to events. There was a strong nationalist right in Germany, but the powers that Hitler accrued during the 1930s — and his clear racist intent outlined in *Mein Kampf* — beg the question of whether anything could have contained him. Once Germany had tasted success in the Rhineland and seen what Mussolini could do in Abyssinia, the Second World War became inevitable. Look also at the influence of anti-war public opinion in Britain during the 1930s and consider what room for manoeuvre it gave to politicians like Neville Chamberlain.

THE CAUSE OF THE SECOND WORLD WAR

What was the responsibility of the world community and the major powers for not dealing with the troublemakers?

There is one simple answer to the question of who or what caused the Second World War — Hitler's aggression. However, you need to look wider and consider all the main countries dealt with above, the failure of the League of Nations and the failure of the ideal of collective security.

Key factors in international relations in the 1920s

- the Fourteen Points
- the Treaty of Versailles
- the establishment of Bolshevism in Russia
- intervention in Russia
- American isolationism
- the structure of the League of Nations
- revisionism of Versailles

- the Rapallo Treaty between Germany and the Soviet Union in 1922
- Chanak and Corfu, which demonstrated how fragile the peace was
- the invasion of the Ruhr by the French
- the Dawes and Young Plans, which modified German reparations
- collective security
- the Kellogg–Briand Pact aimed at ending war
- the Washington Naval Conference to limit navies

Key factors in international relations in the 1930s

- the Manchurian crisis
- Japanese aggression
- the disarmament talks of 1933 and their failure
- the direction of Italian foreign policy — the Stresa Front
- Italy and Abyssinia
- Italy and Spain
- Italy and Germany
- Italy and the Balkans
- the changing attitude of Stalin to Hitler
- Stalin and collective security
- Stalin, Spain and Munich
- the Nazi–Soviet Pact
- Britain, France and disarmament
- Britain, France and collective security
- the Anglo–German Naval Agreement and the Stresa Front
- the Hoare–Laval Pact, when Britain and France let Italy keep Abyssinia
- the Rhineland and the *Anschluss*
- the Munich Crisis
- the invasion of Czechoslovakia
- the Polish guarantee against German attack by Britain and France
- the failure of negotiations between Britain, France and the Soviet Union in 1939
- the role of the USA

A The causes of the American Civil War

Key questions

How substantial were the differences between North and South on the eve of the Civil War?

How did events after 1848 lead to increasing sectional tensions between North and South?

What were the motives behind secession and why did this lead to Civil War?

WESTWARD EXPANSION

The attitude of the new states towards slavery was fundamental to the South.

The pioneers' drive to the west continually kept the issue of slavery to the fore as the new agricultural states linked with the industrial North to oppose slavery. With the slave and non-slave states fairly evenly balanced in the Senate, the attitude of new states was vital, particularly after the acquisition of Texas and James Polk's presidential victory in 1844. The Mexican War resulted in large gains in territory, and the defeat of the Wilmot Proviso thwarted attempts to ban slavery in the new territories.

SLAVERY IN THE NEW TERRITORIES

Note the inability to find any compromise on this issue.

Slavery was the great national issue by the late 1840s and it split the Democrats and Whigs. Senator Calhoun of South Carolina supported a Platform of the South to allow slavery in the new territories, and he tried to deny Congressional authority with the argument that the issue of slavery should be left to the new territories to decide.

THE 1848 PRESIDENTIAL ELECTION

The issue of secession was a live one by 1848.

Zachary Taylor, the Whig candidate, won, in an election campaign dominated by the slavery issue. The growth of the Free Soil Party showed the depth of feeling. With the arrival of California and New Mexico as new non-slave states, the fear of non-slave domination of the Senate led the South towards thoughts of secession.

THE CLAY COMPROMISE

The slavery issue was not going to go away.

The Clay compromise of 1850 was a serious attempt to end the quarrels over slavery. It dealt with factors such as new territories, fugitive slaves and popular sovereignty over the issue of slavery, and it was accepted, with reservations, by both North and South. However, the compromise postponed rather than prevented conflict and the Union gained because — while secession might have worked in 1850 — the North was in a position to win a war by 1860. The compromise should be seen as a truce.

A COMPARISON OF NORTH AND SOUTH IN THE 1850S

Note the differing attitudes in the South.

Although the American Civil War is seen as a clash between two differing social

UNIT 6   The United States of America

and economic systems, there were many similarities in areas such as language and law. The South was smaller, poorer, in more scattered settlements, less diverse economically and more socially stratified. There was less immigration, fewer changes and a more rural, agricultural atmosphere. The population was one-third black slaves, who worked in a plantation system amid a more violent society than in the North. This Southern society had strong military traditions, a romantic self-image with duels about honour etc., and a tendency to glorify agriculture at the expense of industry.

FACTORS WHICH LED TO SECESSION

There was a strong degree of unity within most of the core southern states. They felt exploited over the tariff issue (tax on imports) and subordinated to the growing economy of the North. The loss of the Senate with the arrival of California was a severe blow and — having dominated the presidency, the Senate, the Supreme Court and the military to this point — the South feared its transition to becoming a permanent minority within the Union. Though slavery was always the fundamental issue, there was a range of other economic, social and psychological factors linked to it.

THE 1850S

An economic boom during the 1850s calmed the issue temporarily, and the presidential election of 1852 was an attempt to quell discontent. However, President Pierce was seen as a tool of the slavers by the North, and an image of incompetence was strengthened after his dealings with Spain over Cuba. In addition, the Fugitive Slave Law of 1850 made it easier to get runaway slaves back to their owners, and the increasingly effective pressure group tactics of the anti-slavers kept the conflicts simmering.

THE KANSAS–NEBRASKA ACT

The Kansas–Nebraska Act, which opened Kansas to white settlement, was vital in the build-up to the Civil War as it ended the truce of the 1850 compromise. Then came Senator Douglas' bill for new territories, and the divide North of 36° 30′. It argued for popular sovereignty, which meant that it was possible for slavery to spread west. Douglas hoped to win southern support while benefiting the rail interests of the North. However, although this was a practical solution, too many in the North now saw slavery as a moral issue for it to work. The Douglas Bill passed, ending the Missouri compromise of 1820. It was hated in the North and further split both the Whigs and the Democrats.

POLITICAL REALIGNMENT

Slavery and associated issues wrought a changed American political landscape as many former Whigs drifted towards the Republican Party's free, white, democratic and capitalistic platform. The arrival of 3 million immigrants in the USA between 1846 and 1854 terrified the South and further added to political and partisan fluidity. Note also the success of the Know Nothings (the nationalistic, anti-alien party). Gradually the Whigs vanished and the Democrats became increasingly South orientated. The Republicans became the party of the North, especially once the Know Nothings declined.

Slavery was the central cause of the Civil War, though there were many other factors involved too.

President Pierce was unable to offer any solution to slavery.

The fact that both major parties were fundamentally split over the issue was also a factor in the lack of any solution.

Note the gradual realignment, partly along racial lines.

A The causes of the American Civil War

Kansas accelerated the USA towards its Civil War by revealing the impossibility of compromise.

THE KANSAS DISPUTE

The issue over whether slavery would be allowed in Kansas was central to the build-up to the Civil War. Both slavers and anti-slavers were deeply involved in it. By 1856 there was virtually a civil war there as both sides armed and formed two separate legislatures. It was a North/South split in microcosm. Bleeding Kansas, as the local civil war was called, with its 200-plus dead, pushed the sides further apart.

THE 1856 ELECTION

The 1856 election was contested between Buchanan, the pro-slavery Democrat, and Frémont, the anti-slavery Republican, with the weak and indecisive Buchanan emerging as victor. Terrified of secession, he made major concessions to the South. The economic depression was beginning to affect the North (the South was largely unaffected) and made the North keener on tariffs and a Homestead Act which — to the intense anger of the South — would have given land free to those who settled in the west.

Note the other issues which divided the two sides.

DRED SCOTT

The Dred Scott case of 1857 was a major cause of the Civil War. Scott was a slave who was assumed to have been free, as he had lived with his master in free territories. The Supreme Court decision on him struck down the 1820 Missouri compromise and ruled slavery as legal in all territories. The return of Dred Scott to slavery clarified that slaves were not citizens, but existed as property.

This was another factor which pushed the two sides apart and made compromise impossible.

KANSAS–LECOMPTON, 1857

A further step towards war came when the pro-slavery group drew up a constitution which would have permitted slavery, and then called for an election based on it. Free settlers boycotted the election, so the pro-slavers initially won and brought in the Lecompton system — with slavery. Although eventually rejected, Kansas–Lecompton created a storm in North and South, and split the remaining Democrat politicians in a sectionalisation of politics which was a vital cause of the Civil War.

By this stage, secession appeared inevitable.

THE LINCOLN–DOUGLAS DEBATES

Abraham Lincoln was a lawyer/politician from Illinois who ran for the Senate in the 1858 election against Stephen Douglas. Lincoln used the campaign to gain publicity against the better-known Douglas and they met in seven separate debates where Lincoln argued that slavery was morally wrong, that there should be no extension of it and that he wanted its abolition. Douglas argued for popular sovereignty, tried to dismiss slavery as an issue and in July 1858 declared: 'I do not think the Negro is any kin of mine at all … This government … was made by white men, for the benefit of white men and their posterity, to be executed and managed by white men.' Although Douglas won, he alienated many Democrat supporters and Lincoln became a national figure.

The Lincoln–Douglas debates had major political implications.

JOHN BROWN

John Brown was a central figure during the violence in Kansas and he organised an armed raid in 1859 into Virginia, a slave state. He hoped for a slave rising —

See John Brown as providing a final spark to open conflict.

one of the South's greatest fears — and was backed by many in the North. The Harper's Ferry assault, when he tried to capture a US army depot, was a failure and he was executed. However, the support he gained from the North convinced the South that slavery was not safe within the Union, and so spurred the secession process onwards.

THE 1860 ELECTION

The 1860 election proved the final straw for the South. The Democrat cause was divided between two candidates, Stephen Douglas (who was hated in the South for his opposition to Lecompton) and John Breckinridge, the former vice president. The Republicans had an outstanding practical politician, Lincoln, as their candidate. He was very much a man of the people, a great debater who had managed the Convention (where presidential candidates are chosen) brilliantly. He was a moderate anti-slaver who also proposed tariffs, further immigration, a Homestead Act and government aid to the Pacific Railroad. While Breckinridge won the South, Douglas' support was too thinly spread to have an impact and Lincoln became president with 40% of the vote. Though the victory was not due to his opponents' divisions and he won the large populous states of the North, Lincoln's was still a largely sectional vote.

> The South viewed Lincoln's victory as the equivalent of a declaration of war.

SECESSION OF THE LOWER SOUTH

The South's view of Lincoln as a sectional northern president culminated in seven states, led by South Carolina, quitting the Union and proclaiming the Southern Confederacy under President Jefferson Davis. The secessionists were very well organised and their more radical members had already drafted a new Constitution for the breakaway South, known as the Secession Ordinances. The Constitution argued that secession was the right of all states, and was permitted under the drafting of the Constitution in 1787. The main reasons for secession given in the Ordinances were the need to defend slavery and the election of a president biased towards the North. Economic issues were not seen as important.

> Note the emergence of slavery as the central issue.

THE FINAL STAGES

James Buchanan, the president from 1856 to 1860, was indecisive and felt that the federal government could not prevent the South's secession. The Crittenden compromise of 1860, which would have permitted slavery in the South, failed. Lincoln was against any extension of slavery, but he was prepared to allow it to remain in the states where it existed in order to preserve the Union. The Fort Sumter Crisis of 1860, where Southern troops fired on federal government forces, ended the indecision and drift. Lincoln then went to war.

> The resolution of Lincoln was vital for both Northern commitment and Southern secession.

THE REASONS FOR LINCOLN'S DECISION TO FIGHT

Lincoln felt he had no choice. Although economics and loss of markets played a part in his political calculation, the primary reason for going to war was that he was not prepared to see the destruction of the United States as a nation. He felt that secession destroyed the ideals of democracy and liberty upon which the USA had been built, and he had a vision for the future of the USA which would not be fulfilled with a 'house divided'.

> Lincoln represented the bulk of opinion in the North.

The key differences between the North and South

- westward expansion
- slavery
- agriculture versus industry
- tariffs
- new territories
- social structure

Key events from 1848 onwards

- the 1848 election
- the Clay compromise, which would have kept slavery in the South
- Kansas–Nebraska — the issue of the expansion of slavery into new territories
- loss of Senate control by the South
- California
- Brown's raid into the South
- Dred Scott and the Supreme Court decision which endorsed slavery
- the election of President Buchanan
- the election of President Lincoln

The motives for Southern secession

- the retention of slavery
- fear of Northern domination
- becoming a minority group
- retention of their own way of life
- protection of economic interests

B The course of the American Civil War

Key questions

What were the relative strengths of the Union and the Confederacy during the War?

How far did methods of warfare change?

Why did the Confederacy collapse and the North win?

THE NATURE OF THE WAR

Perhaps the American Civil War was the last of the old-fashioned wars.

The American Civil War was fought on a massive scale and over 650,000 died. As always with civil wars, bitterness and savagery were laced by incidents of chivalry. In the end it was force of numbers and industrial might that won. There was limited technological innovation: cavalry was still important; the bayonet was much used and the old single-shot rifle was the main weapon; artillery made little advance on the Napoleonic Wars; and battles tended to be large numbers of men thrown at each other. Medical care was limited and wounds frequently meant death through infection.

THE BALANCE OF THE TWO SIDES

The North had a population of 22 million, the South had 9 million (and slaves). The North had industrial potential and was largely self-sufficient in food and war materials, whereas the South had to rely on imports. Military leadership was competent with Robert E. Lee and 'Stonewall' Jackson effective for the South, and Ulysses Grant, Philip Sheridan and George Thomas equally effective for the North. The North's industrial strength was countered by the South's advantage of fighting a defensive war with shortening communication lines. Luck and good judgement in the early days brought the four key border states — Maryland, Delaware, Kentucky and Missouri — into the Union and this proved to be of vital strategic importance.

> The main reasons for Northern victory were apparent from early in the war.

POLITICAL BACKING

Initially Lincoln had to deal with the disunity of the Copperheads (Northerners who would have allowed secession) and the anti-abolitionists. He also had problems with opposition to his war powers and the suspension of civil liberties. However, he received full backing for his economic policies, such as the Homestead Act (free land in the west to settlers), the Morrill Land Grant Act (designed to develop agriculture), the Tariff Act, the Pacific Railroad Act and the National Bank Act. An agricultural, commercial and industrial boom in the North was vital for Lincoln's support and for his military success. The North actually benefited economically from the war.

> Lincoln eventually had both numbers and industrial might behind him.

THE SOUTH

The South had major economic problems, for the fighting was mainly in its territory and an economic blockade left it fewer resources than the North. As the war progressed, the Confederate political leadership under Davis had less backing than Lincoln. Davis — although an experienced soldier, planter and senator — was not a strong leader and he had a poor-quality Cabinet. He got too involved in military details and had a real power struggle with Vice President Stephens and the governors, who opposed his central direction of the war and his conscription policy.

> In terms of internal politics, Lincoln had a much easier task.

THE CIVIL WAR, 1861–62

The Unionists' basic policy was defined in the Anaconda Plan as being to starve and blockade the Confederates. It was a sound strategy that eventually ensured a Northern victory. The North, however, made some strategic errors by responding too fast to public pressure for action. It invaded Virginia, which led to the disaster for the North at Bull Run. As a result, General McDowell was replaced by the cautious General McClellan. The new man was a good organiser who was inclined to overrate enemy strengths, and he was strongly criticised for his inaction over the winter of 1861–62. Many argue that the events of 1862 in the west were critical. Note the work of Northern Generals Buell, Halleck and Grant in the west. In spite of the bloodbath of Shiloh (23,000 dead on both sides), New Orleans and the Mississippi were Northern gains in late 1862. Although Jackson and Lee proved to be successful against McClellan in the north, they did not have the capacity to destroy his army. At the fiasco of Antietam, McClellan failed to defeat the South in spite of his superior numbers, and he was sacked.

> The only hope for Southern military victory lay in a pre-emptive and successful strike in 1861–62.

EMANCIPATION

Lincoln disliked the emancipation of the slaves. He had been pledged to non-interference on the issue earlier and had opposed the Crittenden compromise as a violation of 'free soil' principles. However, there was substantial pressure on Lincoln from Congress — note the Confiscation Act of 1862, whereby the slaves of rebels would be freed. Lincoln adopted emancipation reluctantly, because he feared it might strengthen the resolve of the South to fight on. However, he hoped that it would win support in Europe. He waited until Antietam, where the Southern advance was halted, before issuing the Proclamation in 1863. It was to be a gradual measure because he did not wish to alienate the four Union slave states. This had little immediate impact in the North, and in fact was opposed in some parts. It had a greater impact on the South in liberated areas, and on Negroes in the Union army in particular.

THE CIVIL WAR, 1863

Victory for the North was simply a matter of time.

The slow-moving Northern General McClellan was repulsed by the less able Southern General Burnside, and the Northern defeat of Chancellorsville followed that of Fredericksburg. Military talent lay with the South, numbers with the North. It was not until General Meade replaced General Hooker that victory seemed for the North more certain, as Gettysburg showed. Only the North had the resources to find replacement troops and Lee could not go on the offensive again.

THE INFLUENCE OF EUROPE

The prevailing neutrality of foreign powers favoured the North.

The South hoped for support and recognition, and reckoned on a British dependency on cotton supplies. However, the British cotton industry had large stocks of raw materials and could import from Egypt and India. Other British industries did well out of the war and there was little need for Britain to get involved. British and French public opinion was split and economic considerations were not sufficient motive for European powers to try intervening. Some argue that Palmerston might have recognised the South if it had more military success, but the *Trent* and *Alabama* affairs — where British-built ships damaged Northern trade — soured relations. Emancipation actually had little effect either on improving relations with European countries.

THE CIVIL WAR, 1864–65

Lincoln's patience in waiting for decisive victory was to have a major impact on the surrender and the results of the war.

There were appalling casualties in 1864, especially in the Wilderness Campaign in the west and at Cold Harbor where a total of 25,000 were killed. Peace talks started amid growing war weariness on both sides. The capture of Atlanta ended peace talks and ensured the re-election of Lincoln in 1864. General Sherman's scorched-earth policy in Georgia finally destroyed Southern hopes and cut the Confederacy in half. The war dragged on until 1865 with Lincoln insisting on Union, no slavery, surrender and the end of the Confederacy in all its forms. The final surrender came at Appomattox.

LINCOLN'S CONTRIBUTION

President Lincoln was criticised both for underestimating the secessionists' military strength and for overestimating the Southern unionists as a political force. He got the military under control by replacing General McClellan with General Grant, and his management of Congress and his Cabinet proved him an outstanding war

UNIT 6   The United States of America

Note the impact that
Lincoln had on the
office of presidency.

Both the issue of slavery
and the relationship
between the states and
the federal government
were seen as solved. The
future direction of the
USA was now clear.

leader for a democratic society. Note the Gettysburg address, plus Lincoln's ideas on reconstruction and the way he harnessed the power and resources of the Northern states to ensure a federal state.

THE IMPACT OF THE CIVIL WAR

In the South, over 25% of the young men were casualties and the war led to the collapse of the economy as ex-slaves deserted plantations. There was starvation in some areas and the age of the carpetbagger (the Northerners who were determined to exploit and rule the South) arrived. Those in the South who would not accept defeat were eventually persuaded to do so by the Jim Crow laws, which institutionalised segregation in the South. However, the United States emerged from the Civil War as emphatically one nation. Federalism had won against state rights, and slavery had gone for good. The race relations issue festered, but the North prospered during a later stage of mass industrialisation.

RECONSTRUCTION

There was military occupation, but no revenge killing or mass confiscation. Congress was less tolerant than Lincoln and that meant a tempering of Lincoln's initial generous intentions at Gettysburg. Make sure that you know the ways in which the South was governed, both initially — when racial equality was insisted on — and then when its own Jim Crow methods were allowed to return.

Why the North won and the South lost
- numbers of soldiers
- population
- quality of generals — eventually
- the border states
- the political ability and power of Lincoln
- the weak economy of the South
- the Anaconda Plan — the slow surrounding and crushing process
- the failure of the South's pre-emptive strike into the North in 1861
- the attitude of Europe
- the economic resources of the North
- the inability of Davis and the other Southern leaders

Factors which helped the South's fight
- incompetence of early Northern generals
- shorter lines of communication
- a clear ideology to fight for
- better generals and stronger military tradition

C Westward expansion

Key questions

Why did so many Americans move to the west?

What was the effect of westward expansion on the native Americans?

What was the impact of the frontier on American politics and society?

THE EARLY REASONS FOR WESTWARD EXPANSION

The ability to settle land was seen as a basic American right.

By the 1862 Homestead Act, which gave land virtually freely in the west to those who wished it, westward expansion became easy. Cheap land was a Congressional article of faith, for easy land acquisition had been one of the most attractive features to new immigrants since European settlers had first arrived. Western migration had been present since colonial days and the attempted closure of the west by the British had been a cause of the War of Independence. The Louisiana Purchase of 1804 fuelled the ability to expand westwards as well. The chance to break away from old European values and get a place of one's own was central to an American Dream that spurred many to emigrate across the Atlantic. Within the new country, land hunger in the east, gold fever, European conscription and factory slavery were further nineteenth-century incentives to move west.

THE GLAMORISATION OF WESTERN EXPANSION

The media and propaganda also played a part in westward expansion.

The gold and silver strikes of California in 1849, Colorado in 1858, Arizona in 1870 and the great Comstock Lode (a huge silver discovery), and the lure of copper in Montana, were great draws west. The profits from cattle farming by the 1860s provided a more reliable incentive for a population made up largely of immigrants who had made a massive move in the first place (say from Ireland, Scotland or Russia) and could therefore contemplate a move a few hundred miles west as a relatively small undertaking. From the beginning, the American media — from the press to the landscape paintings of Remington and Beadle — consistently portrayed western expansion as a romantic enterprise that defined the essence of being an American.

THE 1860S

Get some idea of both the pace and the size of the fresh settlement.

During the 1860s, the Plains, the Rockies and the Great Basin were settled, and there was real hope that democracy and equality would thrive there. Big companies anxious to capitalise on the silver and copper added their pressure and helped order to follow the chaos of initial settlement. The ranges were wired off, the Texas/Kansas/Chicago cow trails converted the Americans from pork to beef eaters and the railway lines followed.

DESTRUCTION OF THE PLAINS INDIANS

Given the different lifestyles of the settler and the Indian, conflict was inevitable.

It is estimated that there were about 300,000 Indians in the west, split among 250,000 Plains Indians, plus smaller groups near the Rockies and among the farmers/ herders in the southwest. The nomadic, buffalo-dependent Plains Indians were the most opposed to westward expansion. They were seen as vicious and barbaric by the settlers and by American opinion, and there were massacres on

both sides, notably at Minnesota in 1862, Sand Creek in 1864 and Fetterman in 1868. The whites were blamed by the Peace Commission of 1867 and Congress offered reservations in 1869. However, the Indians were reluctant to comply with an imposed system that disrupted a traditional way of life.

THE END OF THE INDIAN 'PROBLEM'

By 1875 conflict between settlers and Indians had died down, only to flare up again during the Black Hills gold rush, leading to battles such as Little Big Horn. The Nez Percés caused problems in 1877, with Chief Joseph trying passive resistance to expansion into his territory. Geronimo and the Apaches were finished by 1886 and the butchery at Wounded Knee ended the 'Indian problem' as far as most Americans were concerned. The gun, the telegraph, the railroad and the destruction of the buffalo all played their part. The attitude of most white Americans was totally hostile: they wanted defeat and reservations for the Indians at best, and extermination at worst. The desire to 'civilise' and educate was in evidence with the Indian Rights Association, but the Dawes Act of Congress, which tried to end the idea of reservations, was more typical.

TRANSPORT AND COMMUNICATION

A trans-American stagecoach service was operating in 1857, and the Pony Express followed. By 1861 the telegraph linked the Atlantic with the Pacific. Then came the Pacific Rail Act of 1862, which — despite widespread corruption — led to a rail link between east and west in 1869. Stimulated by federal grants, cheap land and cheap loans, there were five separate trans-American rail links by the turn of the century.

REASONS FOR THE WESTERN SETTLEMENT

The whole process of moving west and acquiring land was made easy; there was simply nowhere else in the world where anyone could go and get prime land for themselves and keep it. The railroads were vital, as was the demand for labour and a growth of technology ranging from wells, ploughs and reapers to the development of barbed wire for enclosing the ranges.

THE CONSERVATION MOVEMENT

With the settlement of the bulk of the United States by 1890, a strong conservation movement was started to protect the environment against further damage. The buffalo had been wiped out, huge areas of forest destroyed and mining had devastated large tracts of land. National Parks were created and major Acts passed by Congress, such as the Forest Reserve Act of 1891 and the Forest Management Act of 1897. Writers such as Gifford Pinchot and John Powell added to the conservationist cause. There was a great deal of opposition from vested interests such as mine owners.

Expansion of the American west
- tradition
- cheap land
- incentives to settle the land, such as the Homestead Act
- personal freedom and independence
- gold and silver

Side notes:

There were signs of genocide in white America's attitude to native Americans.

The railroad was fundamental to westward expansion.

Note that some of the richest farming land in the world was up for grabs.

Conservation became a major divisive issue in the 1890s and has remained so.

- money to be made out of cattle and farming
- the railroads
- part of the American character — the Turner thesis stressed the role of the frontier in forming American democracy
- the glamorisation of the west

Impact of western expansion
- the destruction of the Indians
- Indian wars
- new states
- railroad empires
- the conservation movement of the 1890s

D Race relations in the South, 1863–1912

Key questions

How much did the position of the blacks change during Reconstruction?

How and why were black freedoms eroded in the South after 1877?

How did blacks, especially their leading spokesmen, respond to their situation after 1877?

RECONSTRUCTION

Emancipation was only the very first stage of a long process.

The Civil War did not solve the USA's racial issue and at first freedom meant starvation for many Southern blacks. The 13th Amendment to the US Constitution abolished slavery and its acceptance was a precondition for admission back into the Union, but President Andrew Johnson's suggestion for limited black suffrage was ignored. The Black Codes of 1865–66 were a Southern attempt to restrict blacks which illustrated the problem well. They made the blacks second-class citizens and were seen by the South as necessary after slavery had gone, and by the North as a reversion to slavery. The Freedmen's Bureau Bill and the Civil Rights Act of 1866 tried to limit the Black Codes and the 14th Amendment was a further attempt to improve black rights. However, even these slow moves to reconstruction resulted in violence in the South, such as the New Orleans race riots of 1866.

DEVELOPMENTS IN THE 1860S

The political gains of the blacks in the South were to be minimal and short lived.

Blacks were in the majority in five of the former rebel states, and therefore race was a major party issue during the 1868 presidential election when the Republicans argued for Negro suffrage and a Reconstruction Act, while the Democrats pressed for state-by-state legislation. The Republicans won. The 15th Amendment, which was a further attempt to ensure black rights, got through in 1870 and a few blacks were appointed to public office. There was some black political control in South Carolina, but little elsewhere. Two black senators and 15 representatives were elected to office in 1868.

UNIT 6

The United States of America

You might consider whether black people made any gains from the Civil War at all.

Note the lack of any change of attitude in the South.

The 1877 compromise opened the way for official segregation.

There was limited scope for any black economic development.

Powerful white Southerners were hostile to any form of black development.

THE IMPACT OF EMANCIPATION AND THE WAR ON THE BLACKS

By 1870 black illiteracy was at least 95% and most black people remained at work in their slave occupations. There was some black demand for land, education and the vote, but the majority became tenants and sharecroppers. Education made some impact in the 1870s and dragged literacy rates up to 30% by the 1890s, and universities such as Fisk and Howard were also developing at this time. The Freedmen's Bureau, set up by the federal government after the war, made efforts to deal with refugees, education and the prevention of black exploitation.

THE REACTION OF THE SOUTH

A strong reaction against the idea of Negro suffrage made the Ku-Klux-Klan active by 1866, and it set out to wreck the pro-black Union League and generally to intimidate blacks and carpetbaggers. Congress retaliated within the Force Act and KKK Act, and the worst of the Klan work had been suppressed by 1871. Northern interest in the black issue was cooling by the early 1870s and the Freedmen's Bureau was gone by 1872. The Amnesty Act of 1872 (which officially forgave those who had fought for the South) and the Depression and Panic Act (which tried to deal with the economic crisis of the early 1870s) took interest away. The Force Bill of 1875 and the Civil Rights Act of 1875 were designed to help black people in the South, but they were never fully enforced. The failure of the Republicans in the South and the Mississippi Plan of 1874 resulted in pressure on the blacks and led to white control of the majority of Southern states by 1876.

THE 1877 COMPROMISE

By 1877 the whites had reasserted control in all Southern states and electoral deadlock threatened. The compromise of 1877 — which allowed the Democrats in the South considerable freedom over racial matters in return for allowing the Republicans to retain control of the presidency — demonstrated that reconstruction had failed the blacks. The North implicitly agreed to abandon its ideas of racial equality and permitted white domination of the South.

RACE IN THE SOUTH FROM 1877

There was limited economic change in the South to influence the race issue because there was virtually no immigration into an area that remained largely rural and dominated by a planter system. Some 90% of USA's black population was still in the South. Few black people owned land and they were sharecroppers or part of the crop lien system (a type of payment in kind). Black poverty was endemic, with a lack of both cash and credit, and no incentive to improve the land that black people worked. However, there was some prosperity as a result of a cotton boom and growing demand for tobacco, sugar and rice.

BOURBON RULE

The ruling caste was known as the Bourbons, the old planter families who believed in white supremacy, white middle-class domination of business and a laissez faire attitude to government and economic intervention. Low public spending — especially on education — was a marked feature, as was corruption in government and a barbaric prison system. Meanwhile, limited developments in coal, rail, iron, steel and textiles created little wealth and, in any case, these industries were mostly staffed by poor whites.

AS/A-Level 19th & 20th Century European & World History

Race relations in the South, 1863–1912

THE EROSION OF BLACK FREEDOM

A few black people kept the vote gained after the Civil War, but increasingly they were prevented from exercising it by white violence. The 14th Amendment and the Civil Rights Acts of 1866–75 were undermined by the Supreme Court, particularly by the Cruikshank ruling of 1875 which prevented any sanctions being taken against those who did discriminate against black people. With no federal government protection against discrimination, segregation spread across the South with a poll tax, literacy tests and residential requirements used to exclude black people from power and influence. The Supreme Court played its part here with the Williams case, which allowed Mississippi to make it virtually impossible for a black person to vote.

> With no federal government and Supreme Court limitations, the Southern ruling caste was free to impose its prejudices.

THE JIM CROW LAWS

The Jim Crow laws imposed racial segregation in the South. They spread all over the South after 1887 and were upheld by the Supreme Court. The key decision here was Plessey vs Ferguson, which permitted segregation provided it was 'equal'. An official toleration of racism encouraged the spread of racial hatred and lynching, which deliberately created a cowed and deprived minority. Apart from a minor improvement in real wages and the growth of a few black businesses, it could be argued that black people had made no real progress since 1865.

> Note the endorsement of the entire Southern establishment in the segregation process. Even many of the churches did not allow black members.

THE BLACK RESPONSE

Booker T. Washington, head of the Tuskagee Institute, advocated black self-help, hard work, enterprise and acceptance of the status quo. He became the most powerful black politician and created a substantial political organisation. He focused on literacy and vocational education, and in the Atlanta compromise was prepared to accept white supremacy. Washington was criticised by men like Du Bois, one of the founders of the National Association for the Advancement of Colored People (NAACP), who wanted political equality and full civil rights. Washington won the debate, but the economic advantages that his approach anticipated did not materialise. Limited progress was made under his auspices, such as including black people on some juries.

> Note the black population's docility in the face of provocation.

NORTHERN MIGRATION

Towards the end of the nineteenth century, black people started moving to the Northern cities, where they found that inequality and unemployment were not just a Southern phenomenon. Northern trade unions could be as hostile as any Southern plantation owner; and while the Southerners might lynch, the Northerners could riot and kill. The anti-black Springfield riot of 1908 led to the formation of the NAACP. Its leader, Du Bois, charted a strategy of using the courts to gain protection for the blacks. The NAACP's attack on the political consequences of segregation included cases such as that against the Grandfather clause in 1915 (another device to prevent black people from voting). The National Urban League, set up in 1910, also worked towards ending black poverty in cities.

> There were some signs of black progress, but they were few and far between.

The impact of reconstruction on the blacks
- the emancipation of blacks
- the Black Codes, which limited black rights
- Freedman's Bureau, set up by Congress to help blacks after the War

- Civil Rights Act, designed to guarantee black rights
- 14th and 15th amendments to the US Constitution
- education
- electoral involvement initially

The erosion of black freedoms

- the Ku-Klux-Klan
- failure of the Force Act, designed to ensure black rights
- failure of the Civil Rights Act
- the Mississippi Plan, which condoned racism in the South
- the compromise of 1877
- Bourbon rule
- the poll tax — a device to ensure that blacks could not vote
- the Jim Crow laws, which institutionalised racism in the South
- the work of the Supreme Court in upholding the Jim Crow laws

The black response after 1877

- Booker T. Washington and his vocational educational ideas
- Du Bois and his more assertive views on black rights
- Northern migration
- the NAACP and its nationwide organisation to help black rights
- the Urban League, designed to help blacks who had emigrated to Northern cities

E American politics, 1877–1900

Key questions

How effectively did politicians respond to the nation's needs in this period?

What was the nature of American politics in the years after the American Civil War?

Industrialisation changed the nature of American society and politics.

THE AMERICAN INDUSTRIAL REVOLUTION

During the last two decades of the nineteenth century, a massive industrial development accelerated the USA to a position where it produced 30 % of the world's manufactured goods. The Civil War proved a stimulus to economic growth, and a unified and expanding country provided a growing domestic market. With vast natural resources, government backing and cheap labour, huge economies of scale were possible. There was also great inventiveness, as the telephone, the light bulb and the typewriter showed. Politics and business intermingled in a prevailing culture that supported industrial growth by filling courts and legislatures with businessmen who supported business.

The American tradition of free enterprise and laissez faire was hostile to any regulation of industry.

ATTEMPTS AT REGULATION

The monopolistic ways of the Rockefellers in oil, the Carnegies in steel and the Morgans in banking were hardly checked. The Interstate Commerce Act of 1887

tried to prevent some of the abuses which came from monopoly control, but its impact was limited. The Anti-Trust (anti-monopoly) Movement made limited headway, especially given the attitude of the Supreme Court. Note the Knight decision (which limited the role of the federal government) of the Supreme Court in this respect.

TRADE UNIONS

Note the limited impact of any movements to improve wages and working conditions.

American trade unionism never attained the power and impact enjoyed by its European counterparts. Though real wages went up in the years after the Civil War, the prevailing culture was hostile to organised labour, and immigration kept labour cheap and replaceable. When unions attempted to organise and strike, employers like Carnegie were able to use force to smash them. The Lochner case was one of several which showed how the courts would back employers against workers. The taint of anarchism and violence, particularly by the Industrial Workers of the World (IWW), gave the unions a bad press. The Haymarket Riots in Chicago in 1886, where seven policemen were killed, also gave unions a bad image. The capitalist and anti-socialist Sam Gompers, head of the American Federation of Labor (AFL), made more progress, but this was still limited to minor changes in hours and conditions.

POLITICS IN THE LATE 1860S AND EARLY 1870S

Note several important factors in the development of the party system and the presidency.

The impeachment of President Johnson and the failings of President Grant damaged the presidency after Lincoln. The Gold Scandal of 1869 and economic depression in 1873 led to over 3 million unemployed and pointed out several fundamental failings in the American economy and its politics. The Republican Party became very much the party of business. Liberal republicanism vanished and attempts to reform the civil service failed. Corruption became endemic in government, as shown by the rise of bosses like Tweed in New York, who embezzled over $100 million of public money.

THE NATURE OF POLITICS AFTER 1875

The tradition of two parties with only mild divisions between them grew.

Major economic issues were usually ignored in the scramble for political office. The great political machines grew and bossism (the dominance of big cities by corrupt mayors), patronage, the spoils system (giving jobs and contracts corruptly) and mediocre presidents dominated American politics. Third parties — for example, the Grangers, the Greenbacks and the Workingmen's parties — came and went. There was great political involvement, but in the end there was a fairly even split between the Democrats and Republicans. Two-party American politics was here to stay.

THE POLITICAL PARTIES

Party divisions tended to be internal and not between the parties.

Few large issues divided the two major parties, though there were serious (and frequently personal) local divisions. The Republicans became identified with the Union, tariffs, wealth, business and central government influence in economics, and they were strongest in New England and the Midwest. The Democrats tended to be supported by the South, Northern immigrants, the Catholics and the States Rightists, and they favoured limited government, tended to be racist and were anti-tariff. Both parties had internal splits on issues and on personalities.

UNIT 6

The United States of America

It is important to note how and why American politics developed in this period.

THE PRESIDENCY AND THE STATES

The inheritance of Grant and Johnson led to a drop in status of the presidency. The lack of activism on the part of most incumbents from 1865 onwards further lowered the prestige of the office. Many holders of the office were products of a corrupt political process. Meanwhile, commercial interests such as the railroads dominated legislatures and the legal system, and formal power lay increasingly in Congress and the local party machines. The power of the corrupt big city bosses grew.

PRESIDENTS HAYES AND GARFIELD

This was not a distinguished period of American political development.

President Rutherford Hayes (1877–81) was a pro-Southern Republican with a reputation for honesty. He tried civil service reform, but failed to win over Congress. Known as a hard money man, Hayes tried to rationalise American currency with the Coinage Act and bimetallism. He terminated reconstruction and, it could be argued, he abandoned black people in the South as the price of his election. President James Garfield, the last president to come from a log cabin, is best known for being shot in 1881. He provoked a huge spoils row over patronage. Hayes and Garfield provide two good examples of the mediocrity of the presidents and you have to work quite hard to say anything about them.

PRESIDENTS ARTHUR AND CLEVELAND

The presidencies of Arthur and Cleveland showed some signs of activity.

Republican President Chester Arthur (1881–85) was a product of the spoils system, yet there are points in his favour, such as the Pendleton Act which radically reformed the civil service. The Democratic President Grover Cleveland (1885–89 and 1893–97) got involved in protection and Catholic issues. Fairly honest by the standards of the time, Cleveland hit out at the harm being done on public lands by western rail, timber and cattle interests. He cleaned up army pensions and at least tried to raise the tariff issue. His work on the Interstate Commerce Act, trying to regulate business, was contentious, as was his limited view of the role of the president and the federal government.

THE 1888 ELECTION OF PRESIDENT HARRISON

It took nearly 30 years for popular pressure to start to turn against the business age.

Republican President Benjamin Harrison (1889–93) achieved power after a corrupt election which also produced the infamous Billion Dollar Congress, named after the staggering wealth of its members. The Harrison regime saw an increase in pensions, public works, subsidies, the McKinley Tariff, the Silver Purchase Act (another attempt to rationalise the currency) and the Sherman Anti-Trust Act, designed to try to regulate monopolies in business. The Republicans performed poorly in the 1890 elections and there was a growing national dislike of a corrupt Congress together with the first signs of an alliance between radicals, reformers and populists.

THE AGRARIAN REVOLT

Agrarian unrest was the first sign of a populist revolt against entrenched economic interest.

In the late 1880s agricultural prices fell, farm debt soared and there was considerable overproduction both in the USA and abroad. The export market collapsed. With high rail freight charges, rising interest rates and manufacturing monopolies, farmers felt that the whole system was rigged against them. They suffered a great loss in income and status, and the aggrieved and hungry farmer was to become a major political force.

THE GRANGERS AND THE PEOPLE'S PARTY

Many groups formed outside the range of the two main political parties. The Grangers supported co-operatives and wished to nationalise the railways and to reform the American banking and taxation systems. They failed because of their limited and negative focus. The People's Party and the Knights of Labor were also part of a protest against unbridled capitalism and they too failed in the 1892 election. However, populism wasn't over and support for it grew again after the panic of 1893 and its resulting unemployment.

Note again the spread of populist groups.

THE SECOND CLEVELAND ADMINISTRATION

The Sherman Silver Act continued legislative concentration on the issue of whether the dollar should be based on silver or gold. President Cleveland, in office for the second time, was — just — able to maintain national solvency, but he was unable to deal with mass unemployment and considerable social distress. With the failure of an income tax and tariff reform, Cleveland was seen as no more than a tool of business. There was an increasing demand from the public for more action by the presidency and the federal government to deal with economic depression.

Note the growing expectation of the public for action on the part of the presidency.

THE 1896 ELECTION OF PRESIDENT MCKINLEY

The election was dominated by William Bryan the Democratic candidate and the issue of silver. The unstable Bryan, with his 'Cross of Gold' speech, was seen as the populist fighting against the exploiter. Business committed itself to the defeat of Bryan and the victory of Republican President William McKinley (1897–1901). In many respects, McKinley's period in office was the swan-song of the gilded age of business opportunity. The Republicans became the party of business and the skilled Northern worker, while the Democrats were divided and populism collapsed as a political force. An economic boom helped ensure Republican domination of both Houses of Congress in 1900, and the tariff of 1897 and the 1900 Currency Act showed how business thinking still dominated the government. McKinley was assassinated in 1901.

McKinley's death was to bring about a huge change in American politics.

Key points in the role of presidents and Congress

- the domination of business interests
- laissez faire
- deregulation
- the rise of monopolies
- the defeat of trade unions
- corruption and bossism
- the spoils system
- the decline of the status of the presidency
- Republican domination of the presidency and Congress
- business control over both Congress and state legislatures

Key issues of the gilded age

- tariffs and tariff reform
- anti-trust legislation
- the Silver Purchase Act and the attempts to rationalise the basis of the currency
- the populist revolt

- populist groups such as the Grangers
- Bryan and the silver currency
- Republican presidents

F The progressive era, 1900–19

Key questions

How effectively did the presidents and Congress respond to the nation's needs?

What was progressivism and what did it achieve in this period?

THE PROGRESSIVES

The progressives formed a wide-ranging reform movement that sought government regulation in a range of areas, the key ones of which were:

- cleaner politics
- government regulation of the economy
- female suffrage
- city and state government reform
- working conditions
- tariff reform
- vice prevention
- conservation
- Prohibition
- child labour
- poverty
- crime prevention

COMPARE AND CONTRAST PROGRESSIVISM WITH POPULISM

Progressivism came in a period of prosperity and focused on national issues, particularly as they affected cities. It was largely pressure group politics which worked inside the existing party structures and thus had no agenda to clean up party politics. Progressivism was middle-class led and inspired, and was never really the socialist movement which some accused it of being.

THE CAUSES OF PROGRESSIVISM

Progressivism was caused by the state of American industry and politics in a society where unbridled capitalism had led to many casualties. The powerful monopolistic trusts and a concentration of wealth in the hands of a few caused a concern that was fuelled by political corruption and industrial strife. Endemic bossism and the poor quality of political leadership were also factors in its rise.

THE PROGRESSIVES

The progressives wanted to restore social harmony and efficiency and tended to be academics, social workers and journalists. They were largely liberal, though they contained reactionary and conservative elements which opposed immigration and extending rights to black people and trade unions. Many progressives had business links; business was both their target and in some cases their sponsor. The tradition of a free press was crucial in stirring consciences, and the work of the so-called muckraker journalists who exposed scandals in industry and politics was vital in raising awareness. In particular, the journalism of Steffens and Tarbell brought to light many abuses in American business and politics.

You need to know the breadth of the demand for reform.

Note the less radical nature of progressivism.

Uncontrolled capitalism was the key cause of progressivism.

The progressives formed a pressure group that had limited social demands.

F *The progressive era, 1900–19*

THE MAIN AREAS OF REFORM

A considerable amount of progressive success was due to state initiatives.

Elective commissions curtailed the force of bossism in the cities. Examples of the reform movement at work in individual states are Governor Hiram Johnson's moves to municipal ownership and rail regulation in California, and Governor Wilson's work on business regulation in New Jersey. Perhaps the most notable progressive success was that of Governor Robert La Follette of Wisconsin, who broke the power of rail companies and brought in educational reform and primary elections. Women began to gain the vote in some states, and the courts were used increasingly to end the worst excesses of child labour.

THEODORE ROOSEVELT

Theodore Roosevelt had a massive impact on American society and politics.

Theodore Roosevelt (not to be confused with his nephew, Franklin Delano Roosevelt) came to power after an anarchist murdered President McKinley in 1901. To the surprise and horror of his Republican backers, Roosevelt proved to be anti-trust, had sympathy with the unions and had an unusual willingness to use the federal government to regulate. Once elected in his own right, Roosevelt saw through the Hepburn Act to limit railroad company power, and introduced food and drug regulation. His work with Gifford Pinchot on conservation was vital. He changed the nature of the presidency by alienating his conservative backers in the Senate, and gave an enormous boost to the progressive movement. Roosevelt's willingness to provide leadership, both domestically and in foreign policy, was a great contrast to his predecessors.

PRESIDENT TAFT

Note how the nature of the presidency had changed.

Although more conservative than Roosevelt, the Republican President William Taft (1909–13) was prepared to act and lead. There were increasing prosecutions under the Sherman Act and the conservation movement made further progress. More power went to the Interstate Commerce Commission (ICC) to regulate business, and the Department of Labor and the Children's Bureau were set to increase government regulation. The role of the federal government and its ability to intervene in the economy was growing. Income tax was introduced, which gave further resources to the federal government, and direct elections to the Senate continued to break up the power of the bosses. The Republican Party split under President Taft over tariffs, progressivism and conservation.

THE 1912 ELECTION

The alliances that Wilson forged ensured his election in 1912.

Taft and Roosevelt clashed over old and the new Republicanism. The old guard won in that Taft was selected as the Republican candidate, but Roosevelt went on to damage the party with his third party candidature. Woodrow Wilson, an academic New Jersey governor with a reforming record, won the Democratic nomination and campaigned under the 'New Freedom' slogan on a platform of reduced tariffs, an activist role and business regulation. He united a divided Democrat Party and won a great personal victory with the backing of the outsiders of American politics in the South and among the poor.

WILSON'S PRESIDENCY: THE ACHIEVEMENTS

President Wilson involved the presidency and the federal government on a large scale in a great range of activities, and continued the work of Roosevelt here. His early ideas on states' rights and laissez faire, designed to appeal to his Southern

Exam Revision Notes

147

supporters, received less attention than they hoped. He passed legislation reforming tariffs, the Federal Reserve Act which helped control the banking system, and the Clayton Act which encouraged the development of trade unions. He also set up the Federal Trade Commission which examined trusts, and introduced federal farm loans, the 8-hour working day, workmen's compensation and limitations on child labour.

WILSON'S PRESIDENCY: THE CRITICISMS

President Wilson went further than many expected, and perhaps as far as American society and government would let him. However, although steps were taken in areas such as working conditions, government regulation and conservation, there was still no American welfare system. Monopoly power existed in several major industries, poverty was deep rooted and the boss system remained a force. Women still had not got the vote and the courts soon revealed the flimsiness of child protection legislation. Nevertheless, like Roosevelt, Wilson showed what the presidency and federal government were capable of.

Key areas where progressivism had an impact
- management of the cities
- reforming the administration of state governments
- making elections less corrupt
- conservation of the environment
- regulation of trusts
- regulation of industry
- working conditions
- expanding the role of the federal government
- enhancing the role of the presidency
- gaining rights for trade unions

> Note the areas in which the presidency and the federal government became involved.

> Both parties produced activist presidents.

G American foreign policy from the Civil War to the First World War

Key questions

Why was the USA able to become a world power in the twentieth century?

In what ways and why did American foreign policy change between 1877 and 1917?

What was the role of the presidency in the conduct of foreign policy in this period?

THE BACKGROUND

The Munro Doctrine, which demanded 'America for the Americans', was crucial in setting the scene for American foreign policy in the nineteenth century. Generally there was little American interest in international events because there were few external threats to the USA's aspirations during the nineteenth century,

Nineteenth-century American traditions are very important.

nor was there a need for large-scale foreign trade or any traditional alliances or hatreds. Isolationism was a deep tradition and the State Department was tiny. The country had military potential, as the Civil War armies and navies of the 1860s had shown, but they were disbanded at once in the face of hostility towards large military establishments.

SEWARD

Seward is very much the exception to the rule. He is really the only nineteenth-century Secretary of State worth noting.

William Seward, Abraham Lincoln's Secretary of State, provides the only nineteenth-century exception to American isolationism. He took a strong line against the French in Mexico, attempted expansion into the West Indies and bought Alaska from the Russians, in spite of tremendous opposition from Congress and the public. Seward also had Canadian ambitions, but again received limited support. After his departure there was a return to the traditional isolationism.

CHANGE FROM 1890 ONWARDS

There was a fundamental shift in American policy and attitudes by the end of the century.

A significant change in American foreign policy occurred with the closing of the frontier and the growth of a more aggressive nationalism. A greater sense of nationhood was stoked up by a more chauvinistic and xenophobic press. The imperialism of the great European powers was increasingly imitated by the USA, although it always saw itself as an anti-colonial power. There was a feeling of manifest destiny — that the USA had a global role to play in addition to its guardianship role of the Americas which the Munro Doctrine envisaged. The ideas of Admiral Mahan had a strong impact when he argued that the USA ought to have a large and powerful navy.

ACQUISITIONS AND DEVELOPMENTS IN THE 1890S

American attitudes and policies began to shift from pure isolationism in the 1890s.

Although isolationist as far as Europe was concerned, there was growing American interest in Latin America, the West Indies and the Far East. The USA acquired its first proper colonies with the naval bases in Samoa and Hawaii. Further aggressive and nationalistic behaviour was seen in the Venezuela affair of 1895 when President Cleveland threatened to use force against Britain. There was a large naval building programme that was never envisaged as being totally defensive.

THE SPANISH–AMERICAN WAR

The Cubans hated Spanish rule, and the harsh treatment of the Cuban opposition by the Spanish was sensationalised in the American press. Agitation for involvement was ignored by President Cleveland and — for as long as he could — by President McKinley. The Maine incident, when the Spanish were blamed for blowing up an American warship, led a reluctant McKinley to war with Spain, and an incompetent Spanish army and navy were easily smashed in 1898. The Platt Amendment, which ensured American control of Cuba, helped the growing dominance of American business interests in Cuba, and also the taking of Puerto Rico. There were other colonial gains, especially in the Philippines.

The USA gradually moved towards becoming a colonial power.

ROOSEVELT'S FOREIGN POLICY

Roosevelt was an activist president, in both national and international politics.

Having risen to prominence in a colonial war and been part of the American navy's expansion, Roosevelt favoured a more active foreign policy than his predecessors and sought involvement in the Russo–Japanese war. Presidents Taft and Wilson were not to follow his activist example.

The fact that the USA was a major Pacific power as well as an Atlantic one was important for the direction of American policy.

CHINA AND JAPAN

The USA was well aware of the business potential of trade with the East and adopted policies to further its commercial interests. Secretary of State Hay came up with the Open Door policy in 1899, where all countries could trade freely with China. In a major change of attitude, the USA demonstrated its willingness to act forcefully abroad when it sent in troops over the Boxer Rebellion in China. Japanese hostility to the USA grew quickly after the Treaty of Portsmouth, when it tried to broker a peace between Japan and Russia. The 'yellow peril' fear of mass Japanese immigration did not help relations; nor did the California education affair, where there was discrimination against Japanese immigrants. The Roots/Takahira Agreement of 1908 brought most outstanding issues to a solution. Roosevelt was sensible and realistic over Japan, and managed the relationship well, but President Taft was less successful and hostility was to grow.

THE PANAMA CANAL

The Panama Canal was to have a major influence on United States foreign policy in Latin America.

The French had tried and failed to dig a link between the Atlantic and Pacific. The Hay/Pauncefoote Treaty of 1901 gave the USA total control over any future canal. There was much debate over the Panamanian or Nicaraguan route. The Panamanian revolt of 1903 against Colombia led to American aid to gain freedom for Panama from colonial rule. The Panama Canal was finished in 1914, but created a lot of hostility and suspicion about the intentions of the USA and its attitudes towards Latin America.

LATIN AMERICA AND THE CARIBBEAN

Note the growth of American power, interests and involvement.

The non-interference and isolationist tradition which had gone back to Munro changed under Roosevelt, and the Corollary of 1904, which announced that the USA would intervene in the Americas if it felt that its interests were threatened, demonstrated this well. There was a growth of 'dollar diplomacy' in the region and then the Dominican involvement of 1905, with American troops being sent in to maintain order. There was also increasing involvement in Nicaragua, with control taken of its finances and the crushing of a revolt in 1912. It became clear that traditional American isolationist policies were not going to apply where direct American interests were threatened. Even the idealistic Wilson felt he had to intervene in Haiti in a policing role in 1913, justifying the intervention as a protection of interests that were close to home.

MEXICO

Consider whether American interests were in fact well served by this policy.

The USA's Mexican adventures of both 1914 and 1916 are further examples of how President Wilson was unable to keep out of the affairs of another country, particularly one bordering the USA. The campaigns were a disaster from Wilson's point of view, for there were few American gains and Latin American hatred of the USA grew.

CHANGES AFTER 1890

In just over a decade, the USA had become a major player in the Pacific, Latin American and Caribbean areas.

The USA became a significant world power in a short space of time. Commercial and popular pressures, a mood of imperialism, activist presidents and a growing sense of nationhood all played their part. Some of the foreign policy thinking was defensive; some blatantly imperialistic and acquisitive. Note the very ambivalent attitude to colonial acquisitions that was prevalent.

Key factors in the rise of the USA as a world power
- the closing of the frontier
- the ideas of Mahan about the need for naval power
- the work of Seward
- activist presidents
- expansion of American business interests
- growth of export markets
- protection of the USA's interests in the Americas
- colonial ambitions

Key changes in American foreign policy
- naval development
- colonial development
- the Spanish wars
- the growth of manufacturing, leading to a demand to export
- developing interests in China
- the developing hostile relationship with Japan
- the building of the Panama Canal
- involvement in Colombia, Haiti and Cuba
- involvement in Mexico
- Roosevelt's more active foreign policy
- the Treaty of Portsmouth ending the Russo–Japanese War

H The USA and the First World War

Key questions

Why was the USA able to become a global power in the twentieth century?

What was the role of American presidents in foreign policy during this period?

Why did the USA become involved in the First World War?

What was the impact of the First World War on the USA?

THE OUTBREAK OF WAR IN 1914

Note the initial, and very important, neutral stance.

At the outbreak of the First World War, American public opinion was divided. German Americans and Irish Americans favoured Germany, and those suspicious of Prussian militarism favoured Britain and France. The official American stance was neutral, though it swayed against the Germans. President Wilson and his main advisers House and Lansing were all pro-British, fearing that a German victory would be bad for American commercial and strategic interests. The fact that the war stimulated American industry and helped end a depression was also relevant. Britain and France were able to borrow freely in the USA, which upset the Germans. The British had command of the seas and the British blockade of Germany caused resentment in many quarters.

SUBMARINE WARFARE

Submarine warfare was always critical as far as American opinion was concerned.

American public opinion became sharply anti-German when American citizens died after German submarines sank the *Lusitania* and the *Arabic*. However, when Bethmann-Holweg — the German chancellor — was able to contain his submarine extremists, American opinion became less hostile to Germany. Merchant and passenger ships were warned not to cross the Atlantic — or be sunk — rather than being torpedoed without warning. The Easter Rising in Dublin against British rule in Ireland fanned anti-British feeling amongst the millions of Irish Americans.

THE CHANGES IN AMERICAN POLICY

A growing impatience with German policy shifted American public opinion.

American policy gradually became pro-British and French, partly through British propaganda that focused on the threat to democracy and the Belgian horrors. Some American rearmament, especially for the navy, was under way by 1916, though President Wilson fought and won the 1916 election on a peace ticket. Wilson's peace missions failed, as did his 1917 attempt for 'peace without victory' and a League of Nations. American opinion generally saw the Germans as being uncooperative.

THE DECISION TO GO TO WAR

Entry into the war altered the USA's status as a world power.

German submarine warfare was the final straw for American public opinion. Germany realised its naval tactics would provoke war, but felt they were necessary for a chance of victory. Armed neutrality was the initial American response, and then there was a pause for the first overt act. German overt acts duly arrived when the *Laconia* was sunk and when, in the Zimmerman telegram, Germany encouraged both Mexico and Japan to take action against the USA. With American merchant ships being sunk without warning, Congress agreed with Wilson and declared war against Germany in 1917.

OPPOSITION TO THE WAR

Opponents to the war had a strong case: were American interests that much threatened?

Most of the American population supported the declaration of war because few realised what would be involved and they had been convinced by a combination of President Wilson's ideals and British propaganda. The war's stimulating effect on the economy also dampened opposition. Such dissent as there was came from Senators Norris and La Follette, who gathered support in the Midwest and among the German, Irish and Jewish communities. But Wilson's determination and the U-boat issue were difficult obstacles for the war's opponents to overcome.

THE IMPACT OF THE USA ON THE FIRST WORLD WAR

It is quite possible that without the USA, the British and French armies would have collapsed. This is one of the great military history debates.

The initial American involvement was limited to North Atlantic convoys, for it had virtually no army, planes, tanks or guns. It mobilised rapidly and 300,000 men fought in France under General Pershing by June 1918, and a total of 1,500,000 were in position for the autumn offensive. This had a huge impact on Allied morale from the start, was important in holding the German offensive of 1918 and vital in the Meuse/Argonne offensive.

THE HOME FRONT

The American government showed itself able to act quickly and firmly in an emergency, thus

Federal controls regulated the supply of food, energy, rail and labour, and imposed taxes on profits and on the rich. Prohibition was extended, women got the vote

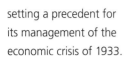

setting a precedent for its management of the economic crisis of 1933.

Note Wilson's mismanagement of the peace process and also the attractive ideals behind it.

Consider the extent to which Wilson should be held responsible for the criticism usually directed against Versailles.

Consider the point that the USA was abandoning its new role as a world power.

and the state played a large part in arousing anti-German feeling. Civil liberties were curtailed by censorship and the Espionage and Sedition Acts. Eugene Debs, the socialist union leader, was jailed for anti-war activities.

THE PEACE

President Wilson's Fourteen Points peace plan was infused with idealism, but he failed to consult Allied powers. When Britain, France and Italy proved reluctant to adopt the Fourteen Points, Wilson threatened a separate peace treaty. He satisfied American public opinion on specific territorial points, such as Poland and Alsace-Lorraine, and by trying to establish principles such as open diplomacy and the League of Nations. Wilson's position was difficult after the 1918 elections, with the Republicans in a majority in both Houses.

VERSAILLES

President Wilson, a Democrat, made the errors of taking no senior Republicans with him to the Versailles peace conference and of failing to understand the needs of Lloyd George and Clemenceau to satisfy public opinion in Britain and France. Nonetheless, Wilson achieved much by ensuring that self-determination applied to most countries, in weakening punitive French demands against Germany and in including the League of Nations in the treaty. However, reparations payments were also included, as were the colonial mandates, and self-determination did not apply to some areas such as China.

THE REJECTION OF VERSAILLES

The Covenant of the League of Nations was not popular within the USA because it was seen as a threat to American sovereignty that required too much commitment on the part of the USA. The bitter opposition led by Senator Lodge and the Senate Foreign Relations Committee mixed personal animosities with a partisan desire to damage the Democrats. American isolationism reasserted itself again and, as Wilson was too ill and tired to argue his case, a separate peace was made with Germany in 1921.

Key factors in American involvement in the First World War

- the Allied blockade
- American neutrality
- American commercial interests
- the U-boats
- the sinking of the *Lusitania*
- British propaganda
- the changing American attitude towards Germany
- the Zimmerman telegram inciting Mexico against the USA
- the Mexican War

The American impact on the war

- convoys
- a boost to Allied morale
- numbers of soldiers
- the German offensive of 1918
- the battles of the Argonne/Meuse

- the work of Pershing
- the changes on the home front

Key factors for the peace
- the Fourteen Points plan proposed by Wilson as the basis for peace
- the threat of a separate peace
- the negotiations at Versailles
- the impact of the Fourteen Points on Versailles
- the importance of the idea of self-determination
- the restraint of Clemenceau and Lloyd George
- the ideas for the League of Nations
- the rejection of Versailles by the Senate

American foreign policy, 1919–41

Key questions

Why was the USA able to become a world power in the twentieth century?

Why did the USA first adopt and then abandon isolation in this period?

VERSAILLES AND AFTER

There was a considerable change of attitudes and policy between 1919 and 1920.

The American consensus after Versailles was that intervention in the First World War had been a mistake. Isolationism grew along with nationalism, the fear of revolution and a reaction against immigration and imports. Events in Russia worried many, and the USA was one of the powers that intervened to try and destroy the Russian Revolution. The League of Nations and collective security were ignored. However, the USA sent observers and joined the International Labour Organisation (ILO), a subsidiary of the League of Nations.

THE WASHINGTON CONFERENCE

The USA was not totally isolationist and the Washington Conference was one of several attempts to maintain peace.

The USA increasingly recognised its role as a Pacific power as a growth in tension in the Far East caused a fear of Japanese aggression. Meanwhile, a strong navy was proving costly to cost-cutting presidents, and the combined pressures of diplomacy and economics led to the Washington Conference. This was a significant part of American diplomacy in the 1920s. The conference, attended mainly by the USA, Britain and Japan, was a first for arms limitation in that it cut military expenditure and stabilised the Far East for a while. Note the details of the Five- and Four-Power treaties and what they meant to the actual navies concerned. They may have helped to keep the peace, but in the light of later events they weakened the USA's relationship with Japan. No attempt was made to limit the size of armies, and the naval treaties had no means of enforcement. They also relied too much on Japanese consent and there was no monitoring. However, the treaties led to the London Naval Conference of 1930 and credit must be given for a sound attempt to ease tension and bring peace.

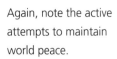

Again, note the active
attempts to maintain
world peace.

THE KELLOGG–BRIAND PACT

This was signed in Paris in 1928. Kellogg, the American secretary of state, and
the French foreign secretary, Briand, led 13 nations in a pledge to renounce war.
Again, note the idealism, the involvement of the USA and the hope that moral
force would bring peace. American public opinion was important in getting it
passed, and there were effective pressure politics and petitions. Denouncement
of war was a great ideal, but there was no means of enforcement. The Senate
passed it, unlike Versailles, but insisted on limits to any American involvement
abroad.

DEBTS

There are merits and
demerits in American
policy on trade and
debts.

The USA's attitudes to its foreign debtors varied, from President Coolidge's
comment that 'they hired the money', to the more tolerant attitudes built into the
Dawes and Young Plans. Debt repayments led to the circularity of the USA
receiving British and French money that came from German reparations that
drew on funds supplied to Germany by the USA. While Dawes and Young did
much to ease tension, President Hoover and his high tariffs did a lot of harm to
trade — and therefore to international relationships.

LATIN AMERICAN POLICY

Note the contrast with
earlier defensive/aggres-
sive attitudes towards
neighbouring states in
the region.

There was more restraint and non-interventionism in the internal politics of
independent Latin American states through the Good Neighbor policy, which
removed troops from Cuba to allow improved relations with Colombia and Mexico.
Note the work of Hoover (President from 1929 to 1933) and the Clark
memorandum, which declared that the USA was not willing to intervene in the
affairs of other American states. An easier attitude towards debts was another
significant change in American policy, and a much more favourable impression
of the USA evolved.

THE FAR EAST UP TO 1933

Note the growth of
tension in the Far East
and consider the
degree of American
responsibility for it.

The Japanese were unhappy about the absence of racial equality clauses in the
League Covenant, and also disliked American immigration policy. The growth of
Japanese militarism and expansion in Manchuria worried the Americans considerably. However, President Hoover was hostile to any action after Japanese aggression at Mukden. In 1932, Stimson, the secretary of state, tried to limit Japanese
aggression by diplomacy and tried to deny Japan access to vital raw materials.
This served to increase Japanese irritation. Meanwhile, other events created
a situation where there seemed to be no alternative but to accept that might
was right: Britain was reluctant to act; the USA was suspicious of the Soviet Union;
there was a world depression; and key nations were not members of the League
of Nations. Kellogg–Briand had failed its first major test and so had the
League of Nations.

PRESIDENT FRANKLIN DELANO ROOSEVELT'S EARLY ISOLATIONISM

Public opinion was a
major factor in the
making of American
foreign policy at this
time.

President Franklin Delano Roosevelt (FDR) arrived in office in 1932, just as world
tension was starting to rise. Always conscious of isolationist American public
opinion, Roosevelt was also pre-occupied with a major domestic crisis and the
Wall Street Crash. The Depression further limited his scope for action. Many felt
that war benefited business and bankers, and that it was a conspiracy of the rich.

It was also felt that no American interests were involved as far as Hitler and Mussolini's courting of the Japanese were concerned. There was a strong isolationist strand in the Democratic Party, as well as among the Republicans. President Roosevelt had to be cautious.

THE PRESSURE TO MAINTAIN ISOLATIONISM

The work of Senator Nye in Congress plus the output of Hollywood and Randolph Hearst's newspaper empire fuelled anti-war sentiment. Even membership of the World Court was impossible. The Neutrality Acts limited presidential power to act in any way abroad, but the USA did manage to sell vital oil to both Mussolini and Franco.

THE EARLY YEARS OF ROOSEVELT

President Roosevelt reflected the prevailing isolationism and gave no leadership in solving either economic or international issues. He avoided both disarmament talks and serious participation in a World Economic Conference which was hoping to deal with depression. He did finally give formal recognition to the Soviet Union, but that was just realism. The non-involvement policy in Latin America continued, even though it led to the rise of dictatorships in countries like Cuba. There was still a strong interest in economic domination of the region, but even in Latin America there was no intervention to protect the USA's interests.

ROOSEVELT AFTER 1936

With the Depression easing at home, Roosevelt had time to look abroad and he became increasingly worried about the Japanese, Germans and Italians. However, public opinion was hostile to any intervention and had its effect: for example, the Panay incident was ignored. The Ludlow amendment to the Constitution, to reduce a president's foreign policy control and military potential, was only just defeated in Congress. Meanwhile, Roosevelt tried to work with Chamberlain in 1938 to defuse European tension. He managed to start some rearmament with the Naval Expansion Act of 1938. However, the Senate was influential in foreign policy, and isolationism was as strong there as among the US public.

THE SECOND WORLD WAR, 1939–41

Although officially neutral, President Roosevelt did as much as he felt able to assist his allies, and the aid to the British was crucial. The fall of France produced a fundamental shift of both American opinion and policy — rearmament moved ahead, conscription came in, lend-lease was accepted and destroyers were deployed to protect British convoys. Though public opinion was hostile to the Nazis, Roosevelt had to be cautious during a 1940 presidential election which was already controversial because he was standing for a third term. Note his campaigning — he had to be strongly pacific. Note also the debates between the Committee to Defend America and the America First group, which was committed to staying out of the war.

THE WAR AT SEA, 1940–41

President Roosevelt knew that Britain could not sustain its Atlantic losses and he offered covert support to the Allies. There were, for example, the illegal repairs to British ships in American bases, and the events in Greenland and Iceland when

Roosevelt wanted re-election in 1936 and so had to heed public opinion on foreign policy.

There is continuity between Roosevelt and his Republican predecessors.

Consider whether Roosevelt should be criticised for American isolationism and the rise of the dictators.

Roosevelt started to play a more positive role in preparing the USA to resist Japanese and Nazi aggression.

Roosevelt showed decisive leadership in foreign policy.

American forces took them over. The Atlantic Charter and the aid against the U-boats bent neutrality remarkably. Note also the Greer, Kearney and James incidents and the end of the Neutrality Acts, as well as the extension of lend-lease to the Soviet Union in 1941. Churchill and Roosevelt's use of executive agreements were also important. Roosevelt was clearly moving ahead of Congressional and public opinion.

THE CAUSES OF THE CONFLICT WITH JAPAN

The actions of the Japanese in 1940–41 have to be studied. Make sure you know the geography of the region.

The USA sent aid to China in 1940, showing the kind of opposition to Japanese expansionism that had always angered the Japanese. The latter went ahead with aggression in China and Indo-China, and in forming an alliance with Hitler. The Japanese fear of conflict with the Soviet Union had ended by the summer of 1941 with the Nazi invasion of the Soviet Union and the subsequent Soviet–Japanese deal. Japan viewed the British — as well as the French and Dutch — as defeated powers and this left the USA as the only real obstacle to Japanese domination of southeast Asia. The American oil embargo was the final straw for the Japanese.

JAPANESE DEMANDS

It is fair to say that the Japanese were determined on war.

Japan wanted total domination of China, a free hand in southeast Asia and the ability to gain all the raw materials it needed. It demanded that American aid to China was stopped, that Japan's assets in the USA were unfrozen and that the oil supply was resumed. Probably only complete agreement with all these demands would have satisfied the Japanese leadership. But there was no way in which the USA could agree.

THE USA'S DEMANDS

Roosevelt's position was made much easier by the fact that Hitler declared war on the USA.

The USA wanted an end to Japanese expansionism, withdrawal from China and Indo-China, and a termination of Japan's alliance with Hitler. Though Roosevelt wanted peace, he was not prepared to sacrifice China to the Japanese. In Japanese eyes, that meant war. The attack on Pearl Harbor was vital in mobilising American opinion, and Hitler's declaration of war on the USA then brought it into another European conflict.

Key points in the development of the US as a world power

- rejection of Versailles
- isolationism of the 1920s
- involvement in the Soviet Union
- the Washington Naval Conference limiting the size of navies
- disarmament
- the Dawes and Young Plans on reparations
- the Kellogg–Briand Pact
- the London Naval Conference further reducing the size of navies
- the Good Neighbor policy

Key factors in the abandonment of isolationism

- China
- growth of Japanese expansionism
- Roosevelt's concerns about Hitler and Mussolini

- the restraining influence of isolationism in Congress
- strength of public opinion
- the naval expansion programme
- the impact of the fall of France
- lend-lease — the critical aid to Britain
- the Atlantic Charter — a statement of principles for future international relations
- Pearl Harbor ·
- Hitler's declaration of war

J The USA and the Second World War

Key questions

How important a role did the USA play in the Second World War?

What was Roosevelt's role as a war leader?

TOTAL WAR

The surprise attack by the Japanese and Hitler's declaration of war were vital for public opinion — the USA was defending itself.

There was less impact on American civilians than on Americans in uniform, with virtually no shortages, no bombing of American cities, an improvement of real wages and full employment — which particularly benefited blacks and women. The federal government increased its control over many areas of life from conscription to censorship. Civil liberties were willingly abandoned, for public opinion viewed this as a just war. There was no internal division. German-American and Italian-American soldiers fought as well as anybody else. American citizens of Japanese origin were interned, even though their young men had proved good soldiers in the fighting in Italy.

THE ARSENAL OF DEMOCRACY

American industry was a crucial factor in Allied victory.

Military production was one of the great American contributions to the war, and its productive capacity was crucial to defeating the Axis powers. One example is aircraft production, which rose from 2,000 a year in 1939 to 96,000 by 1944. The Liberty ship dominated the Atlantic, the Sherman tank dominated the battlefield, Soviet soldiers were ferried to the front in Ford lorries and British soldiers ate American beef. The Axis powers simply could not compete.

THE IMPACT OF THE SECOND WORLD WAR ON THE BLACKS

The war had a major impact on black attitudes, less so on white ones.

Millions of black people migrated north to the munitions factories and shipyards, and for the first time the American federal government took active steps to ban racial discrimination in defence projects. The ghettos expanded and there were race riots in northern cities. A million blacks joined the armed forces. Though a few became officers, there was still tremendous discrimination within the military. The real problems came when black soldiers came home and were expected — particularly in the south — to resume a subordinate role in society and tolerate the traditional discrimination.

The decision by the Japanese to attack the USA was a fundamental error.

WAR IN THE PACIFIC

Details of the various Pacific campaigns are not expected to be known. Pearl Harbor was vital in mobilising the USA against Japan and by the end of 1942 the Japanese advance had been halted. In early 1943 the tide turned, but the terrible battles of Leyte Gulf, Okinawa and Iwo Jima showed that military commitment was as important as sheer weight of resources. The bombing of Japan and the decision to use the A-bomb brought final defeat to the Japanese.

OTHER AMERICAN CAMPAIGNS

American resources, in both men and material, were crucial factors in all the major campaigns against the Axis powers.

The USA played a central role in campaigns other than the one against Japan. It provided important support to the Chinese which tied down many Japanese troops. It was key to the invasion of North Africa. Sicily and Italy followed, with General Mark Clark entering Rome in 1944. The American navy helped defeat the U-boats, and the American airforce mounted daylight raids on Germany. The Spaatz offensive was vital in the defeat of the Axis powers in Europe. Remember that 10,000 bombers were lost and that only the USA could replace aircraft and men in such numbers.

EISENHOWER'S ROLE

General Eisenhower's ability to get men from many nations to work together was exceptional.

Given the American dominance in men and material, it was natural that an American should command the re-invasion of Europe. Although criticised by some for his tactics, General Dwight Eisenhower commanded the Allies in their defeat of the Germans in Europe and did it with comparatively low casualties. His success as Supreme Allied Commander — and giving control to one man was a major factor in winning the war — led to Eisenhower's successful presidential campaign in 1952.

ROOSEVELT'S ROLE

Roosevelt was an exceptional statesman.

Roosevelt's foresight ensured an adequate level of American preparation for war, and helped Britain to survive Nazi attacks. Although the American war effort was disorganised at first, Roosevelt soon brought about effective command and control systems both for the military and for the economy. His ability to work with difficult allies — and from the American viewpoint the British, Soviets and French were all difficult — was important. Roosevelt's vision could allow no repeat of the Treaty of Versailles and his insistence on postwar planning from an early stage was vital. He made a major contribution to founding the United Nations, the International Monetary Fund and the World Bank.

ROOSEVELT AND STRATEGY

Roosevelt's role in deciding the USA's Second World War strategy was crucial.

Roosevelt's relationships with General Marshall, his chief of staff, and Churchill were excellent, and the early agreement on the 'Germany first' policy had great benefits for Britain. It was less easy to explain to an American population which was angered by the fact that it was the Japanese who had attacked the USA first. The North African campaign and military action against the 'soft underbelly' of Italy were Roosevelt's decisions, and were taken against the advice of many of his advisers. He played a crucial role in vital planning conferences at Casablanca, Quebec and Tehran during the war. He also led the demands for unconditional German surrender after D-Day. Roosevelt had a difficult relationship with Stalin, and was criticised for being too soft on the Soviet leader.

Roosevelt played a
central role in the
planning of the
postwar world.

YALTA

The Yalta Treaty of 1945 was Roosevelt's final contribution to world politics. The treaty, where Roosevelt met with Stalin and Churchill, dealt with the future of postwar Gemany and Eastern Europe. It also played a critical part in the creation of the United Nations Organisation. Roosevelt was able to manage Stalin particularly well — but Stalin was to break most of the agreements he made at Yalta.

POTSDAM AND THE DECISION TO DROP THE ATOM BOMB

The policiés started by
Roosevelt were largely
followed by Truman,
with the exception of
the relationship with
the Soviet Union.

With the death of Roosevelt in 1945, Harry Truman took over as American president. Truman had a simpler view of politics than Roosevelt, and Potsdam completed the work left by Yalta. The United Nations was set up, the division of Germany was agreed and reparations were finalised. Lend-lease was ended. Don't get too enmeshed in the merits or otherwise of dropping the atom bomb, because the generally accepted view is that the way in which the information was presented to Truman by the military gave him no choice.

THE MERITS AND DEMERITS OF ROOSEVELT AS A WAR LEADER

Do Roosevelt's critics
lose the debate?

Discussing President Roosevelt's qualities as a war leader offers historical revisionists plenty of scope for argument. He was seen as too favourable to Churchill and the British, and a bad manager of Stalin. Was he too much of a politician and only a limited statesman? He is said (particularly by the Chinese and the Poles) not to have understood China or Poland. Was the decision at the Casablanca Conference in 1943 to push for unconditional surrender a mistake? Did it keep Germany fighting to the bitter end? These questions aside, Roosevelt did lead the Allies to victory and held together an alliance which contained many differing agendas. He coped well with the difficulty of dealing with Stalin. Roosevelt also achieved consensus at home, and his focus on the high ideals of the United Nations was important.

Key factors in the impact of the USA on the Second World War

- the Arsenal of Democracy
- the development of the black movement
- the Pacific war
- support for China
- the North African invasion
- the invasion of Sicily and Italy
- the bombing of Germany
- the invasion of France and Germany
- the work of Eisenhower as Supreme Allied Commander
- the building and the use of the A-bomb
- the strategic planning of General Marshall

Roosevelt's influence as a war leader

- his strategic direction of the war
- his relationship with Churchill and Stalin
- lend-lease — the critical aid to Britain in 1940
- the initial survival of Britain
- American preparedness
- postwar planning

- the harnessing of American resources for war
- the high level of domestic support for the war
- his input into the conferences of Casablanca, Tehran and Yalta

K The USA in the 1920s

Key questions

What were the main social and economic changes in the 1920s?

What were the reasons for the Republican ascendancy in the 1920s?

Why did the American economy boom and then bust in the 1920s?

THE IMPACT OF THE FIRST WORLD WAR

There was a widespread disillusionment with participation in the war, and a growing desire to forget all foreign entanglements in an era of nationalism, isolationism and the absence of reform. At the same time, there was major social and economic change. War helped create an economic boom and boosted technology in areas like electrification and production lines. The innovations helped to ensure full employment during the 1920s in a relatively easy adjustment to peacetime.

The war had an impact on both the American economy and society.

RACIAL CHANGE IN THE 1920S

The 1920s was a period of limited racial progress and the aspirations of returning black soldiers were dashed. White hostility was strong in the north, where fear for jobs caused real tensions. The northern migration produced ghettos in the cities and while more black people in the north were able to vote, they were outnumbered by the whites. The parts of the south where blacks were in the majority still largely excluded them from the vote. The National Association for the Advancement of Colored People (NAACP) and the Urban League — which was created to help blacks in northern cities — made limited headway and received limited black support. One significant development was the Back to Africa movement led by Marcus Garvey, but that collapsed by 1923 and was intensely disliked by other black leaders.

Although war had some beneficial economic effects on the blacks, there was no change of attitude by white society.

IMMIGRATION

Although the USA still accepted more immigrants than most countries, its 'open door' policy went and never returned. Immigration quotas were imposed in 1921, and there was a change in attitude towards asylum seekers as well. The hostility to foreigners was linked to a broader reactionary atmosphere, of which the Ku-Klux-Klan and the prohibition of alcohol are examples. Note the literacy tests (designed to keep out less intelligent immigrants), the Red Scare (with its attacks on socialists and communists) and the hostility to the trade union, the Industrial Workers of the World (IWW).

Attitudes towards immigration underwent a change.

THE KU-KLUX-KLAN

The Ku-Klux-Klan aimed to destroy the status of the blacks and was also anti-Semitic and anti-Catholic. Its hostility to all minorities attracted a 2 million strong

Note the breadth of reactionary forces in this period.

membership and its use of violence was opposed with violence, particularly by some white minority groups. Membership of the Ku-Klux-Klan declined after the Stephenson scandal of 1925, when the leadership was discovered to be corrupt. It was part of a broader movement, hoping to return to what were defined as true American values. The Scopes Trial — when a teacher was prosecuted for teaching evolution as opposed to the biblical version of creation — and the Hays censorship of the film industry were a part of this strand of 1920s American fundamentalism.

PROHIBITION

Prohibition is remarkable in two ways: one, in that it actually happened; two, in the damage it did to American society.

Prohibition gives a good example of the power of pressure groups to influence local US legislatures and Congress. The banning of alcohol was a pious hope, enforcement was limited and Prohibition never won popular acceptance. Its impact on encouraging breaches of the law and organised crime was crucial. The ease with which it came to an end in such a short time illustrates how quickly it was seen as a mistake.

SOCIAL CHANGES

There were fundamental social and cultural changes in this period.

Increased leisure and wealth for many brought about large social changes. There was more personal freedom for the young, and women — who were no longer seen as male property — had the right to an independent existence. Divorce was easier and the birth rate declined. The impact of the radio and Hollywood was vast; note also the literary explosion with American writers like H. L. Mencken, Sinclair Lewis, O. Henry, Scott Fitzgerald and William Faulkner.

THE LAST YEARS OF PRESIDENT WILSON, 1918–20

There was a considerable contrast between the peacetime administrations of Wilson.

President Wilson's hostility to trade unions and the return to older laissez faire attitudes marked an era of deregulation and a move away from progressivism. Illness limited Wilson's power, and the attorney-general, 'Red Scare' Mitchell Palmer, had a free hand. The Democratic defeat in 1920 was an indictment of the last years of Wilson, with interventionism and the League of Nations losing out to what was known as 'normalcy'.

THE RED SCARE

The American liberal tradition came to a halt — temporarily.

The successful revolution in Russia (and the failed American intervention), coupled with the growth of socialism and communism in the USA, led to a largely irrational fear of all aliens. Public opinion concentrated on the fact that some of those involved in radical movements were foreign born — but then so were many other Americans. The strikes of 1919 (which even included the police) raised fears of anarchism and revolt. Attorney-General Palmer led a popular attack on radicals, and serious repression followed. The destruction of civil liberties for many was upheld by the Schenck decision of the Supreme Court. The Sacco Vanzetti affair, where two men were executed really for being foreign aliens rather than guilty of any crime, should be seen as part of this general trend.

PRESIDENT HARDING

President Warren Harding was the product of a Republican cabal, and was perhaps not as bad a leader as is sometimes made out. He pushed through farm reforms,

introduced the 8-hour day and made sound appointments, such as Hughes as secretary of state, Hoover as secretary for commerce and Taft as chief justice. Other appointments, like the corrupt Ohio Gang, were a disaster. Harding's was a pro-business administration, with tax cuts, deregulation and protection. Federal attitudes to strikers were hostile, as with the suppression of Virginia miners. The Supreme Court was also anti-labour, striking down many of the gains of President Wilson, especially over child labour. Harding's downfall resulted from many unwise appointments and — distraught but still popular — he died in 1923.

Note the policies that became associated with the Republican Party.

PRESIDENT COOLIDGE

The ascetic, popular and honest Calvin Coolidge took over from President Harding, and won re-election in 1924. He implemented little, which was what the public wanted. President Coolidge advocated traditional values, laissez faire and a non-interventionist role for the federal government. The presidency became a ceremonial office, in contrast to the roles evolved by Roosevelt and Wilson.

Under Coolidge, the presidency reverted to a non-interventionist role.

THE ECONOMIC BOOM OF THE 1920S

The main causes of economic boom were a growing domestic and international market for American goods spurred on by tax cuts, technological development and scientific management. The culture was supportive, with business seen as a creditable activity; businessmen were welcome in the White House. New industries could develop easily with cheap credit and cheap energy. New products were in high demand, especially electrical goods, radios, cinemas, cars and oil products. Roads had to be built and maintained to cater for the millions of cars coming off Henry Ford's production lines. Real wages improved as did working conditions. There were still some areas of poverty, however, especially in farming and the old staple industries of textiles and coal.

Consider how sound the American economy was in this period.

PRESIDENT HOOVER

Herbert Hoover had a remarkable career prior to the presidency. As a self-made millionaire and a successful engineer, and with a record of public service, he was a strong candidate in the 1928 elections. It was a revealing election, in that Hoover's opponent, Al Smith, was a Catholic social reformer who made a considerable impact in the northeast and the cities. This should have told the Republicans to be more thoughtful in their policies. However, President Hoover adopted a similar approach to the hands-off President Coolidge.

A key factor in the choice of Hoover was his reputation as a problem-solver.

THE CAUSES OF THE DEPRESSION

The economy had insecure foundations, and production had outrun consumption with too many people too poor to buy the products pouring off the production lines. There was a badly flawed banking system and a lack of regulation of insurance companies, local banks and the stock markets. The investment trusts were too self-centred and profit orientated. Too much investment had been unwise and there was too much credit available. Extensive exports were not balanced by any imports because protection was too strong, so fewer countries could afford American goods. The Florida land crisis of 1926, when there was a collapse in property prices, and the steady decline of housing and car sales, were all signs of economic crisis which were ignored. By 1928 investment was down, exports were down and speculation had taken over.

Consider whether any preventive action could have been taken to avoid the Depression.

The social and economic devastation caused by the Wall Street Crash was widespread.

THE WALL STREET CRASH

Early 1928 is most often suggested as the time when Wall Street lost touch with reality and share prices became ludicrous. The USA got lost in a speculative mania so far-reaching that — when it crashed in October 1929 — it brought down the economy with it and then infected the world. Bank failures led to deflation, which led to mass unemployment. Industrial production plummeted. With no welfare system the 25% unemployed faced a bleak future, and the banking and insurance collapses hit the middle class by destroying their savings and pensions.

Hoover's reasons for his policies — or lack of them — were mainly ideological.

HOOVER'S REACTION

President Hoover came to office with a reputation as the man who had fed Europe in 1919. When the markets started to tumble, Hoover stuck by his belief that it was not the role of federal government to take the initiative. His political philosophy dictated that the bulk of recovery work had to be done by individuals and firms. He held that the problems were not economic and could be solved with individual determination. He blamed foreigners, demanded loans back and worked for a balanced budget. He did set up the Reconstruction Finance Corporation (RFC), but resolutely gave no help to individuals. The work of General MacArthur in breaking up the war veterans' marches for higher pensions illustrates Hoover's views well.

Key social factors in the period
- the reaction to the First World War
- racial progress
- immigration and the Red Scare
- Prohibition
- the role of women
- the changing pattern of leisure
- the growth of the entertainment industry
- progress in literature

Key causes of the boom of the 1920s
- the First World War
- the effect of the First World War on European commercial rivals
- technological change
- high demand — especially domestic
- the laissez faire tradition
- new industries
- cheap credit

The key causes of the 1929 crash
- a fall in consumption
- the banking system
- lack of regulation
- the role of the trusts
- speculative mania
- the collapse of overseas markets
- Wall Street
- the role of Hoover and the federal government

L Roosevelt and the New Deal

Key questions

What did the New Deal achieve?

What form did opposition to the New Deal take?

THE 1932 ELECTION

The rich, aristocratic Franklin Delano Roosevelt was the nephew of former President Theodore Roosevelt and the governor of New York. FDR was an astute politician and he had the right credentials, the right name and experience in administration in the US Navy Department as well. However, his election campaign offered little in the way of a New Deal and his only specific promise was to end Prohibition. The final bank collapse and the fact that he was not Hoover or Republican ensured a resounding victory, and Congress also became largely Democratic in the strong anti-Republican tide. Hoover had totally failed to sense the desire among the public for action by the federal government, as the individual states had failed to cope with the impact of the Depression.

THE SOCIAL IMPACT OF THE DEPRESSION

The Depression caused poverty and malnutrition, a rise in infant mortality and a falling birth rate. In many states, local government collapsed with schools closing and essential services failing. Many dropped out of college and school as education cuts hit hard. Insecurity and nomadism became endemic, and the Midwest was devastated by drought and the growth of the Dust Bowl. John Steinbeck's novel *The Grapes of Wrath* gives an account of the suffering. Black people were hard hit, particularly when the New Deal actively discriminated against them. However, many blacks still supported Roosevelt, and some were to get welfare for the first time. For those in work, deflation meant an increase in living standards.

THE FIRST NEW DEAL

A special session of Congress gave President Roosevelt immediate backing to extend federal government's power to implement new regulations to cope with the banking crisis. The range of issues taken on in the first 'Hundred Days' programme embraced unemployment, industry, agriculture, labour relations, welfare and currency. The new attitudes towards government spending and 'pump priming' amounted to a remarkable experiment in government, which was revolutionary in American terms. Roosevelt marketed his policies well and used the radio to deliver his 'fireside chats', explaining that his objective was to save capitalism.

KEY LEGISLATION

- The first New Deal comprises a list of acts which all had their impact on economic recovery.
- The Reconstruction Finance Corporation (RFC) provided much of the credit needed for the New Deal.
- The Federal Emergency Relief Agency (FERA) provided relief to the devastated farming states.

Note that in the election campaign Roosevelt offered no clear policies for overcoming the Depression.

The sheer number of those affected, both rich and poor, was to make the USA more prepared to accept the changes that Roosevelt brought in.

Changes in the roles of the federal government and the presidency are fundamental to this topic.

You should know the broad terms of New Deal legislation.

- The Civilian Conservation Corps (CCC) provided work for over 250,000 men on conservation projects.
- The Public Works Administration (PWA) spent federal money on building roads and other projects.
- The Tennessee Valley Authority (TVA) was a hydroelectrical job creation scheme.
- The Securities and Exchange Commission (SEC) was set up to reform the stock markets.
- The Agricultural Adjustment Act (AAA) gave help to American farmers.
- The National Industrial Recovery Act (NIRA) gave the federal government considerable power to regulate business.

OPPONENTS OF THE NEW DEAL

The rich saw the New Deal as an attack on their wealth and influence. Inevitably the Republicans led the opposition to the interventionist New Deal with criticisms that concentrated on the cost to the taxpayer and the risks of an unbalanced budget. The Liberty League was created to reduce the role of the federal government. Many people were left out of the New Deal's drive for prosperity, particularly in rural areas. The Townsend Clubs promoted the needs of the elderly. Father Coughlin led a populist attack from the right, while Huey Long and his 'Share our Wealth' campaign attacked the New Deal from a left-wing populist standpoint.

Opposition was hostile, but divisions weakened its impact.

THE SUPREME COURT CONTROVERSY

President Roosevelt's actions over the Supreme Court were ultimately seen as an error. The Schechter and Butler decisions of the Supreme Court were key ones, and undermined much of the work of the NIRA and the AAA. Roosevelt was furious, and there was public criticism of the role of a conservative and unelected body in striking down the actions of an elected president and Congress. The court packing plan, when Roosevelt attempted to break the power of the courts, was a major error which aroused unnecessary fear and antagonism about the increase in presidential power. The court issue played an important part in alienating the southern Democrats from the Roosevelt coalition.

The constitutional role of the Supreme Court has to be known here.

THE SECOND NEW DEAL

The growth of progressivism in Congress, the Supreme Court rulings and the fact that unemployment was still high prompted a second New Deal. There was less focus on recovery and more on reform. A new agency, the Works Progress Administration (WPA), created work and stipulated the areas where work was to be done in hospitals, artistic projects and so on. There were changes in social security, welfare and pensions, though nothing on health care. Greater taxation of the rich was an important part of this process, as was the Wagner Act which gave trade unions increased bargaining rights. Roosevelt easily won re-election in 1936, in a campaign characterised by rich-versus-poor debates and class antagonism.

See the 1936 election result as a public endorsement of the New Deal.

THE END OF THE NEW DEAL: 1937 ONWARDS

Note the rise of the Congress of Industrial Organisations (CTO) and the growth of industrial strife. There was a gradual alienation of the middle class from the New Deal, as prosperity returned to them and concerns about their status and wealth came back to the fore. The economy dipped in 1937, and the federal

There was a change in direction of the New Deal, particularly in social issues.

government's solution of more spending worried many. There were further reforms in farm security, housing, minimum wages and working hours, but they were not enough to prevent Roosevelt doing badly in the mid-term elections of 1938.

MERITS OF THE NEW DEAL

The threat to capitalism was avoided. Manufacturing industry recovered quickly and became the basis of a flourishing economy. Some responsibility for welfare was taken on by government, and destitution declined. Labour regulation helped many working-class men, and the Securities and Exchange Commission (SEC) and banking regulation reduced the likelihood of another financial meltdown. Morale was raised and most minorities benefited. The Democrats began to dominate the political process, and the role of the president developed to enable the incumbents to take on and advocate the policies that the USA needed.

Consider whether it was the restoration of confidence that was Roosevelt's main achievement — not the actual legislation.

You should be able to make a clear case for both the merits and demerits of the New Deal.

DEMERITS OF THE NEW DEAL

In the end there was only partial recovery, for 17% were still unemployed by 1939; as in Britain, it took a war to ensure full employment. Agriculture was still inefficient and poverty stricken in places. The National Industrial Recovery Act (NIRA) never worked efficiently and welfare reforms did not reach very deep. Responsibility for housing was still blurred, the relationship between the federal government and the states became even more complex, and wealth remained in the hands of a dominant few. In the longer term, critics saw the rise of an imperial-minded presidency.

Key points on the achievements of the New Deal

- the restoration of business confidence
- the development of the role of the president
- the development of the role of the federal government in managing the economy
- reduction of unemployment
- the growth of government regulation in business and banking
- welfare and social security improvements
- conservation
- labour relations improved
- farming was helped
- housing aid to the homeless
- minimum wages and working conditions
- the restoration of manufacturing industry

M Civil rights in the USA from 1945

Key questions

Why was progress in civil rights so slow in this period?

What were the main reasons for progress in civil rights in this period?

THE ROLE OF TRUMAN, 1945-52

Note the signs of the federal government beginning to act and the growing use of the courts.

Although a southern Democrat, President Harry S. Truman was a New Dealer and was therefore committed to the ending of poverty — blacks included. The need for re-election in 1948 was also an incentive to win over the black vote. Remember Truman's courageous (for the time) special message to Congress to end segregation in federal trials, to end lynching and to set up a Fair Employment Practices Commission. These attempts were to fail, but his effort to help the NAACP with lawsuits was productive. He ended segregation in the armed forces, but saw his Civil Rights Bill filibustered in the Senate. The frightening atmosphere of McCarthyism in the background did not encourage tolerance, but the federal government had made its stance clear.

THE BROWN CASE

The role of the Brown case in the evolution of civil rights must be considered thoroughly.

President Dwight Eisenhower had not been enthusiastic about integration in the army and was not a man primed to take civil rights initiatives when he came to power in 1952. However, his appointment of Chief Justice Earl Warren, coupled with the legacy of Roosevelt's appointments to the Supreme Court, had a dramatic effect. The Plessey decision, which permitted segregation, was overruled un-animously and the whole concept of 'separate but equal' was gone for good. The new activist Supreme Court was to play a dominant role in the ending of segregation and the American army was used to stop open defiance in Arkansas. In spite of Brown, the famous Supreme Court case which banned segregation, progress was slow. Force was still used in states to prevent voter registration and school integration. The two Civil Rights Acts of 1957 and 1960 had limited effect — they would not have passed through Congress otherwise. Education and voting were still a major problem for blacks, given the hostility of both Congress and the states. The operation of the Senate gave disproportionate influence to a few senators from the racist South.

THE GROWTH OF PUBLIC PROTEST AND CIVIL DISOBEDIENCE

Compare the role of the protest movements with those of the courts and the federal government in bringing about social justice for American blacks.

The gradually improving educational opportunities of the blacks, particularly in the South, as well as the growing sense of deprivation, led to a rising hostility to the Jim Crow laws still prevailing in the South. Martin Luther King used the ideas of Gandhi to mount peaceful protests that attracted support and good publicity. The Alabama bus protest, when blacks refused to accept segregated transport, was followed by successful Supreme Court rulings. Meanwhile, the bad publicity gained by the police and state governors encouraged further federal involvement to assist the rights movement.

THE KENNEDY PRESIDENCY

Did President Kennedy do much of real value to help the position of American blacks?

President Kennedy was seen as a leader who might bring an end to the institutionalised racism of the South and end the poverty which affected many of the northern urban blacks. Kennedy, however, achieved little for the blacks and some accuse him of mere tokenism. In 1963 Martin Luther King criticised him for his timidity and for his appointment of racist judges to the federal bench. Kennedy failed to manage Congress well and did not wish to offend southern Democratic supporters in the Senate. However, with Warren on the Supreme Court — and by following Eisenhower's example of sending troops to enforce the law at Mississippi University and in Alabama — there was some progress.

His brother Robert Kennedy, at the Justice Department, achieved more by using federal courts to pursue issues such as desegregation, equal access to public transport and voting rights.

THE JOHNSON PRESIDENCY

President Lyndon Johnson came from the South, knew its ways and was a good enough manager of Congress to achieve legislative breakthrough with his Great Society programme. His Civil Rights Act of 1964 had an effect on racial discrimination, voting rights and education. An Equal Opportunities Commission was created to enforce an Equal Opportunities Act. The Voting Rights Act was also vital, as was the 24th Amendment of 1964 which prevented states from using a poll tax device to stop blacks from voting.

Compare the impact of the work of Martin Luther King with that of President Johnson and his Great Society programme.

THE BLACK REVOLT

The work of Johnson and the Supreme Court was not enough to defuse black people's anger at the lack of progress. The poverty of many blacks, the failure to bring about a change of attitude on the part of many whites, the disproportionate numbers of blacks sent to Vietnam and the disproportionate numbers of blacks in jail and on death row were obvious indicators of the gap between black and white. Black youth turned increasingly to violence and the anti-integrationist ideas of the Black Muslims, the SNCC, Carmichael, the Black Panthers, Malcolm X and Eldridge Cleaver. Rioting broke out in the Watts ghetto in Los Angeles and spread to other cities in 1967–68. The assassination of Martin Luther King and President Johnson's distraction over Vietnam exacerbated a difficult situation.

Consider whether the black revolt achieved as much as or less than the non-violent movement in the advance of black rights and status in the USA.

PROGRESS SINCE THE 1960S

The move to the northern cities continued, the ghettos grew bigger and the white middle class went to live in the suburbs. The white flight lowered city tax income, which increased urban poverty. The number of black people living below the poverty line dropped, but black family income remained on average 40% below that of whites. Black mayors were elected and a black middle class started to emerge, but poverty, unemployment and bad housing remain endemic amongst blacks. The Los Angeles riots over the Rodney King affair in 1991–92, when police officers who had been filmed beating an innocent black man were acquitted by a white jury, show the depth of feeling. Note also the impact of the affirmative action programmes, and their decline after the Bakke case, which ended positive discrimination. Consider whether positive discrimination has actually had a positive effect.

Consider how much real progress has been made.

Key points

- Truman and the end of federal desegregation
- the Brown case, when the Supreme Court ended legal segregation
- Eisenhower's use of troops to enforce the Brown decision
- the civil disobedience programme
- the work of Martin Luther King
- the role of the Warren Supreme Court in key cases such as Brown and Baker
- Johnson's Great Society programme
- the black revolt